THE PAINTING

A NOVEL BASED ON A TRUE STORY

Published under consultancy of Emerson Agency LLC., Baltimore, Maryland.

Cover design: Monique Sterling
Cover Art: "El Saxofonista" 1953, 13" x 10" by Carlos Sobrino
Book Layout: Sophie Erb

Library of Congress Control Number: 2022932257

ISBN (hardcover): 9781662925443
ISBN (softcover): 9781662924941
eISBN: 9781662924958

"TO THE BRAVE AND WONDERFUL PEOPLE OF CUBA"—MR

THE PAINTING

A NOVEL BASED ON A TRUE STORY

MICHAEL REID

Havana Cuba 1982

I

"Roberto. Roberto!" said Carlos from the kitchen, a little louder the second time.

Carlos was always anxious and today his anxiety was worse than normal as he had promised to help his elderly friend Julio move from his house of 65 years. Julio was 92 and had outlived his wife and all his children and was no longer in need of the large 5-bedroom house in Santos Suarez. He was moving to an apartment in the same neighborhood, where he would be closer to the market and to the chemist.

Carlos knew that this move was going to be difficult and emotional for his friend Julio and wanted to get it over with as quickly as possible.

"Roberto!" Carlos shouted once more, this time even louder.

"What do you want, Carlitos?" Roberto replied.

He was annoyed that his brother had woken him and did not remember that he had promised Carlos that he would help to move Julio's belongings.

"You don't remember that today is the day we move Julio?" Carlos asked him.

"No, I forgot, I'm sorry, Carlitos."

Roberto rarely became angry with his older brother and loved him dearly. He understood how profoundly difficult it had been for Carlos growing up with autism, and he saw daily how he suffered.

"I'm coming now, Carlitos, but first I need some coffee and

something to eat." Their mother made the best *coladas* and *pastelitos* in the neighborhood, he thought to himself. The strong sweet coffee and guava pastry was all he needed to make it through the day.

"Yasiel is coming with the car in twenty minutes, and he told me he could only help for one hour. We need to move as much as possible with the car. I want to move all the heavy furniture first. After Yasiel leaves we can move the rest with the *carro de bueyes*," said Carlos.

"The car is only available for one hour?" Roberto asked.

"Yes, and you need to hurry. Take your coffee with you," said Carlos.

"The *carro de bueyes* is for animals," grumbled Roberto.

"I understand but that is all we have," Carlos replied. "I don't like it much either. We can pull the cart together. And besides it is mostly downhill."

Yasiel was very proud of his 1950 Chevy Sedan Delivery and only reluctantly agreed to let the boys use it to help Julio move. It was large and they could move many pieces of furniture in a single trip.

Julio had practiced general medicine in Havana for more than sixty years, helping poor families in the boys' neighborhood with all their medical needs as well as food and clothing, both always in short supply, along with many common goods. Of course, these shortages were never acknowledged by the Castro regime and only talked about in private settings.

In recent years, as Julio's family had passed on, Carlos chose more and more to look after his aging friend, helping with many of his daily tasks. He felt sorry for Julio without his family and was very protective of him.

As they approached Julio's house, they could see him waiting by the front gate. The house was old and in need of repairs. It had once been a magnificent house and a remarkable example of neoclassical architecture, deserving of much better care. The tropical sun and climate had taken their toll on the old house over the years. It was a typical large home in Santos Suarez, no doubt owned at one time by a wealthy American family who used Havana as a winter playground. Unfortunately, as Julio grew older and more frail, it had become impossible for him to do all but the most simple repairs. Everyone in communist Cuba made the same monthly salary. Even a highly trained doctor received just $40 a month, which was barely enough to live on, so paying anyone to help repair the house was not an option.

"*Buenos dias*, Julio. *Como tu ta*?" asked Carlos.

"*Buenos dias*, boys." Julio was always cheerful and possessed none of the anger and bitterness many older people in Cuba felt toward the regime. "Yasiel will be here soon. I'm sorry we cannot use the car for more than an hour."

"That's okay," replied Carlos. "We'll manage and we can work fast."

"We need to finish before the afternoon rain." Roberto reminded his brother.

It was midsummer, very hot and very humid, and that meant heavy tropical squalls would likely form over the high land to the south of the city, always moving north toward the sea in the late afternoon.

The brothers worked fast moving the heavier pieces of furniture out of the house and down the steps to the street in front of the old man's house. If they could make several trips with the Sedan Delivery then all that remained to move using the oxcart would be small household items.

Yasiel arrived on time and the boys made short work of filling the massive old American car. The brothers were grateful to Yasiel for having offered to help.

By the time Yasiel had to leave with the car they had finished the second load and most of the large heavy pieces had been moved to Julio's new apartment. Yasiel said goodbye and the boys walked behind the old man's house where he kept the oxcart.

The cart was old, large, very heavy, and made of fine-grain Caribbean mahogany.

"It's beautiful," remarked Roberto. Since he was a little boy, he had always loved anything old. He didn't know why, maybe it was the feeling of authenticity intrinsic in anything made by hand.

"But I think the cart will be too difficult to pull through the cobblestone streets."

"That is all we have," said Carlos. "Here, you take the shaft on one side and I'll take the other."

As they pulled the cart around to the front of the house Roberto, rather surprised, remarked at how easily the large wooden wheels rolled over the stones.

"The large wheels make it easy. Maybe it will not be so bad," he said.

"We'll see," replied Carlos. "Remember, right now it is empty."

The old man, though frail, was doing what he could to help, bringing some of the smaller items out of the house. He was moving to an apartment and didn't have room for many of his things and so he kept only what he needed as well as his most treasured possessions, the paintings.

Roberto and Carlos knew nothing about art but they could see that Julio was taking great care when handling the paintings and so they did the same as they began to load the rest of the old man's items into the cart.

The distance to Julio's new apartment was little more than ten blocks downhill to the north, and even though the cart was full as it could hold, it was easier to pull than they had expected. Occasionally, as they passed through the surrounding neighborhood, young children from each block, all too eager to help and thinking it was a game, would come out to help push the cart along.

It was late afternoon by the time they unpacked the final load and there was little time to spare before the first of the afternoon rain squalls, that built steadily over the hills to the south, reached the southern edge of Havana.

The cool wind from the advancing thunderheads and the expected rain were a welcome relief to the boys. They were tired but also felt good about having helped their friend Julio. Now, they looked forward to getting paid.

As they sat on the front stoop of the apartment building, waiting for the old man, they talked about what they would do with the money.

Carlos loved to read and planned to buy books. He especially enjoyed reading to his father, who had grown up poor in the countryside and could neither read nor write. His father, Guillermo, was very proud of his son, despite the boy's struggles with autism. Carlos would read to his father in the evenings, on the terrace after the sun had set, when it was cooler and more comfortable to sit outside rather than in the old concrete house.

Roberto, on the other hand had only one plan. That was to scrape together enough money to buy a pair of black-market American jeans. The money from Julio would go a long way to making his dream come true. He was only 17. With this new pair of jeans, he would surely be able to get the attention of even the most beautiful girls in his neighborhood.

Julio appeared in the doorway behind them carrying one of the small paintings they had moved in the cart.

"I'm sorry, boys, but I do not have the money to pay you for your work today."

Roberto looked at Carlos as if to say, "you were the one who arranged this deal that I agreed to be a part of and now we will not be paid?"

"I can give you this painting as payment," Julio told them. "I know you wanted the money, but I am no longer working and this is all I have. It is very valuable and was done by an old friend, Carlos Sobrino."

"Are you sure you don't have any money?" Roberto asked, feeling compelled to pressure the old man but not wanting to be disrespectful.

"No, I have no money," replied Julio. "But if you want you can easily sell the painting for more money than I was going to pay you."

The boys could see that Julio was upset, rather embarrassed and in an impossible situation. So they agreed to take the painting, intrigued by what Julio had said about its value. Like everyone in Cuba, particularly for the older people, Julio was doing the best he could, barely getting by day to day.

"I'm sorry for the trouble," Julio said. "Carlos Sobrino was a good friend of mine and a very important artist here in Cuba. I purchased the painting from him in 1953."

"Does it have a name," Roberto asked.

"Yes, it is called *El Saxofonista*. Carlos Sobrino loved music of all kinds, and in particular, American jazz. He never told me who the saxophonist in the painting was. Carlos was forced into exile after the revolution and moved to Spain."

"Why did he have to leave Cuba?" Roberto asked Julio.

"The government considered the subject matter of what he chose to paint incompatible with the ideals of the Revolution. He left the country nearly twenty years ago and died in 1971. In Spain, I think. Anyway, you will have no problem selling the painting should you choose to do so. But I do hope that you keep it. If you sell it the money will soon be gone and then you will have nothing. It is worth much more than I could have paid you," Julio reminded them once again.

"How do we determine the value?" asked Carlos.

"You can go to the Cultural Assets Institution and ask there. They sometimes purchase art works from individual citizens, so they would know what it is worth. I remember, after he won the National Painting award in 1957, the National Museum put several of Sobrino's works on display in the museum, but I haven't been there in years. Good luck and thank you again for your help and kindness today. You better hurry home, it will be raining soon."

Julio bid the boys farewell, turned and went inside the apartment, closing the heavy wooden door behind him.

"We'll go to the Cultural Assets Institution tomorrow," Roberto said to Carlos excitedly. "I think I may know someone who might buy it."

"No one we know has any money, Roberto. You're dreaming. I would rather Julio had paid us today. And besides this painting has sentimental value to Julio. I don't think we should sell it."

"You'll see, Carlitos, this could change our lives!" Roberto said. Not really listening to his brother's concerns about how Julio would feel.

As the brothers made their way toward home, people stared from their terraces and balconies, no doubt wondering why two teenage boys would be carrying a painting. The boys paid no attention to the people, thinking only that they needed to make it home before the rain came.

They were nearly home when the first large raindrops began to fall, and they had to run the last 100 meters to their parents' house to keep the painting from getting wet. When they arrived at the house their father had not yet come home from work, and their mother Rosa was in the kitchen preparing dinner for the family, so they took the painting upstairs without speaking to her.

Roberto carried the painting directly to their room where they found a place to hang it, just above the small desk where Carlos kept his books.

"You know, Carlitos, if we sell the painting our financial problems will be over."

"Maybe for a few days, but you heard what Julio said. We sell the painting and soon the money is gone. Then once again we have nothing. And besides I know you could see how much the painting meant to him. I felt bad even having taken it as payment. We'll talk about it tomorrow. We can visit the Cultural Assets Institution. Julio said they can tell us anything we want to know about our painting and Sobrino."

It was getting late, and the brothers were tired from the day's work. All they could think about was getting something to eat and having some much-needed rest. They took turns showering and went to have dinner with their parents, as they did every evening on the terrace behind the house.

In the morning when Roberto awoke and went downstairs for a *colada*, his brother was already in the kitchen talking with their mother about the previous day's events. He had told her about the painting and that they were going to research the work and the artist.

Their mother reminded them that they needed to be careful who they spoke to about the painting, especially anyone in the government.

"There is a government institution that buys paintings from individuals," Roberto told her. "It's not a crime to own a painting. Julio has many paintings."

"Julio is an old man. The government doesn't bother old people, and you don't know that to be true, Roberto. Many artists, writers, and intellectuals have left the country under protest or have been sent to prison. And some of the ones in prison were never heard from again. I'm telling you to be careful."

The brothers could see the conversation was upsetting their mother, so they changed the subject to baseball and, of course, to fishing. Both of the boys loved to fish and planned a trip the following weekend with their friend, Maykel. He had an old eight-meter-long, wooden boat that he fished regularly in the Gulf Stream just outside Havana Harbor beyond the Morro.

"When you go fishing with Maykel, make sure you catch something this time," their mother quipped. "I'm beginning to think both of you are Jonahs. Maykel, I know, is not *salao*, but the two of you, well. We could use some fresh fish, and remember I like *dorado*. If you catch *dorado* I will make you fish cakes and sweet plantains!"

Roberto turned to Carlos and said, "We should be going Carlitos. Julio told us the Cultural Assets building is on the other side of town near the Palace of the Revolution. We'll be back later this afternoon," Roberto said to his mother.

As the brothers approached the building where Julio had directed them to research the painting, Roberto could see his brother's anxiety level beginning to rise. He put his arm around him, which seemed to help and said, "We don't have to do this if you don't want."

"I'm okay, Roberto, I'll be fine."

The building looked intimidating, like government buildings tend to look, mostly by design. But once inside they quickly began to focus on the reason why they were there.

"We are here to research a famous artist from Havana," Roberto told the clerk at the front desk. The guards posted near the front of the hallway looked at the brothers suspiciously but said nothing.

"You need to go to the Office of Culture on the second floor." The clerk barely looked up from her desk and clearly did not seem to enjoy her work.

Once inside the dimly lit office, they were greeted by an elderly woman with whom they immediately felt at ease.

"*Buenos Dias, señora*," said Roberto, taking the initiative. He knew his brother's difficulties with social interactions and communication would be too much in this case.

"*Buenos dias*. What can I help you with?" the woman replied.

"We are here to research a painting and the famous artist who painted it, Carlos Sobrino," Roberto proudly answered.

"Well, I will have to look through our catalogues since I have never heard of the artist. Is he from Cuba and do you know when he lived?" asked the clerk politely.

"Yes, of course he is from Cuba," Roberto answered, a bit surprised she had never heard of Sobrino. "From Havana. He was born here in 1909 and died in Spain in 1971," Roberto said, trying to appear as confident as possible. One thing Roberto was not wanting for was confidence, and it often got him into trouble.

The brothers waited patiently while the clerk searched through numerous catalogues and publications, all but a few appearing to be old enough to contain any information about Sobrino or photos of his work.

After more than an hour the clerk returned to where the boys were sitting. She looked disappointed and they thought even a little embarrassed.

"I'm sorry," she said. "But I was unable to find any information about this artist. Are you sure of the name?"

"Yes, we are sure of his name. The painting is signed very clearly at the bottom," Roberto told her. "It is entitled, *El Saxofonista*, and it is very valuable. The former owner is a good friend."

"Well, I would suggest you go to the National Museum. It is on Calle Agramonte, and if anyone can help you, it will be the people there. If the artist is famous, like you have said, you will probably find some of his works in the Museum. Good luck."

"Thank you," Roberto said. Carlos nodded to the woman, and they headed down the stairs to the lobby and out of the building.

"I am sure we will find something at the Museo Nacional," said Roberto, as they made their way down the narrow streets of old Havana.

"I don't think so," Carlos replied. "If Sobrino is so famous, the woman at the Cultural Institution would have heard of him."

It was very hot and a long walk to the National Museum, so they stopped along the way for a cold coconut water and a cane juice. The thick cane juice instantly gave them the shot of energy they needed, and they felt optimistic again about their search.

When they arrived at the museum, Carlos suggested they first look in the gallery of early modern art. Often Roberto wondered how his brother came to be so intuitive. Carlos had been a poor student in school but a voracious reader and was naturally instinctive.

"The paintings here are similar to *El Saxofonista*," Carlos said. "If we don't find something in this gallery then we can look in the portraits."

After nearly an hour of searching the brothers found nothing by Sobrino.

"Let's look through the portraits," Carlos said to Roberto.

After looking carefully at every portrait they could find in the museum they began to think that maybe Julio had imagined his friend to be famous and the painting, although beautiful and interesting, was not worth much after all.

"Maybe we can ask at the office of the director," Carlos said.

"I think your friend Julio is an old man and he is sentimental about the painting and his friend Sobrino," said Roberto.

"It doesn't matter to me if it is not worth anything. I like it because it was my friend Julio's and it makes me feel good when I look at it."

"I suppose feeling good is important," Roberto replied, feeling a little confused by his brother's comment. "Maybe even more important than money, especially when you are poor. Anyway, it's late, Carlitos. We should be heading home. The rain will be coming soon."

As they turned the corner onto their street they could see their father, Guillermo, sitting on the steps in front of the house talking with the neighbors. It was Sunday, so he wasn't working and always enjoyed idle conversation with his many friends in the neighborhood.

"*Buenas tardes,* Father," Carlos said.

"Where have you been?" Guillermo asked the brothers.

"We needed to go to the Cultural Assets Fund building and then to the National Museum of Art," replied Roberto.

"What for?" asked Guillermo, clearly not expecting Roberto's answer.

"Well, yesterday we had the job to move Julio to his new apartment and when we finished he could not pay us for the work," Roberto explained to his father. "So he gave us a valuable painting as payment. We went to research the value of the painting to see if we could sell it. But, unfortunately, no one in either place seemed to know anything about the painting or the artist."

Roberto could see from the look on his father's face he was not happy about or impressed with his answer.

"Roberto, is this Julio the doctor? asked Guillermo.

"Yes, why?" Roberto answered.

"And this painting was in Julio's house in Santos Suarez?"

"Yes, we moved all of his furniture and belongings from there to the new apartment," Roberto said nervously.

"Come inside, boys, I need to ask you a few more questions," Guillermo instructed, slightly agitated.

Not wanting to involve the neighbors, Guillermo said good evening to his friends and walked inside and through the house to the terrace in the back.

As the brothers followed their father to the terrace they could smell the evening meal of *pargo frito* their mother was preparing. As they passed through the kitchen she looked up at them but said nothing.

"You should not have taken the painting," Guillermo said.

"Why? We did the work and Julio paid us with the painting," Roberto explained.

"You have the painting now? Here, in my house?" asked Guillermo

"Yes, we have it hanging in our bedroom. Why?" asked Roberto

"I don't want it in my house. It is a bad omen. Everyone who lived with Julio in his house, died in that house. I don't want it here. You need to get rid of it first thing tomorrow. That's all I have to say."

Guillermo turned and went inside to have dinner.

"I am not surprised," Roberto said. "He has always been very superstitious."

"What should we do with the painting, Roberto?" asked Carlos.

"I don't know, but we're not getting rid of it. We can hide it in the bedroom for now and figure out what to do later. I'm hungry, Carlitos."

And with that the brothers prepared to have supper with their parents, not speaking any more about the painting that evening.

The next morning when Roberto awoke, he felt an overwhelming feeling of excitement and went immediately to look at the painting, examining closely every detail of the small painting. The man playing the saxophone, the colors, the lines, and the geometric shapes the artist used to create the images.

Staring intently at the painting he was suddenly overcome with a profound sense of calm and peace of mind, something he had never felt before. He didn't understand why he felt as he did. He had many questions and wanted to know everything about the painting.

"Who was the saxophonist? Where did he live? Was he still living and why did Sobrino paint him the way he did?" Roberto wondered. He knew at the very least he had to learn more about the artist. Remembering now how upset his father had been the night before, and that he had told him to get rid of the painting, he decided to hide it under his mattress before going downstairs for breakfast. It was well protected there and would be safe.

Carlos had been awake for some time and was already in the kitchen having coffee. He didn't sleep much that night and had been thinking about the painting and what to do with it.

"Roberto," Carlos said excitedly. "I have an idea about the painting. I think we should go to the Jose Marti Library and search there for information about Sobrino."

"How do you know about this library, Carlitos?"

"I take books from there all the time. It's one of my favorite places."

"You know, Carlitos, you are smart. I wish sometimes I knew about such things. I am ready to go whenever you are."

As they walked out the front door, down the stone steps and onto the narrow street in front of the house, Carlos turned to Roberto and asked, "What about the painting? We can't leave it in the house!"

"I hid it under the mattress," Roberto said. "It is small, and he will never think to look there. It will be protected underneath the mattress."

It was another long walk to the library and as they came around the bend in La Avenida Paseo, walking east in front of the Memorial to Jose Marti, they could see the library building off to the left. Both the memorial to the famous poet and writer Jose Marti, and the National Library building, were towering modern structures that looked out of place in a city full of classic Spanish colonial architecture.

"When we go inside, Roberto, let me do the talking. The people will recognize me," Carlos said. "And besides, I think I know where to look first." After entering the fifteen-story, square, grey block building, the brothers went up to the front desk, signed in, and walked over to the directory on the wall in the lobby. "There," pointed Carlos. "I think we need to go to the Historical Data Department. It is on the fourth floor. We can take the elevator."

As the elevator door opened on the fourth floor they were confronted with row after row of shelves containing thousands of black binders all looking the same. "I don't know, Carlitos. Where do we even begin to look?"

"Roberto, it's simple," Carlos said, sounding slightly frustrated with his brother. "Everything is by the year. We know when Sobrino was born, when he died, and when he left Cuba for Spain after the Revolution. Julio said Sobrino was already famous when he bought *El Saxofonista*, so we can start looking through the years just before that and up through 1953."

Walking down the first aisle, they quickly found the section containing the years between 1940 and 1949, mostly official government issued periodicals containing historical accounts of the time period. There were no more than forty of the black binders all together, one for each quarter of the year.

"I think we will find something here, Roberto," Carlos said excitedly. "In 1940, Sobrino would have been thirty and just beginning the peak of his career."

"You are amazing!" exclaimed Roberto. "This should take no time at all."

Quickly the brothers began taking each binder down one by one, looking at every page for any bit of information about Carlos Sobrino or one of his paintings. As they carefully went through each one, they saw many references to important Cuban artists, poets, writers, and musicians of the time period, some of whom they knew from classes in school. When they came to the end of the section, they had found nothing about Sobrino.

Two hours had passed and they had become very frustrated once again at not finding any information about Sobrino. They were tired of looking through the binders and wanted something to eat.

"Carlitos," Roberto said. "We should go home now. We can come back and try again tomorrow. We should look in the years after 1949. By the way, did you remember it is my birthday tomorrow?" Roberto asked.

"We can go now, but I will be ready to look again tomorrow. I'm not discouraged. And yes, of course I remembered it is your birthday tomorrow. We can celebrate with our fishing trip on Saturday with Maykel. Eighteen, that is a big deal, Roberto," Carlos said, trying to be congratulatory.

Roberto could see that his brother was disappointed and was beginning to have doubts about the painting and about Julio's story, but out of respect for his brother, and his brother's friend Julio, he didn't let it show.

When they arrived home their mother was in the kitchen, as always, preparing supper. She did not look up when they came in and they could tell immediately she was upset about something.

"*Paso algo, Madre?*" Roberto asked.

"No, nothing happened, but you received this in the mail today," Rosa said.

"What is it?" Roberto asked, a little surprised.

"It is from the military. You are seventeen and you turn eighteen tomorrow. It is probably your conscription papers. I'm surprised the government didn't send them sooner."

"Let me see it," Roberto said. He opened the letter and read it to himself. When he looked up his mother was crying. "What are you crying about mother? You knew this was coming."

"I know, I know. But now it is real. Everyone who enters the military now goes to Angola, and they don't come back," said Rosa.

"I am not going to Angola mother. If I tell them I refuse to go then I simply have to stay in for additional time. I know how it works. You'll see," said Roberto.

"You are always so sure of everything, Roberto," Rosa said. "One day it is going to get you in to trouble. I hope you are right this time. You and your sister and your brothers are all I have."

Roberto realized it was no use trying to console his mother. He walked outside to the back terrace, sat down, and read the letter again to himself. Whatever happened, he thought, he was not going to Angola to fight in another senseless war in Africa. Too many young boys from Havana, many whom he knew personally, had been killed in the war. He saw firsthand how devastating it had been to their families.

He walked back inside, stopped, hugged his mother, but said nothing and went upstairs to his room. When he walked into the bedroom Carlos was sitting on the bed. He had taken the painting out from beneath the mattress and was staring at it intently.

"Carlitos. I don't think we will have time to go back to the library tomorrow. This is my conscription notice." Roberto said quietly, showing the letter to his brother.

He sat down next to his brother on the bed and they looked at the painting together, saying nothing.

After several minutes Roberto looked at his brother and said, "You know something, Carlitos. It's strange, but every time I look at this painting, if I am worried about something, depressed about money or feel that we are trapped and have run out of possibilities, I always begin to feel better. It is like a little window to a place where I can live and think freely."

"When do you think we can go to the library again?" asked Carlitos. "I don't want to give up our search."

"Well, maybe not tomorrow if I am going to the Ministry of Armed Forces, but we can go on Thursday and stay all day, and if we do not find anything on Thursday we will go back on Friday morning. I will be ready to look again tomorrow. I am not discouraged. I have Taekwondo training in the afternoon on Friday, but remember we go fishing with Maykel on Saturday."

"I will not forget your birthday trip, Roberto. I hear the weather is supposed to be perfect on Saturday with a light northeast wind. The *dorado* always bite when the wind is from the northeast and if there are *dorado* you know there will be a marlin or two, and if we're lucky…."

Interrupting his brother, Roberto said, "Carlitos, maybe we should put the painting back under the mattress now. It is hot up here in the bedroom. I am going down to the terrace where it is cooler."

He walked back down the stairs, through the kitchen, and as he opened the door to the terrace, he felt the cool evening air coming down out of the dark clouds to the south, and saw that it was starting to rain. He was beginning to sense that their quest for information about the painting and its artist was taking on a life and a power of its own, and he felt excited.

Roberto woke up early the next day, nervous about his appointment to register for the Army. He got dressed quickly, gathered his identification papers together, had a cup of coffee and left the house right away, speaking to no one.

When he arrived at the Ministry of the Revolutionary Armed Forces, there was already a long line that had formed outside the building, so he took his place in line with the other young men and women waiting for the ministry to open.

After the Ministry finally opened everyone with conscription notices was directed to the registration office to fill out the required paperwork and given a specific date when they were required to report for basic training.

Roberto had fifteen days until he had to report. During his initial interview at the Ministry he was told that—because of his background in self-defense and his national Taekwondo championship the previous year—once he completed basic training it was possible he would be assigned to the Secret Service division in the Department of State Security, an elite division charged with protection of high-level government officials.

It was a long walk home and he had a lot to think about, more than he could ever have imagined less than two days ago. He thought about his mother and how she would manage the stress. It seemed as though, at least for now, he may not be assigned combat duty in Africa, a relief to his mother no doubt, but there were no guarantees. He thought also about Carlos, who because of his autism had been exempted from military service the previous year and who struggled daily to cope with his affliction and who depended heavily on Roberto. Everything had changed for Roberto and he was becoming anxious.

When Roberto arrived home Carlos was waiting for him.

"Are we still going to the library tomorrow, Roberto?" asked Carlos.

"Yes, of course we are."

"What did they tell you at the ministry?" Carlos asked.

"Well, I have two weeks until I need to report and after that I go to basic training for six months," replied Roberto. "I'm not worried about the training. I train all the time in the gym. I know how to suffer," Roberto hesitated, "and to enjoy it. It will be easy. Anyway, let's talk about tomorrow and our trip to the library."

"Yes, let's talk about tomorrow. I have some ideas."

With that the brothers went inside, Roberto needing to tell his mother about the day's events and perhaps ease her anxiety about his future.

After supper the rest of the evening was spent with family on the terrace enjoying each other's company and making small talk. Neither brother mentioned anything about the painting in front of their father, nor their planned trip to the library the next day. It was a lovely summer night, the rains keeping well to the south and the westerlies light from the northeast, bringing in some drier air over the city and relief from the heat.

The next day the brothers left home early for the library. As they entered the building and headed back to the fourth floor where they had been searching several days prior, Carlos remembered Julio telling them Sobrino had won the National Painting Award in 1957.

"You know," Carlos said, as they entered the library. "If Sobrino won the National Painting Award in 1957, it means the museum thought he was the best painter in the country at that time, the best. They must have information about him. We should search all the catalogues between

1950 and 1957 when he won the award."

With renewed enthusiasm they once again went straight to the archive room on the fourth floor, and immediately went to work carefully looking through every catalogue from the 1950's. After three hours of careful searching they again found no references to Carlos Sobrino nor his works. It was an enormous disappointment to the brothers. They simply could not understand how a nationally recognized artist was not represented in the archives of the National Library.

"I don't know, Carlitos. I think we are wasting our time. Maybe we should go. It's nearly 1:00 and I need to be at the gym by 2:00. I'm sorry."

"We can leave now, Roberto, but I am not willing to give up."

Frustrated and saddened by their failure to uncover any information, the brothers headed home.

They would not have another opportunity to return to the National Library for more than six months, after Roberto had completed his basic training. Refusing to fight overseas in Angola and having qualified for acceptance in the Cuban special forces, Roberto would eventually be assigned full time duty in the Secret Service, stationed at the Palace of the Revolution, tasked with protecting El Presidente, Fidel Castro, a turn of events that would change his life forever.

Roberto, sleeping little that night, was up well before dawn, preparing for the much-anticipated day of fishing on the ocean. Together with their good friend, Maykel, they would celebrate Roberto's eighteenth birthday. Maykel was in his 60's now and considerably older than the brothers, but full of passion and always the first one to the dock in the morning before sunrise. He genuinely seemed to love taking the brothers fishing, enjoying their youthful exuberance and optimism.

"*Buenos dias*, Carlitos," Roberto greeting his brother as he sat down at the kitchen table for some coffee. "I hope you got a good night's sleep and are feeling strong. We are going to catch a lot of fish today."

Fishermen are eternally optimistic. No matter how poor the fishing was the day before they are always certain that today will be the day.

"I will be ready when Maykel needs me," said Carlos.

"I saw his son, Aroldis, yesterday afternoon on my way home from training. He said Maykel had a good day yesterday and caught a nice bull *dorado* of twenty-five kilos."

"How many fish did he catch?" Carlos asked.

"Aroldis said his father fished in the bight and caught twenty-five and two big wahoo," said Roberto.

"Was he fishing alone?"

"I think so, yes," replied Roberto.

"He must have been very tired. We will reel in all the fish today," Carlos said confidently.

"We should be going, Carlitos. I hate being late to the dock. Maykel told me 4:30. He will be waiting."

The brothers gathered the lunch Roberto had made, along with two jugs of fresh coconut water. Leaving the house through the back door, they headed to the sea front.

When they arrived at the dock Maykel had untied the boat and was waiting for the boys with the engine running in front of the steps leading down from the sea wall along the Avenida del Puerto.

"*Buenos dias, Pescadores*," Maykel said cheerfully.

"Maykel was always in a good mood," Roberto thought to himself.

"*Buenos dias*, Maykel. I heard from Aroldis they were snapping pretty good yesterday," Roberto said.

"Yes, I fished alone and caught twenty-five and two wahoo. Fortunately no marlin." Maykel was not interested in catching marlin when the *dorado* were running. They required too much time and effort to bring to the boat and often threw the hook before he could bring them close enough to reach with the gaff.

The brothers quickly stepped from the dock to the washboard as Maykel gently eased the old wooden boat out into the harbor, the coming quarter moon giving them just enough light to safely navigate the Canal de Entrada and out into Havana Bay.

Maykel always left the dock before the other fishermen, refusing to fish behind any other boats. He believed it improved his chances and he regularly outfished the bigger boats.

"Carlitos, take the wheel while I rig some baits," Maykel said, knowing it made Carlos feel important and gave the older brother confidence. Having passed beyond the reef and out into open water, Maykel knew there was no risk of hitting bottom.

With a faint sliver of yellow light beginning to brighten the horizon and a flat calm ocean, they began trolling to the northwest, putting out all four baits, one on each outrigger at the sixth wave made by the boat's wake, and two flatlines half the distance off the stern. Maykel's preferred bait was a pink and white feathered trolling lure with a small ballyhoo rigged inside.

The Gulf Stream normally flowed close to the Morro just outside Havana Harbor and even though it was still too dark to make out its distinctive dark blue color, they could easily tell when they reached the edge of the current, which was pushing steadily into the early morning northeast breeze, making the waves a little steeper and forcing them closer together.

"Look Maykel!" Carlos shouted. "Three war birds, off the port bow, and one is on the water!"

"I see them. For sure they're on fish!" said Roberto. "I see the flying fish now coming out of the water underneath the birds!" he said excitedly.

"They are right by that big patch of Sargasso. Check the baits for weed, boys. Make sure they are clean," Maykel said as they closed in on the birds.

"I see the *dorado* breaking!" Carlos said.

"The current is pushing the fish toward us," Maykel said, responding to Carlos.

"See the *dorado*?" yelled Maykel. "See him there, see him there. Get ready, he's coming, he's coming!"

All four lines went off at once, the outriggers bending under the weight of the fish before releasing and snapping back loudly from the force of the strike. Quickly each brother grabbed a flat line rod and slowly leaned back as the line went out, each one feeling the weight of the fish. Maykel eased off the throttle just enough to help keep the lines tight and to ensure the hooks would hold, and then picked up the starboard outrigger rod.

"The fish on my rod is a big bull, boys," Maykel said. "After we gaff one of the smaller fish one of you needs to fight this fish for me. He's heavy and my back is still bad from yesterday."

Holding the rod with his left hand and steering with his right he slowly brought the boat around so they could fight the fish off the port side.

It wasn't long before Carlos had his fish alongside the boat and ready to gaff.

"Roberto!" yelled Maykel. "Grab the hand line and a bait. There are three more with your brother's fish." *Dorado* often run in schools and will follow the fish that is hooked all the way to the boat.

"There is another big bull, Maykel!" said Roberto.

They could see the free-swimming bull *dorado* just below the fish on Carlos's rod, clearly visible in the clear, cobalt colored water, its pectoral and tail fins glowing a brilliant neon blue.

"Tie the hand line off and throw him the bait, Roberto!" said Maykel.

After securing the heavy nylon hand line around the port stern cleat he threw the baited hook overboard with the remaining line, just in front of the big fish. Holding the line with both hands he braced his knees against the wooden apron on the inside of the boat, waiting for the fish to take the bait.

"He's got it, Roberto, he's got it!" yelled Maykel.

"Set the hook," shouted Carlos, trying to remain calm.

Roberto felt the weight slowly begin to build on the line as the big bull *dorado* with the bait now in his mouth, swam parallel to the side of the boat. He tightened his grip on the heavy nylon fishing line and gave a quick pull, low and hard in the opposite direction the fish was swimming.

When the fish felt the sting of the hook it turned away from the boat and made a burst toward the surface, every inch of his six-foot length coming clear of the water.

With everything he had, Roberto tried unsuccessfully to horse the fish back in the direction of the boat. Maykel, seeing that Roberto was overmatched by the power of the fish, immediately grabbed the line to help, realizing if the fish made it to the end of the hand line it would snap from the force of the run and the weight of the fish.

The old bull, probably having been hooked before, then tried going deep but failed to take any line, instead changing direction once more, coming up and out of the water right beside the boat, splashing Roberto and Maykel with a mixture of sea water and blood.

Fully out of the water the fish had nothing to push against and they quickly pinned the massive blunt head of the fish against the side of the boat.

Carlos, ready with the long gaff in hand, instantly sunk the six-inch, semi-circle tip into the fish's soft under belly.

"We don't have him yet!" Maykel grunted, holding onto the line with both hands and straining to maintain control of the fish. "Throw him in the boat. Now, NOW!" he yelled.

With one last supreme effort the brothers and Maykel pulled the massive bull into the boat, stepping quickly out of the way as the fish began slapping its powerful tail against the inside of the stern, spraying blood over the interior of the cockpit.

"All right, let's get these other fish in," said Maykel. "Roberto, gaff Carlitos's fish. I'll crank yours in. The other big bull is out far. Leave him until last."

Working frantically the brothers and Maykel managed to quickly bring the other three smaller fish to the boat, successfully gaffing each without incident. Once the fish were in the cooler both brothers sat on the lid to prevent the fish from flopping back out onto the deck.

Again Maykel picked up the rod with the other big bull on it, still hooked. Reeling steadily, he slowly began to gain line, synchronizing his movements by pulling back and reeling down with the rise and fall of each swell.

Maykel continued fighting his fish while the boys, each dipping buckets of sea water from the ocean, began cleaning the blood splatters caused by the fish they had caught on the hand line that covered nearly everything on the inside of the stern of the boat.

"He's close now. Get the long gaff, not the small one. Have the small one ready if we need it. I want him on this side," said Maykel, pointing toward the port side.

Keeping the rod tip low and making one or two turns at a time on the reel, Maykel made steady progress easing the fish closer to the boat. Roberto readied the gaff and as the fish slid slowly on the surface gently bumping the side of the boat, he drove the point into the thick part of the fish's shoulder behind the head, piercing the spine, killing him instantly.

"Nice job, Roberto. Let's get him in the cooler," said Carlitos.

"We keep this up we'll be to the dock by noon," Maykel said, laughing out loud. "These are big fish. A few more and the cooler is full."

"I know *Madre* will be happy," Carlos said.

With the sun now well above the horizon, and having trolled a good distance to the west, Maykel decided to turn back into the sea, heading to the east in the direction of Havana. Trolling east, the sun would now be at their backs as they watched the baits trailing behind the boat to the west, making it easier to see the fish when they came into the spread.

Maykel and the brothers managed to catch a few more small *dorado* and a good-sized sailfish as they fished their way back toward the city. By the time they could see the outline of the buildings along the western sea front, they had filled the cooler and decided to call it a day.

Trolling to the edge of the drop-off at the mouth of Havana Bay, and into the shallows, Maykel backed off the throttle to make it easier for the brothers to pull in all the lines. Tired, wet and with his clothes stained with blood, Carlos, remembering it was his brother's birthday, turned to Roberto and said, "*feliz cumpleanos hermano*, it was a good day."

"Thank you, brother. For certain, it was a good day. I will never forget my eighteenth birthday."

Returning to the dock the boys began cleaning the boat while Maykel saw to the job of filleting the fish, which he was very particular about. When he finished cleaning the last fish, the boys divided up their share of the meat, filling a full kit bag. Turning to Maykel the brothers each gave him a hug, thanked him again, and headed home. They were proud and knew how happy their mother would be to have so much fresh fish in the house. It would be many years before Roberto would have another opportunity to enjoy time together on the ocean with his brother Carlos.

II

The following two weeks went by quickly after their trip with Maykel, and soon the day came when Roberto was required to report for military basic training. He planned to leave early that morning for the Ministry of the Revolutionary Armed Forces, not wanting to further upset his mother with an unnecessarily long goodbye.

However, all four siblings, along with his parents, were gathered in the living room waiting to say goodbye, when he came down the stairs from his bedroom. Roberto knew how difficult the separation and time away would be on the family, and in particular for Carlos, so the tearful goodbyes were intentionally brief.

"I'll see you in six months," Roberto said, trying to sound as cheerful as possible. "The time will go by quickly. You'll see."

"Do what you are told Roberto, and remember, don't be cocky," Rosa said sternly.

"Yes *Madre*, I'll remember. I know how to stay out of trouble."

As he left the house and headed toward the Ministry, he felt calm and not particularly nervous about what lay ahead, knowing that the physical part of the training would be easy for him, and that he had a good chance of being stationed in Cuba, after the training was complete, and most likely in Havana.

The discipline he had learned and the confidence he had gained from his years of high level training and competing in Taekwando would prove invaluable over the next several years, becoming, in fact, the critical element in what would ultimately become a fight for survival.

The following six months in basic training passed quickly and uneventfully for Roberto. He encountered little trouble meeting all of the physical requirements for entry into Special Forces and was well respected among his fellow trainees. He was proud of his accomplishments, and—having been recognized for his exceptional abilities in self-defense, as expected—he received a special assignment at the Palace of the Revolution.

After receiving an additional two weeks of Secret Service training, special Palace uniforms and the necessary credentials, Roberto was granted two weeks of much anticipated military leave. After signing out at the base entrance he nodded to the attending officer and walked through the gate. As he made his way through the streets of Santos Suarez nearing home, he became increasingly excited about seeing his family, and especially Carlos. Roberto's brother depended on him heavily for emotional security and he hoped the time away had not been too hard on Carlos.

He remembered also the painting from Julio and wondered if Carlos had made any more attempts to research the painting at the Jose Marti Library. Roberto realized then how much he had missed looking at the painting and he began to feel excited about continuing their search for information about the work and the artist.

Reaching home he wasted no time going inside, dropped his military duffel bag in the living room, and went straight to the kitchen, knowing his mother would be there waiting for him.

"*Hola, Madre, como estas?*"

"I'm fine, Roberto," said Rosa, as she embraced her son. "The question is how are you? You look thin. Fidel doesn't feed you?"

"Yes, he feeds me, but I train hard every day. It's hard to keep the weight on, but I feel good," said Roberto. "Anyway, it's official mother, I don't have to fight in Angola. I have been assigned to the Palace. I am a member of the Secret Service."

"I don't believe you."

Roberto slowly and deliberately reached into his back pocket and pulled out his wallet, carefully revealing to his mother the shiny new SS identification badge he had been issued the day before.

"I wouldn't joke about something so serious, Mother. You know that."

"Carlitos will be happy," Rosa said. "He has missed you terribly. He is in his room. You should go and see him."

"I will go see him now."

"Roberto," Rosa said, as Roberto turned to go upstairs to see his brother. "Don't be long. Supper is nearly ready."

"What are we having?" asked Roberto.

"Baked corvina and sweet plantains."

"I love you, mother," said Roberto.

"Go see your brother, he's been waiting for you all day."

When Roberto opened the door to the bedroom and went inside, Carlos was sitting on his bed looking at the painting propped up against the wall at the foot of the bed.

"You know, Roberto, I have an idea where we will find the information we are looking for about Sobrino," Carlos said, not bothering to formally greet his brother.

"I missed you, Carlitos," said Roberto, sitting down next to his brother on the bed.

"I missed you as well brother. How long will you be home? Are you going to Africa?"

"No, I don't have to go to Africa. As a matter of fact I am stationed here in Havana, working at the Palace of the Revolution, and I have military leave every three months. So when I am home we can go fishing with Maykel. I don't have to report for duty for two weeks!"

"Tomorrow, can we go to the library?" Carlos asked.

"Absolutely. Tell me about your idea. Actually, we should wait until after supper. Mother is cooking corvina and sweet plantains. Let's eat now and we can sit outside on the terrace later and you can tell me."

"Okay, Roberto."

Before leaving the bedroom, Carlos carefully placed the painting under the mattress at the foot of the bed and went downstairs with Roberto to the kitchen for supper.

Their father had not spoken to the brothers again about the painting, and they were careful not to talk about it when he was at home, knowing how upset he would be to find out it was still in the house.

Excited about the opportunity to renew their search for information about Carlos Sobrino, and wanting to make the most of his time on military leave, Roberto left early the next morning with Carlos for the library. With a portion of the money Roberto had been paid for military service, the brothers made time to stop along the way at Cafe El Escorial, for a *colada* and *empanada*.

The quiet little cafe, located on the Plaza Vieja, was the perfect place to sit and relax in the early morning.

"Carlitos, you said your plan for when we arrive at the library is to go to the archive room where they keep all of the pre-revolution newspapers, like Diario de la Marina, right?"

"Exactly. If Sobrino won the National Painting award in 1957, two years before the revolution, there has to be a news article about him . . . something. It's too important," said Carlos.

"We asked about the newspaper archive room when we were there before and they said we were not allowed in there," said Roberto.

"I remember, but I think we should try again."

"All right. We have nothing to lose."

And with that the brothers finished their coffee and left for the library, putting the remainder of their pastry in a small sack to eat later.

Arriving at the library the brothers signed in, went past the military guards in the lobby, and straight to the newspaper archive room on the seventh floor.

Walking into the archive room Roberto noticed that it was the same clerk on duty behind the desk that had denied them entrance the first time they had been there.

"Roberto, it's the same man as before. He isn't going to let us in," said Carlos.

"I'll do the talking, Carlitos," whispered Roberto.

"*Buenos dias, senor,*" said Roberto.

"You have identification?" the clerk asked.

Taking out his wallet, Roberto slowly handed the clerk his military ID.

"I'm sorry but you need specific permission from the local Committee for the Defense of the Revolution to use this part of the library," the clerk said, handing the ID back to Roberto. The CDR was the principal counterrevolutionary investigative arm of the regime.

"You will have to leave," the clerk said.

Roberto taking his ID and putting it back into his wallet, remembered his Secret Service badge. Without responding and with no hesitation, he took the silver SS badge out of his wallet and held it directly in front of the clerk's face.

"We are here to do an investigation," said Roberto, continuing to hold the badge where the clerk could clearly see it. "I am going to need your name and ID number."

The clerk, clearly stunned, said nothing.

Roberto, trying not to appear surprised that his scheme seemed to be working, leaned forward placing both hands on the desk, and looked straight at the man.

"I said, I need your name and identification," said Roberto.

Incredibly, the impromptu plan worked. Saying nothing, the clerk handed his ID to Roberto, who pretended to study it intently.

"Thank you, *senor*," said Roberto. "Now if you would please let us in."

"What is the investigation concerning?" the clerk asked.

"It's classified," said Roberto, responding bluntly to the clerk. "We are not authorized to reveal anything about the investigation."

With that the clerk stood up from behind his desk, walked over to the archive room, unlocked the door, and let the brothers in.

"How long will you be?" the clerk asked.

"I will let you know when we are finished our investigation," said Roberto.

Not wanting the clerk to eavesdrop on their conversation, the brothers walked past several rows of shelving to a point in the room where they knew they would not be overheard.

"I hope this doesn't get us in trouble," said Carlos. "What if he tries to verify your story? I can't believe you did that."

"I'm not worried. Come on, let's see what we can find. Where do you want to look first?"

"Well, we know that Sobrino won the award in December of 1957, so let's start looking through everything we can find from December 1st and later. I'm certain it would have been in the news."

"I don't know how you know these things, Carlitos, but let's start looking," he said.

The brothers easily found the section that contained Diario de la Marina newspapers from December of 1957. As they methodically went through each one, beginning with December 1st, they were astonished to find numerous articles highly critical of the revolutionary forces fighting to overthrow the Batista regime.

"Roberto," whispered Carlos, "Look at these articles!"

"This is why they don't allow anyone in here," said Roberto. "The government doesn't want us to see any of this. Look, I'll start at the end of the month and work backwards. That way it will take only half the time. We need to work quickly."

No more than twenty minutes had passed when Roberto heard his brother drop one of the boxes containing the old, yellowed newspapers. He looked up to see Carlos holding a single paper, his eyes scanning quickly back and forth as he silently read to himself. When Carlos finished, he slowly raised his head and stared momentarily at his brother.

"I found something, Roberto."

"Let me see."

Roberto carefully took the paper from Carlos's hand and read the article.

"This is exactly what we have been looking for, Carlitos. It says where he lived in Havana, that his paintings were in the National Museum, mentions his family, and even gives their names. Write down the names of his children. His parents are probably no longer living. And don't forget the name of the neighborhood," said Roberto.

Carlos suspected the clerk might check to see that they had left everything in order and was careful to make sure the newspaper was in the correct box. After placing the newspaper back in its box, he then slid the document box into the shelf, exactly where he had found it.

Returning to the front desk, they thanked the clerk and informed him that they had completed their investigation and would be preparing an official report on their findings.

The man at the desk still seemed nervous and said nothing, choosing instead to immediately lock the door to the archive room. The brothers, thinking it might be best to avoid any further conversation with the man, took the elevator down to the lobby, signed out, and quickly left the library.

"I can't believe we found something," said Roberto. "I could never have done this without you."

"I believed in my friend Julio. I just knew he was telling us the truth. We should let him know."

"If we do, I think we should tell him not to talk with anyone about this," said Roberto.

"The article said that Sobrino was living in La Rampa Barrio at the time of the award. That is a small neighborhood, so I believe it will be easy to find someone there who knew him, maybe even a family member. The paper said he had children and that one of the daughters was also an artist. Here, I wrote her name down," said Carlos.

"We can go tomorrow with the painting . . . first thing in the morning," said Roberto.

"I don't think we should tell anyone, not even Mother. She'll worry too much," said Carlos.

Walking briskly now toward home the brothers spoke little. They could somehow sense the significance of their discovery and could scarcely believe their good fortune.

The following morning they awoke at sunrise, and before going down to the kitchen for coffee and something to eat, they decided not to leave the house until their father had left for work. If he were to see that the brothers still had the painting, there would be no chance of them going to look for Sobrino's family.

After coffee and pastry, and with their father safely out of the house and on his way to work, they carefully wrapped the painting in newspaper and then in a small burlap sack. The painting, only 20 by 30 centimeters, was inconspicuous and would not draw the attention of anyone as they made their way through the streets of Havana. Believing their mother would ask too many questions about their plans for the day, they uncharacteristically left the house without saying goodbye, thinking it might be easier to explain their way back in when they returned.

La Rampa Barrio was an hour walk or so from their home in Santos Suarez. After arriving they planned to go directly to the neighborhood post office, knowing the postmaster would have the names and addresses of anyone living there who had a permanent address.

The post office in La Rampa was a small, dilapidated concrete building directly across the street from the Mariana Grajales memorial park.

With only a few older people waiting outside for the daily mail to arrive, and no one inside, the brothers walked up to the counter where they were met by an elderly woman, the only employee on duty.

"*Buenos dias, senora,*" said Roberto. "We are trying to find the family of a friend of ours who has passed away and we understand they live in this barrio. We have something we need to return to the family."

Roberto showed the burlap sack to the woman, and said, "Our friend was a famous painter, and this belongs to his daughter."

Carlos, looking more than a little surprised upon hearing his brother's cleverly concocted story, tried to remain calm and said nothing.

"What is the name of this person?" the attendant asked, seemingly not the least bit suspicious.

"Her name is Anabela Sobrino. But I do not know if she is married. Sobrino is her maiden name," said Carlos.

"There are two Sobrino families in La Rampa, one on Avenida Paseo and one on Calle 15. I can give you the addresses if you like."

"Thank you, *senora*. We appreciate your help," said Roberto.

Back on the street in front of the post office, the brothers quickly decided to go first to the address on Calle 15, which was a little closer.

"I can't believe you just made up that story!" said Carlos as they began to walk the three blocks toward Calle 15.

"People are very suspicious, Carlitos. She probably wasn't going to give us any information unless we had a good explanation why we were looking for the Sobrinos."

"Well, it worked. Here is the street," said Carlos, as they turned the corner on to Calle 15. "We need to go to the right, maybe two blocks."

"Here is the house, 1465. Doesn't look like anyone is home," said Carlos.

Roberto knocked loudly on the wooden door and stepped back on to the street, looking up at the old facade with its faded yellow paint and crumbling iron balcony railings.

After several minutes a middle-aged woman dressed in a brightly colored, floral dress appeared in one of the second-floor balconies.

"Who is it?" she asked, leaning over the rusted iron railing and looking down at the brothers.

"I am Roberto Ramos, and this is my brother, Carlitos. We are looking for Anabela Sobrino, the daughter of Carlos Sobrino, the painter. Do you know her?"

Momentarily staring down at the brothers, the woman didn't answer and suddenly disappeared back into the building.

"I told you, Carlitos, people are suspicious. What do we do now?"

Noticing an older gentleman sitting in front of a house several doors down the street, Carlos suggested they ask him if he knew who lived in the house at 1465.

No sooner had they begun walking in the direction of the old man, the brothers heard the door to the house behind them unlock. They turned around to see the woman in the floral dress from the balcony, standing in the doorway with one hand on her hip and the other holding the door open slightly.

"Do you work for the government?" she asked.

"Uh, no, no we don't. We are friends of Dr. Julio Martinez from Santos Suarez. We are looking for the family of his friend, Carlos Sobrino. This is a painting that Mr. Sobrino painted in 1953." Roberto, taking the painting out from under his arm, held it out so the woman could see it. "We are trying to determine its authenticity and value. It was given to us by Mr. Martinez. He said it was quite valuable, but in researching Mr. Sobrino, we've found very little about the artist. Do you know the Sobrinos?"

The woman stared at the brothers for a moment. "Come inside," she said.

Following the woman inside, they passed through the doorway into a dimly lit hallway and into the living room.

"Sit down, please," the woman said.

As the brothers sat down and began to look around the room, they noticed hanging on the walls, numerous small paintings done in a style that appeared to be identical to *El Saxofonista*.

"Roberto, look at these paintings," whispered Carlos.

"Were these paintings done by...."

Roberto, curious to know if the paintings in the room were done by Carlos Sobrino, was suddenly interrupted by the woman.

"I am Anabela Sobrino," the woman said.

Roberto looked at Carlos who was staring at the woman.

"Anabela, it is a great pleasure," said Roberto. "Your father, through this painting, has inspired us to learn about the great artists of Cuba."

"It is a pleasure, Roberto," the woman said, beginning to relax somewhat. "Unfortunately, there are a lot of important artists from Cuba that you will never know."

"What do you mean?" asked Carlos.

"The government doesn't want you to know about certain ones whom they consider to be counterrevolutionary," said Anabela.

"You mean like your father?" asked Roberto.

"Yes, like my father. He hated Fidel and he hated communism. He wanted to be free. Free to express himself through his painting. So he left Cuba in 1969 and never returned. I never saw him again."

Taking the painting out of the bag and unwrapping the newspaper, Roberto handed Anabela the painting and asked, "But why would the regime object to a painting of a musician?"

"What is the title of the painting?" she asked Roberto.

"*El Saxofonista*. It is written on the back," replied Roberto, showing her the back of the canvas.

"Saxophonists play jazz music, the freest form of creative music, and jazz is American. Fidel hates America."

"Music? They're threatened by music?" asked Roberto.

"Well," said Anabela, gesturing with her hands, "painting, music, dance, literature, film, theater—anything in their opinion that could deliver a counter-revolutionary message."

"My brother and I had great difficulty finding out any information about your father or his work," said Roberto.

"I'm not surprised. You see my father chose exile over living under communist rule, and the result was he became persona non grata in the eyes of the regime. His paintings were removed from the National Gallery and there was no longer any mention of him in the public record."

"Then you must know of many other artists, writers, or musicians that have found themselves in the same situation as your father," said Roberto.

"Yes Roberto, there are many. Unfortunately, too many to remember," she replied.

Looking in the direction of his brother, Roberto could see that Carlos was becoming uncomfortable and had reached his limit.

"Anabela, I think we should be going. It has been an honor, truly. We will never forget this moment, and we'll forever cherish this amazing work of your father's," said Roberto.

"It has been my pleasure, boys. You should know something though. It is illegal to buy or sell the work of people like my father, who have been banned by the government. You need to be very careful."

"We will be careful," said Carlos.

With that the brothers stood up, each warmly embracing Anabela, and after carefully repacking the painting in the burlap sack, they left the Sobrino family house and headed back down the street toward home.

"Remember, be careful, and keep in touch," said Anabela, waving goodbye from the doorway.

"I can't believe what just happened," said Carlos.

"I know, I know. We would have never found Anabela though if not for your idea to look in the newspaper archives, Carlitos," said Roberto.

"Yeah, and you showing your Secret Service badge to the clerk, pretending to be doing an investigation," joked Carlos.

"This has been a good day," said Roberto.

"I don't ever want to sell the painting," said Carlos.

"I don't either, Carlitos. You know, tomorrow I believe I would like to go to the National Art Museum," said Roberto.

"What for?" asked Carlos.

"I want to look at all of the other paintings there, and I also want to ask them why they no longer have any Sobrinos on display. You know, to see what they say. Obviously, now I know why. Remember the newspaper article from the library said they had three of his works hanging in the museum."

"I don't think that is a very good idea," said Carlos.

"What are they going to do? Arrest us for asking about an artist that no one seems to know anything about? I just want to see what sort of answer they give," said Roberto.

"Yeah, and if they do try to arrest you, then you can just show them your SS badge," laughed Carlos.

When they arrived home the brothers quickly made their way to the bedroom, carefully hiding the painting again under the mattress. Late in the day and nearly dark, their mother had just finished preparing supper for the family. It was a lovely evening with no sign of a late day shower and there was a light, north breeze coming in off the ocean. With only a few days remaining on his military leave, Roberto and Carlos chose to spend the rest of the night enjoying the company of the family on the terrace under a brilliant autumn full moon.

Sometime during the early morning, just before dawn, a strong norther blew in off the ocean and across the city, bringing with it a torrential downpour of rain, lightning, and heavy tropical thunder.

Awakened by the noise from the storm, Roberto had already dressed and had quietly made his way in the dark down to the kitchen. He was sitting having coffee with his mother when Carlos joined them.

"What do you think, Carlitos? You going with me to the Museo Nacional today?" asked Roberto.

"I don't think so. The thought of asking why the museum removed the work of Sobrino makes me nervous, and besides we already know why."

"It's not right though, Carlitos. The people of Cuba should know who Carlos Sobrino was, and that he was a great artist. He is part of our heritage. What right does Fidel have to say that Carlos Sobrino never existed?" said Roberto, raising his voice.

"Roberto!" Rosa said sharply.

"Someone is declared an enemy of the state because he paints an American jazz musician? It's ridiculous," said Roberto, as he stood up behind his chair. "You know," Roberto said, pausing slightly, "you can wipe out your opponents, but if you do it unjustly you become eligible for being wiped out yourself."

"Roberto, I don't want you saying things like that," said Rosa.

"I didn't say it, I am only repeating it."

"I guarantee whoever said it is no longer living in Cuba," said Rosa.

"The person who said it is dead. But at least he died on his own terms," said Roberto.

"And so who is that?" asked Rosa.

"Ernesto Hemingway. I'm leaving for the Museum!"

Rosa, by now clearly upset by the conversation, followed Roberto to the front door and watched him as he walked down the street.

"You be careful!" she said loudly.

The museum was not yet open when Roberto arrived, so he decided to wait in the Granma Memorial Park across the street. The park was established as a memorial to "La Granma," the 60-foot-long vessel Fidel Castro used to transport 82 fighters from Mexico to Cuba in November of 1956 as part of the effort to overthrow Fulgenico Batista. Coincidentally, it was built by the same shipyard that built the deep-sea fishing boat, the Pilar, for Ernest Hemingway in 1934.

When the doors to the museum opened, Roberto, along with several groups of uniformed school children, who had also been waiting patiently in the park, entered the building. He decided to spend his time looking through the handful of rooms containing paintings from the late Spanish Colonial era through the Republican period.

Having previously searched unsuccessfully for works by Carlos Sobrino, and having been told firsthand by Anabela Sobrino that everything done by her father had been removed from the museum, he was curious to see what sort of subject matter the Communist regime had approved for exhibition.

Passing from one dimly lit room of paintings to the next, Roberto began to realize intuitively that all he was seeing were poorly done paintings glorifying early attempts by the communists to overthrow Batista, along with idealized depictions of rural life in Cuba from the early years of the Republic.

Remembering as a young child the stories told to him by his grandparents about the 19th century Independence Movement, the Spanish American War, and the Sergeant's Revolt, during the time when the family lived on a farm in the countryside outside Havana, he felt certain that surely there must exist many works done by the great artists from that time that should have been here in the National Museum of Cuba.

I have seen enough today, he thought to himself. Not having eaten since early morning and feeling hungry, he decided to leave the museum and make his way back home without confronting anyone about the Sobrino paintings. He had only one more day before he needed to report for duty at the Palace of the Revolution and wanted to spend the time with his family.

As he passed by the receptionist at the front of the hall near the entrance to the museum, she looked up briefly. "*Buenas tardes, senor,*" she said. "I hope you enjoyed your visit, and please come back."

"*Gracias, senora,*" replied Roberto. "I'm sure I will come back, and you know, I learned a lot more today about my country than I expected. *Buenas tardes.*"

Because it would be a little cooler near the ocean, Roberto chose to walk the short distance to the sea and make his way home by way of La Avenida Malecon. It was one of his favorite places to walk in Old Havana. The late day breeze always blew from the north this time of year, making it feel cooler by the sea wall on the northern edge of the city.

Soon the fishermen would be coming in from the Gulf Stream, he thought, and if his friend Maykel had been out fishing, stopping by the harbor would give him an opportunity to see what Maykel had caught.

As Roberto neared the area of the harbor where Maykel docked his boat, he could see at a distance a group of locals gathered in front of the sea wall along the Malecon. Many of the people living in the area enjoyed going down to the docks in the late afternoon, checking to see what the fishermen had caught that day.

Making his way through the small crowd of people, many of whom were talking loudly and pointing in the direction of the boat, Roberto could finally see why the people were so excited. Wedged against the inside of the washboard on the port side was the steely, blue-colored tail of an enormous blue marlin. The massive head and bill were leaning vertically against the washboard on the opposite interior side of the cockpit.

The fish looked disproportionally large for the size of Maykel's boat, Roberto thought.

"*Hola,* Maykel," said Roberto. "I can't believe you were able to bring that fish onboard, just the two of you."

"Fortunately the sea was a little choppy today. We were able to slip it over the stern at the bottom of a steep swell with the help of the block and tackle," replied Maykel.

Maykel and his elderly friend had already begun to fillet the fish, realizing it would have been impossible to lift the fish out of the boat and onto the dock before cleaning it.

"Maykel, I thought you didn't like to catch the blue ones?" Roberto said.

"I don't when the *dorado* are biting. They take too long to land. I kept hoping he'd throw the hook, but it never happened. I could have used your help today Roberto."

"I'm sorry I missed all the fun. Any chance I could have a few steaks for the family?" asked Roberto.

"*Por supuesto que si.* You know that," replied Maykel. "Gregorio, can you give Roberto a bag of steaks? Roberto, do you know my old friend Gregorio?"

The old man was lean and dark. He looked directly at Roberto with piercing blue eyes, and his skin had the appearance of thick old leather, the result of countless days spent fishing under the intense tropical sun, in the Gulf Stream, off the north coast of Cuba.

"*Mucho gusto, Senor* Gregorio. We have never met but I know that you are a legend here and in Cojimar," said Roberto.

"*Mucho gusto,* Roberto. Maykel tells me you are a good fisherman. Here, take this. This fish was healthy, thick, and quite heavy, and the meat is dark, full of fat, and very sweet. Perhaps some day we can fish together with Maykel," said Gregorio.

"It would be my dream," said Roberto. "I need to be going, Maykel. It's late and tomorrow I return to military duty. It was my pleasure *Señor* Gregorio, and thank you for the fish," said Roberto.

As Roberto turned to pick up his bag of marlin steaks, Maykel shouted. "Don't forget about your old friend Maykel. We need to go fishing before I am too old and no longer able to do battle when the big ones come."

"I will not forget. Next time I am on leave, we'll go out. We'll take *Senor* Fuentes, and catch an even bigger one, Maykel. *Abrazo!*"

III

The next several months of military duty for Roberto were uneventful and passed quickly. Roberto was reassigned to security duty at Punto Cero, the lavish private residence of Fidel, located in the former Havana Biltmore Yacht Club, west of Havana, that was completely unknown to ordinary Cubans.

Security at Punto Cero was a massive and complicated affair, made up of three concentric security rings consisting of nearly five thousand armed personnel. The size and scope of the security operation was a direct reflection of Fidel's increasing level of paranoia and fear.

Much of Roberto's free time was spent in training for the annual National Taekwondo Championships held in Havana. The national team was strong, but typically fell short when competing on the international stage against countries like North Korea, China, or Iran. Due in large part to the lack of collective national experience, Cuba simply didn't have the coaches and trainers needed to prepare their athletes for the next level.

Recognizing the need for better coaching, President Castro turned to Kim Il-Sung of North Korea for help in developing the Cuban team. President Kim was more than happy to help his good friend and communist ally in Cuba, immediately sending the top two Taekwondo coaches in North Korea to Cuba.

Roberto, now having access to advanced high-level training techniques, was excited for the opportunity. He quickly realized this would mean he would be able to improve his conditioning and competitive skills much more quickly. He would ultimately realize unimaginable benefits outside of the organized competitive arena as well.

Late one afternoon after a long training session Roberto was ordered to report to security headquarters where he was told that the head of security, Colonel Alejandro Charon, wanted to see him. He had never met Colonel Charon and couldn't imagine why he was being summoned.

When he entered the office there were two men in the room. A tall, well built, Afro-Cuban man was sitting behind a large desk. Roberto immediately recognized him as the Colonel by the insignias on his uniform. Roberto thought he recognized the other man, but he couldn't be sure.

"Ramos, thank you for coming. Please sit down," said the Colonel.

"Thank you, sir," replied Roberto.

"Ramos, this is Antonio Castro."

"Sir, it is a pleasure," Roberto said, as he stood to address the son of the President.

"My pleasure, as well. Please sit down. There is no need to be formal here," replied Antonio.

"What do you want from me?" Roberto asked nervously, more than a little confused by the sudden and rather casual nature of the meeting.

"Relax, Ramos," the Colonel said, seeing that Roberto was uncomfortable. "Antonio is a serious athlete and is in need of a personal trainer."

"But what does that have to do with me?" Roberto asked.

"I understand that you are serious as well. Very dedicated and disciplined. And, like Antonio, are a talented footballer. Antonio needs a trainer. What do you think?" asked the Colonel.

"I would be interested, certainly. But I am not sure if I would have the time. My security duties here don't leave any extra time."

"That will not be a problem, Roberto," said Antonio. "We will have time every day to train. Along with time for matches on the Palace field."

"When would you like to start, Antonio?" asked Roberto.

"We can start tomorrow morning if that's okay," said Antonio. "8:30, at the gym?"

"I can put together a training program, but I need to understand what you want to work on. What areas you are weak in," said Roberto.

"I need to improve my speed and explosive power, and of course my overall fitness level," said Antonio.

"I understand. We can make that happen, but you need to work hard. You need to suffer if you want to be good," replied Roberto.

"Okay then. See you tomorrow," said Antonio.

With that Roberto thanked Antonio and Colonel Charon and turned to leave.

"Roberto, I will not disappoint you," said Antonio.

Roberto turned around, paused for a moment, looked directly at Antonio, and said "I trust that you will not Antonio. Until tomorrow."

Their training session the following morning went better than expected and Roberto was excited for the opportunity to work so closely with the son of the President.

Antonio was a willing student and quickly realized that with Roberto's knowledge and the disciplined approach he demanded, he couldn't help but become a better footballer.

Roberto and Antonio had much in common besides athletics. Antonio was just a few years younger than Roberto and they were both the fourth of five sons. Their fathers had both fought against the Batista regime, although in different organizations, and with differing political philosophies.

Roberto's father, Guillermo, was a member of the violent anti-Batista group known as the Directorio Revolucionario Estudiantil. The DRE was a Catholic student group opposed to the Cuban dictator Fulgencio Batista. Guillermo had been tortured by the Batista regime in 1956, at a time when Fidel, after returning to Cuba by sea on the Granma, was just beginning his guerrilla campaign against Batista from the Sierra Maestra in southeastern Cuba.

Following the death of the DRE's leader, Jose Antonio Echeverria, who died in a shootout with police, shortly after delivering his now famous speech in 1957, "Three Minutes of Truth", on the National Radio Station of Cuba, the group joined forces with the 26th Of July Movement in the Escambray Mountains under the leadership of Che Guevara.

However, soon after the revolution, the original principal members became disillusioned with the Castro regime and reformed the DRE at the University of Havana. Their opposition to communism, and in particular Castro's increasing political alignment with the Soviet Union, led to their expulsion by Castro from the University, and ultimately the country, eventually setting up a new headquarters in Miami, Florida, where the group developed connections with the Central Intelligence Agency.

These events would leave Roberto's father very bitter and forever opposed to the regime, and Fidel in particular. Guillermo never spoke to Roberto about the DRE, Fidel, or the communists. It was extremely dangerous to do so. And even though Roberto's father rarely spoke about his early anti-Batista efforts, Roberto somehow knew, even from the beginning of the revolution, that his father had never trusted Fidel, a fact that would eventually influence Roberto's own opinion of Fidel.

Over the following months Roberto and Antonio Castro spent countless hours together, in the gym and on the football field. The field was a private, meticulously groomed playing field near the palace, available only to high-ranking officers and anyone fortunate enough to be invited by Fidel. It was the finest football field in Cuba, and ordinary Cubans, even though they had paid for it, knew nothing of its existence.

Roberto's commitment to excellence and his attention to detail in every aspect of his training was contagious. Antonio was eager to show Roberto that simply because he was the son of the Prime Minister, he did not expect any sort of preferential treatment. From the beginning of their friendship, it was clear they both genuinely enjoyed each other's company, and they quickly became good friends.

Roberto was careful at first not to talk politics with Antonio, and never spoke about Antonio's father, Fidel. Even though Roberto trusted Antonio, he was still unsure about Antonio's commitment to the ideals of his father's regime, that is until one day, Antonio, clearly upset about something, mentioned he'd had a disagreement with his father, and that it had turned into a serious argument. It became clear to Roberto from that point on that Antonio did not enjoy the same sort of close relationship with his father that his four brothers did. Roberto could sense that things were different in their friendship as a result of the conversation. Roberto could tell that Antonio trusted him implicitly, and that he was a deeply loyal friend. It was a critical turning point.

Several days had passed and Roberto couldn't stop thinking about the conversation he'd had with Antonio regarding Antonio's disagreement with his father, Fidel. It was beginning to affect his mood and Antonio took notice.

After a long week of training and several hours playing football late one Friday afternoon, Roberto and Antonio decided to drink a couple of Cristals together in the officers' club.

The officers' club was located in a wing of the old Havana Biltmore Yacht Club and was decorated with a bizarre mix of 1920s' pre-revolution ostentation and poorly done portraits of the principal characters from the communist revolution in 1959.

Roberto was uncomfortable sitting among the officers. He had little in common with any of them. Strangely, upon sitting down, he immediately thought about all of the old Cuban Master works of art that must have hung on the walls in the great room. His discomfort only added to the uneasiness he felt as he sensed that Antonio knew something was troubling him.

"Roberto, you're not yourself lately. Is it Charon? He can be difficult, I know. I've had issues with him from time to time."

"No, it's not Charon. I agree he's a difficult person, but that's not what's been bothering me. I've been thinking about your father and the problems you have with him."

"My father?" asked Antonio. "The problem I have with him is, he thinks he's always right, about everything. He'd make a terrible philosopher. Always gathering evidence to support his political theories rather than developing theories from the evidence. And if you challenge him, it immediately becomes personal."

"You know Antonio, everyone has ideas, theories as you say. But here, in Cuba, you're not free to express those ideas. You can't write whatever you want. You can't play the kind of music you want. I know you can't paint what you want. Nothing, without approval from the government first."

"What do you mean paint whatever you want? Artists are free to express themselves any way they want. Most simply chose revolutionary subject matter," said Antonio.

"That's absolutely not the case, Antonio. I know this for a fact. I have a painting done by an artist named Carlos Sobrino. He won the National Painting Award in 1957. At one time he was famous here. All over Cuba. And now no one knows who he was or anything about his work."

"Why is he no longer famous. Is he living here in Cuba?" asked Antonio.

"No, he died in Spain in 1971. He had to leave Cuba because he was opposed to much of the regime's ideology. And because he left Cuba, he was deemed *persona non grata* by the regime, and his paintings were removed from the National Gallery. Now it is nearly impossible to find any reference to him or his works."

"From what you are telling me, Roberto, this Sobrino was a traitor."

"A traitor to what?" asked Roberto, slightly annoyed. "He loved his country, his homeland. But not in the way the government demanded. You can't question his loyalty to the country he loved simply because his political philosophy is not aligned with yours. Sobrino was not a traitor. Your father is the traitor." Roberto paused slightly, gaging Antonio's reaction to his bold characterization of Fidel, before continuing. "He is a traitor to the ideals of freedom for the Cuban people. He doesn't care about the average Cuban. He cares about absolute power and money. Just look around you. This was all paid for by the hard work and sweat of the ordinary Cuban worker. But the average Cuban will never see the inside of these walls. He professes to be a communist and he's living like an 18th century king. If he believed in freedom for Cuba, why did he change the motto on the peso from, *Patria y Libertad* to *Patria o Muerte*?"

Antonio ignored the question, choosing instead to warn Roberto against publicly denouncing his father.

"Roberto, you need to be careful what you say. And lower your voice. Whatever you do, don't talk to anyone about this. You remember the two officers that died recently in Nicaragua? And when their bodies arrived home they were given a public funeral with full military honors? My father had them killed. I don't know the details, but they did or said something that angered him. That could easily happen to you. I'm telling you, no one is safe. You need to be careful."

"I understand." Roberto paused, peeling the paper label from his beer. "But do you understand Antonio, that in Cuba now, today, everyone is condemned to silence. And if you disagree with Fidel, even if you are popular among the people, you end up like Cienfuegos."

"Camilo Cienfuegos' death was an accident. You know that," said Antonio.

"Sure, and everyone that disputed the governments claim of it being an accident also wound up dead. You just said yourself, no one is safe. Look, I understand you are in a difficult situation. You need to play the part. But I need to know, where does that leave us? I mean he's your father."

"As I have told you recently, I don't have much of a relationship with my father. Honestly, as a person, I don't particularly like him. But he's my father, so I guess I need to play the part, as you say. Listen, you are my brother, Roberto. I take our friendship very seriously. I will never do anything to jeopardize your safety. I mean that."

"I believe you, and I appreciate your loyalty as a friend. I have a hard time hiding my feelings sometimes. I suspect that Colonel Charon has noticed," said Roberto.

"He's a bad person. Be careful around him," said Antonio. "I'm sorry, but I don't think we should talk about this any more. Especially in here."

Roberto and Antonio never again spoke about Fidel, the Communist regime, or Roberto's increasing disillusionment with the Communist ideology. They continued to remain close, with both men careful never to do anything that would jeopardize their mutual pledge of loyalty.

Fortunately, his upcoming scheduled military leave could not have come at a better time. Feeling like he was at an emotional crossroads, he looked forward to time away from military duty, and even his athletic training with Antonio. Thinking the much-needed break would help him to clear his head, Roberto left Punto Cero, excited to see his family, and especially his older brother, Carlos.

As he made his way toward home, through the dusty streets of Old Havana, he thought about the painting he and Carlos were given by Julio. The painting had inspired him to look at the world around him in a way that he had never known.

He noticed the little things now that he had previously overlooked and often took for granted. There was the old woman in the Parque Cervantes he passed on his way home, who patiently swept the vermillion-colored poinciana flower petals that had fallen overnight, from the sidewalks in the old park. The curiously stylized graffiti that began showing up on the walls of numerous abandoned buildings throughout Old Havana. The late 20th century urban street art that contrasted starkly with the formal looking Cuban baroque and Neoclassical architecture. And the dignified elderly man entering La Bodeguita del Medio, with a worn out looking but still wonderfully functional double bass preparing for an evening of traditional Afro-Cuban jazz.

Roberto realized that even though he was not an artist, he was beginning to see the world as an artist sees it. The feeling he realized, was powerful and he felt an overwhelming sense of freedom, similar to the way he felt the first time he examined closely the painting from Julio.

Arriving at the house of his parents just as the sun was setting, Roberto quietly made his way around to the kitchen door at the back of the house, wanting to surprise his mother whom he knew would be preparing an elaborate end-of-the-week Friday supper for the family.

When he reached the opening, he carefully peered around the edge of the open door jam. He could see his mother slowly stirring a large pot of *arroz congri*. The Cuban black beans and rice was one of his favorite dishes. Her back was to him, and she had not heard him as he approached the house. Standing to the side and just out of sight, he threw his military garrison hat through the open door onto the kitchen floor just behind her.

This startled her, but only for a moment, realizing who had thrown the hat into the kitchen. She carefully picked the hat up and pretended to dust it off. Looking up and toward the door she threw it back outside and said, laughing slightly, "I'll let you know when you can come in."

Roberto knew she was not serious, and he stepped into the doorway where his mother could see him. "What about now? Can I come in?" Roberto asked, smiling.

"Of course, *mi hijo*. We missed you terribly," said Rosa.

"I missed you as well, *Madre*. I would rather be here, fishing with Maykel and studying art and literature."

"Studying art?" asked Rosa, a bit surprised. "You told me the military is an easy life, especially at Punto Cero."

"Yes, it's easy for me, but the work is meaningless. I'm protecting someone who doesn't deserve to be protected," said Roberto.

"Don't start with that Roberto. You're home now. You need to relax. Have some cold coconut water," said Rosa. Reaching into the old, rusted icebox Roberto's mother pulled out a large fresh coconut. With a well-worn, wooden-handled coconut reamer she deftly opened the coconut and poured the cold, fresh, somewhat cloudy liquid into a glass for her son.

"Here," she said, as she handed him the glass of coconut water, "this will calm you down."

"You forgot something, *Madre*," said Roberto.

"Let me guess, the Havana Club," said Rosa sarcastically. "Enough with the rum Roberto. You are obsessed with the rum."

"The best ideas come while sipping rum."

"Another one of your silly quotes, I am sure."

"Yes, another one of my silly quotes. But it's a good one, don't you think? And besides, it's true."

"There is some in the cabinet beside the ice box."

"Some day," said Roberto, as he added some of the dark amber rum to his coconut water, "I am going to have a *coleccion de ron*. A big one."

"Everything you are going to do is always the biggest, Roberto."

"The world is a big place and there's a lot to learn. Many wonderful things to experience."

"Yes, but you live in Cuba, and Cuba is an island. You can only go so far," said Rosa as she turned and attended once more to the large pot of black beans and rice.

"I can go as far as I want," said Roberto.

"By the way, Carlitos said a woman stopped by here the other day looking for you. He said it was about some paintings," said Rosa. "She thought maybe you knew someone who might want to buy them. Anyway, something like that."

"Stopped by here, at the house? What was her name?" asked Roberto.

"I think he said her first name was Anabela. I don't remember her last name," said Rosa.

"Was it Anabela Sobrino?" asked Roberto excitedly.

"It might have been. I don't remember. You need to ask your brother. He should be coming home soon. I asked him to go to the market for some fresh bread," said Rosa.

Roberto could scarcely believe what his mother had just told him. He had been thinking recently about the painting Julio had given him and his brother, and thought there must be many more people like Julio, who loved art and in particular art from the time before the revolution. Surely, he thought to himself, there must be many old paintings in Havana from the time before the revolution.

"You should take your things upstairs, Roberto," said his mother. "If you have laundry to do, leave it with me."

"Thank you, Mother," said Roberto.

Just as Roberto turned to go up the stairs to his bedroom, he noticed, even before his brother came into the kitchen, the unmistakable smell of the warm, fresh loaves of bread his brother had brought home from the corner bakery.

"Roberto!" Carlos shouted. "When did you arrive?"

"Just now. I was talking with *Madre*. She said Anabela Sobrino stopped by. Was it her?" asked Roberto.

"Yes, it was Anabela. I was a little nervous speaking with her. She wanted to know if we knew someone who might be interested in a couple paintings from her father's collection," said Carlos.

"What did you tell her?" asked Roberto.

"I told her I didn't but maybe you knew someone. I remember she said it is illegal to buy and sell paintings, so I was a little worried," said Carlos. "And besides, I don't have that kind of money."

"I trust her, Carlitos. She isn't going to put us in any kind of danger. You know, it's funny but I have been thinking a lot recently about Julio's painting. There must be many artists like Sobrino whom the government has labeled counterrevolutionary, you know . . . enemies of the state . . . because of their political views. I would like to meet with her," said Roberto.

"I told her you would be home this weekend. We could call her. I have her phone number," said Carlos.

"Wait a minute, boys," said Rosa. "I believe you should think this through a little more."

"All I want to do is speak with her and find out what she wants," said Roberto. "You worry too damn much mother."

"You don't need to swear. This isn't a military barracks, and I don't need a commentary from you on what I need or need not do," Rosa said sternly.

"Sorry, I'm just a little excited," said Roberto.

"I don't understand where all this passion comes from," said Rosa.

"Like I said, the world is a big place, a wonderful place, and I want to experience as much as possible," said Roberto.

"We can talk about this later. How about a beer, Roberto?" asked Carlos.

"Sure. We will call Anabela later this evening," said Roberto.

After supper, Roberto spent the remainder of the evening with his family, catching up on all of the news from the neighborhood. It felt good to be in the company of the people who truly loved him and away from the pressure he felt from the people in the military who were always suspicious and who trusted no one.

Before going to bed Roberto called the phone number Anabela Sobrino had given Carlos earlier in the week. Upon calling a young boy answered the phone and said nothing except to confirm that Roberto had in fact called the number for Anabela. When she came to the phone and said hello, he could immediately sense she was a bit nervous and perhaps had second thoughts about meeting with Roberto. She did not know Roberto was now in the military working security at Punto Cero.

"*Hola*, Anabela," said Roberto. "My brother told me you stopped by our house the other day. He said perhaps you were interested in selling several paintings from your father's collection."

"I was thinking about it, yes," said Anabela. "I have very little money, and aside from some family jewelry I inherited, which I would like to keep, the paintings are all I have left."

"Are you still interested in selling any of them?" asked Roberto.

"I didn't know you were in the military," she said.

"I understand your concern, but you have nothing to worry about Anabela. You remember the painting my brother and I brought to your house when we first met? It means everything to me. I think about it nearly every day when I am away in the military. If I can afford to buy a painting from your father's collection it would be a great honor," said

Roberto.

"I appreciate you telling me this. My father was a great man, Roberto. His work deserves to be recognized here in Cuba. I can meet you tomorrow and we can talk about what I have to sell. I go to La Bodeguita del Medio sometimes to listen to music. Do you know where that is?" asked Anabela.

"Yes, it is on La Calle Empredrado. In fact, it is near the Museo de Arte Colonial," said Roberto. "Since my brother and I acquired your father's painting, we have been to the museum many times."

"We can meet in the evening, at 6:00, if that's okay. The music starts then and people will be less likely to eavesdrop on our conversation with the music playing," said Anabela.

"I'll see you then. And Anabela, I am very grateful for this opportunity. You have no idea."

"Okay, we'll talk tomorrow.," said Anabela.

With that, Roberto hung up the phone. Excited about his meeting with Anabela, he had trouble sleeping that night and kept trying to imagine what the paintings looked like that she was interested in selling, and who the artists may have been.

The following afternoon when it came time to leave for his meeting with Anabela Sobrino, Roberto was unable to find his brother Carlos anywhere in the house. He finally found his mother sitting outside on the front stoop, talking with his sister Ana, and their cousin, Grisele.

"*Madre*, have you seen Carlitos? I'm leaving to meet *Senorita* Sobrino, and he said yesterday he wanted to go with me," said Roberto.

"He told me this morning he changed his mind. You know how nervous he becomes when he has to go out in public. I think it was too much for him to deal with. When will you be home?" asked Rosa.

"I don't know. Probably late. I'll have something to eat at La Bodeguita. I'll see you tomorrow," said Roberto.

Roberto was in a hurry to leave. Having spent time looking for his brother he would now be late for his meeting. He wanted Anabela to know he was serious and being late was not going to convince her of that.

When he arrived at La Bodeguita del Medio, he found Anabela sitting alone at a small, dimly lit table near the foot of the stairs in the back of the bar underneath a large red banner on which was printed the iconic photograph of Che Guevara, wearing his black beret. Hanging on the wall just behind the table was an old, yellowed photograph of Ernest Hemingway, along with his wife Mary, and Spencer Tracy, the actor who played Santiago in "The Old Man and The Sea."

Anabela was staring down at her mojito and did not notice Roberto when he walked up to the table.

"*Buenas noches*, Anabela," said Roberto. "Sorry I'm late."

"That's okay," said Anabela, looking up from her drink. "Thank you for coming. It's not as though this is an unpleasant place to be, so I didn't mind waiting. I love this place. It reminds me of my father somehow. It makes me happy. Please sit down," said Anabela.

"The music is amazing. This is the first time I have been inside La Bodeguita del Medio," said Roberto.

"They only play traditional music in this place. I've heard many famous musicians play here. All the great ones. Ibrahim Ferrer, Ruben Gonzalez, Compay Segundo, Eliades Ochoa, all of them. You want something to drink?" asked Anabela as the waiter approached the table.

"Yes, I'll have a Havana Club, *Anejo Especial*, with a little coconut water, and two cubes of ice. *Gracias, senor*," Roberto said to the waiter.

"Roberto, I'll be honest with you. I don't want to sell any of my father's paintings, but I have little money. If you can pay me a fair price, I have three paintings I would be willing to part with," said Anabela.

Just then the waiter returned to the table with Roberto's drink. Anabela quickly changed the subject back to the music.

"Yes, I have heard this group before. They're fantastic," said Anabela.

The waiter, looking briefly at Anabela, said nothing and placed Roberto's drink on the table in front of him.

"You are worried about the waiter overhearing our conversation?" asked Roberto as the waiter left their table and returned to the front of the bar.

"I trust no one Roberto, especially in a bar. Anyway, I have three paintings. I brought photographs of each one to show you," said Anabela.

Anabela carefully took the 3"x 5" photos out of her purse and handed them to Roberto without looking at them.

Roberto took the photographs from Anabela, and before placing them on the table, moved his drink to one side, being careful to wipe up the small pool of condensation left by his glass on the table with one of the paper napkins the waiter had given him.

One at a time he spread the photographs out on the table. Not speaking, Roberto slowly examined the three photographs lying in front of him. After several minutes he looked up at Anabela, who was staring at her mojito and had not noticed that Roberto was looking at her.

"Anabela, are you certain you want to sell these paintings? I mean they are magnificent. You would never be able to replace them," said Roberto.

"I realize that, but I've had them a long time, ever since my father left for Spain twenty years ago. And like I said, I need the money desperately."

"What can you tell me about them?"

Pointing to the one on Roberto's left, she said, "This one is the best. It is entitled, *Bembe a la Caridad*, and was done by Manuel Mesa Hermida, in 1951. It is very small painting, Roberto."

What about this one?" Roberto asked, pointing to the one in the middle. "What is the name of this one?"

"It is simply called, *Un Retrato de Nina*, done by Oscar Garcia Rivera, painted in 1945."

"And the third one?" asked Roberto.

"It is entitled, *Retrato*, by Leopoldo Romanach. I believe it was done in 1930. Romanach, as you may know, was considered the father of Cuban painting. My father bought the painting from him in the 1930's."

"I would like to buy them from you, Anabela, but I'm not sure I am able to pay you what they are worth."

"I don't expect you to pay me what they are worth. This is Cuba. No one has money. Well, except for Fidel and his family."

"And I don't think he would pay you what they are worth, either."

"Can you pay me twenty-four hundred pesos for all three?"

"I don't think so, not with my salary from the military. I give most of it to my family and the little bit that is left I spend here and there when I am on leave. I wish there was something I could do. I'm very sorry."

"I understand. If something changes, maybe some day you will have the money to buy them. Maybe one of them anyway."

"Perhaps. I should be going now," said Roberto.

"What about the music? They play all night. You can stay if you'd like. I wouldn't mind the company," said Anabela.

"Sure," said Roberto. There was a tone of desperation in her voice and he felt sorry for her. "I'd be happy to. Maybe another mojito?" asked Roberto.

"Thanks, and yes I'll have another mojito. Agustin, the bartender, he makes the best mojitos in Havana."

"You mean the guy you don't trust?"

"No, not the waiter. He's a kid, he couldn't make a glass of water. Agustin has been here forever. I remember when Senor Hemingway would come here and Agustin would make him mojitos. Maybe 25 years ago. Hasn't really changed much since then, thankfully. Although there are more tourists now."

"Why do you think so many come to this place? I mean it's small, not very fancy, no air conditioning. You know, not what they're used to at home in Europe, I'm sure."

"They're looking for authenticity and most of the people who come here, they don't understand what it means to be authentic. Or even where it comes from."

"I'm sorry, Anabela, but I don't understand what you mean."

"The average tourist, they have money. You know, they come from means. They spend their entire adult lives accumulating money in order to be comfortable, to feel secure and safe, rather than actually living. And then when they retire, they're too damn old to do anything."

"Safe from what?"

"Existential terror. Which is a waste of time."

"I have no idea what you're talking about."

"Roberto, the average person is terrified of risk, any sort of risk. They want to be certain of the outcome before doing anything. Living and having a meaningful life is directly proportional to the risks you're willing to take. My father, he led a meaningful life. Anyway, these tourists, they come here looking for something meaningful to experience and to be a part of. It's all an illusion, and none of them will ever understand that. You can't acquire authenticity, and you sure as hell can't buy it. But you know, most of them leave here happy, I guess. Ironic, don't you think?"

"How so?"

"Think about it. Most people want the latest this and the latest that, and they're not happy until they get it. They come here looking for a little piece of the past. And like I said, when they leave here they feel satisfied and they are happy. At least for a little while."

"So why do you come here, Anabela?"

Anabela turned away, looking for a moment at the musicians. When she looked back at Roberto her eyes had turned red and they were beginning to tear.

"I come here to be happy. Unfortunately, it doesn't last very long," she sighed, looking back toward the musicians.

"I hope some day I can help you, Anabela. Buy the paintings I mean. Unless you are able to find a buyer somewhere else."

"I know where there are some buyers, and with plenty of money," said Anabela.

"Well, why don't you get in touch with them?"

"Because they live in Spain. Expats. I have no way to get the paintings to Spain and no way to receive the payment. And besides it's too dangerous. If you get caught you go to jail."

"There must be some way to make it happen. Cuba has trade connections with Spain," said Roberto.

"I admire your optimism, Roberto. It's a good quality," said Anabela. "But like I told you, buying and selling artwork is illegal."

"Well, who are these people?"

"Why? It's not as though you have anything to sell."

"No, but you never know what may happen in the future."

"You figure out a way to get something out of Cuba safely and we can talk."

"I will make it happen someday, Anabela. I have no idea how, but I am not easily discouraged. I should be going, Anabela. It's rather late and I have to report for military duty first thing Monday. Thank you for your trust."

"You're welcome. And thank you for listening. There is no one in my life who is interested in art, and the few friends I have, they don't understand why these paintings are so important to me."

"I think I understand."

And with that Roberto finished the last bit of rum in his glass. He and Anabela stood up, briefly hugged each other, and said goodbye.

As Roberto began walking home through the dimly lit streets of Old Havana, he couldn't stop thinking about his conversation with Anabela and the wonderful old paintings of her father's. The revelation that Cubans who fled to Spain after the revolution would still be interested in collecting works of art from their homeland was particularly intriguing to Roberto. Finding a way into that world was going to be difficult, he thought, trying to imagine who it was that Anabela knew in Spain and what their collections were like. He began to envision a future where he was free to pursue his developing passion.

Arriving home after midnight he found the front door locked, so he went through the narrow alley way between his parents' house and the neighbors to the back of the house and into the kitchen.

As he entered the kitchen and shut the door behind him, he turned around and found his brother Carlos sitting at the kitchen table. Opened up in front of him on the table was a large book. Roberto walked around the table and stood behind his brother and looked over his shoulder.

"What are you reading, Carlitos?"

"It is a book about the work of Leopold Romanach. He was one of the most important Cuban painters of the last 150 years."

"That's incredible! One of the paintings Anabela wanted to sell was a Romanach. Where did you get the book?"

"The library. Lately I have been reading a lot about the history of Cuban art," said Carlos as he laid the book down on the table, careful not to place it in the ring of condensation that had formed under his now empty beer bottle. "I always feel better about myself when I am reading. You know, Roberto, I realize there is nothing I can do to change the way I am. I mean no one grows out of autism. It's not like an allergy. Reading is all I have at this point."

Roberto chuckled and said, "You're special, Carlitos. You have gifts that no one else has. If you read this book, a year from now you'll remember eighty per cent of what you read. If I were to read it, I'd be lucky to remember ten per cent."

"The only way I know how to feel free from the oppression here in Cuba is to read. The more I read and the more knowledge I have, the more powerful I feel."

"I'll remember that, Carlitos."

"What happened with Anabela Sobrino?"

"Like I said, she had several paintings from her father's collection she wanted to sell."

"How much did she want for them?"

"Twenty-four hundred pesos for all three. Obviously, I couldn't buy them. She's desperate and needs the money. I felt sorry for her."

"Do you think it was a fair price? I mean did you like them?"

"Yeah, more than fair, they were truly beautiful. She said if she had a way to get them to Spain, she could sell them to wealthy Cubans who had fled after the revolution and who collected art from the period of time before the revolution."

"If anyone could figure it out, it would be you, brother," Carlos said with a smile.

"Someday, Carlitos, maybe you and I, we'll be art collectors, and we'll have a gallery, with paintings by this guy. What was his name?"

"Leopoldo Romanach! Jesus, Roberto, I just told you his name, and Anabela told you his name, and you have already forgotten it."

"That's why you'll be in charge of the history department and I'll deal with the customers," Roberto said with a laugh.

"When do you return to duty?"

"Tomorrow, early. So I probably won't see you again for some time."

"What about going fishing? I thought we would have time to go out with Maykel."

"Next time. I promise, Carlitos. And besides, when I am off again in three months, the fishing will be better."

"I'll be waiting. I would go with Maykel without you, but it makes me a little nervous."

"I know, Carlitos. Don't worry, we'll go. I need to get some sleep. I leave very early tomorrow. Keep studying that book."

IV

Returning to his life in the military, Roberto was beginning to imagine living a life outside of conscription. A life, he thought, in which art would be the key to a future of unlimited possibilities, a future where he was free to determine his own destiny.

The more alluring the notion of a life of freedom became, the more his frustration began to build. It was difficult to hide, especially within the strict confines of the military.

Shortly after reveille one morning during formation before duty, Roberto's commanding officer, Colonel Alejandro Charon, instructed Roberto to report to the parade grounds outside of his office.

Thinking little of the request, Roberto, needing to speak with Antonio Castro about an upcoming training session they had planned for the afternoon, stopped briefly to speak with Antonio before continuing on to see the Colonel.

When he arrived at the parade grounds he was surprised to see only the Colonel and three of his junior officers. As he approached the Colonel, he could see by the look on his face that he was unhappy about something.

Charon was a tall man, powerfully built, and seemed to enjoy his ability to intimidate people with his physical presence. The three men with Charon were similar in stature. Roberto was acquainted with two of the men whom he saw regularly while training with Antonio.

"Ramos, I told you to report directly to the parade grounds," said Charon, now clearly annoyed.

"I'm sorry, sir, but I needed to speak with Antonio," said Roberto.

"You like making your own decisions, don't you Ramos?" asked Charon.

"Yes sir, sometimes I suppose I do," said Roberto.

"You're not entitled to make any decisions and I don't appreciate your tone of voice," said Charon, as he stepped directly in front of Roberto. "This is the military. You don't have any special privileges because you're assigned to train Antonio."

"You asked me to train him," said Roberto sharply.

"You don't talk until I tell you to!" yelled Charon.

Roberto said nothing. Without blinking Roberto stared directly and deliberately into the eyes of Charon, and he could feel the adrenaline beginning to surge in his body as Charon took another step closer.

Charon was now standing within inches of Roberto. As Charon stared down at him, Roberto could smell his breath, a hot, dry, stale mixture of last night's Havana Club rum and expensive cigars occasionally handed out to ranking officers as a token for their loyalty to Fidel.

"I don't care for the way you've been acting lately, Ramos," said Charon, poking his right index finger into the chest of Roberto. "You need to change your attitude before it gets you in trouble," again poking Roberto in the chest with his right index finger, this time a little harder.

"Well then I'll work on changing it," Roberto said in an intentionally sarcastic tone of voice. "And if you don't mind, please do not touch me again."

"What did you say, Ramos?" yelled Charon, furiously.

This was it for Roberto. He wasn't going to back down.

"I said, if you don't mind, please do not touch me again. I'm warning you," answered Roberto, knowing full well that Charon was out of patience and was likely to turn violent.

Charon towered over Roberto and knew he was easily Roberto's superior in strength. He would suffer the consequences of this miscalculation.

"You are warning me? Who the fuck are you?" yelled Charon, spitting into the face of Roberto.

"Don't touch me, Charon," said Roberto defiantly, calling him only by his last name.

The enraged Charon instantly slapped Roberto across the face with the open palm of his right hand. The smacking noise from the blow to the side of Roberto's face drew the attention of several officers entering a nearby barracks, who upon hearing the sound, stopped and looked in the direction of Roberto, Charon, and the three junior officers.

The force of the blow twisted Roberto's head and torso down and to his right. Although bent slightly at the waist, Roberto remained standing in place. Charon leaned over slightly and glared down at Roberto but said nothing. The much larger Charon, now confident he had put an end to Roberto's insubordinate behavior, had not moved from where he had been standing when he struck Roberto.

Out of the corner of his eye Roberto could see that Charon had not moved. Roberto's years of Taekwondo training immediately took control and he instinctively reacted in the only way he knew how. Giving Charon no time to react or prepare for his response, Roberto simultaneously leapt off the ground while spinning in mid-air and landed a crushing blow to the left side of Charon's neck with the top of his right foot.

Charon crumpled to the ground from the force of the blow in a limp heap, only semiconscious and severely injured.

Roberto readied himself, quickly turning his attention to the three junior officers who were now rushing past Charon, who still wasn't moving, and toward Roberto. Judging by the size and power of the three men, Roberto knew the coming fight was going to be brief and would not likely end in his favor.

With his body turned sideways and to the right and his weight positioned over his back foot, he slowly elevated his hands to shoulder height. The first of the men to reach Roberto foolishly threw a punch at Roberto's head, missing wildly, throwing himself off balance. Seeing the other man was in a vulnerable position, Roberto immediately launched a counter-attack, landing a heavy solid blow with his right foot to the man's midsection, cracking two ribs and knocking him to the ground gasping for air. The other two men, realizing now what they were up against, backed off slightly with one of them circling around behind Roberto, knowing if they were to come at him from both sides at once, it would improve their chances of getting him on the ground where his superior skill in self-defense would be neutralized.

It was impossible for Roberto to keep his eyes on both men at the same time, and sensing that the man behind him had made a move toward him, Roberto wheeled around only to find the man behind him had backed off. The third man, now in a position behind Roberto, seized the opportunity, and launched himself at Roberto from several feet away, managing to place Roberto in a choke hold from behind, easily lifting him off the ground. Unable to gain any leverage, Roberto's attempts to flip the larger man around to the front of his body failed, giving the other officer the time he needed to land several heavy blows to Roberto's head, leaving him slightly stunned and unable to fight back.

It was over. The two men had Roberto pinned face down on the ground with both arms twisted behind his back to the point where both shoulders were in danger of becoming dislocated. Charon still lay on the ground nearby, now moaning unintelligibly, and still unable to move. The injured deputy officer, with both arms leaning on one knee, was alternately yelling profanities at Roberto and coughing uncontrollably, attempting unsuccessfully to stand up.

The military police arrived on the scene within minutes and took control of Roberto from the two junior officers. After placing him in handcuffs and lifting him up off the ground, they immediately threw him in the back of the military police van. Roberto hit the hard wooden floor of the police van, groaning slightly, unable to use his arms to blunt the force of the impact.

Since warning Charon not to touch him, Roberto had said nothing either to the junior officers or the military police. He sat on the floor of the police van in silence. He could feel his face beginning to swell and he had trouble opening his mouth, which had become dry. His heart, still pounding from the adrenaline left over in his body, was forcing him to breath heavily. The blood dripped from his nose and mouth onto the floor, running slowly into the cracks between the old wooden boards between his legs. He thought only of his family, wondering if this was it, and if he would ever see them again.

With only a few air vents along the top of the inside of the van, Roberto was unable to see where they were taking him. After what seemed to be half an hour of driving the road surface changed to what felt and sounded like a cobblestone street. He could hear the sound of car horns and there was an increasing odor of diesel fumes entering the van.

When the van stopped Roberto heard both doors from the front of the vehicle, open and then shut. He then heard the officers walk to the back of the van. Unlocking the doors, they slowly opened one and then the other. As Roberto's eyes adjusted to the bright sunlight, he could see one of the officers holding an automatic weapon and the other a pair of leg shackles.

Roberto sat motionless, not taking his eyes off the officer with the gun, while the officer with the shackles stepped into the van and placed them around Roberto's ankles.

As the officer stepped back out of the van he turned to his right and motioned for someone to come to the back of the vehicle. Two men appeared wearing dark blue uniforms unfamiliar to Roberto.

"*Vamos*," said one of the men as they both stepped into the van, each grabbing Roberto by an arm, dragging him to the edge of the back of the van where they lifted him onto the ground.

Roberto, looking around, realized he must be somewhere in Old Havana, but didn't recognize any of the buildings. They were made of large, square, hand cut stone with few windows and there was a high stone wall that appeared to surround the entire complex. There were no trees, only bare earth and he could smell the ocean but couldn't see it.

"Where am I?" asked Roberto.

"Somewhere you don't want to be," said one of the men who had lifted him from the van, with a laugh.

The military police officers closed the doors to the van and walked back around to the front of the vehicle. One of the officers opened the passenger door and reached in, picking up several papers off of the seat. Returning to the men holding Roberto, he handed one of them the papers, nodded, walked back to the van which the other man had started, stepped in, and drove away.

The man with the papers looked at them briefly and then looked up at Roberto.

"Take a look around, Ramos," said the officer.

"What for?"

"You'll see, Ramos. All right, let's go."

The two officers then proceeded to lead Roberto toward the entrance to one of the old buildings. Roberto had difficulty walking at first due to the short length of chain between the two shackles, stumbling slightly every few steps.

Nearing the building Roberto noticed a sign just above the door on the outside of the building which read, Departamento Tecnico de Investigaciones, known to Cubans as DTI. He immediately recognized the name, remembering being told by his father the name of the prison where his father had been tortured.

The prison was built in the early 19th century by the Spaniards. It was impossible to escape from DTI. Dark, damp and smelling of rodent feces and mildew, the prison was unimaginably primitive. It was notorious for the conditions under which the prisoners were forced to live and under constant pressure from Amnesty International to be shut down.

Upon entering the crumbling old stone building the officers immediately took Roberto past another group of guards just inside the entrance to a small room at the end of the first hallway leading from the entrance way.

Sitting behind a small desk in the room were two men wearing slightly different, somewhat lighter colored uniforms. The attending officer who had been given the paperwork from the military police, then handed it to one of the men sitting behind the desk, who slowly and carefully read each page.

"Ramos," one of the men said. "Assaulting your commanding officer. Anything you'd like to say?"

"Sure. Charon, *ele es una mierda cabeza*," said Roberto.

"The situation you are in now, Ramos—calling your commanding officer a shit head—it's not a good idea," said the other man sitting behind the desk.

"I'm certain you would not want me to lie to you about Charon, so

I am telling you the truth. I am trying to be honest. He is a shit head," said Roberto emphatically.

"Ramos, this is Lieutenant Guerra and I am Colonel Torres. I am the warden here.

"You realize you're in a lot of trouble?" said Torres.

"I'm not stupid," said Roberto.

"Maybe you just need a little time to think about it," said Torres. "Put him in number 8," he said, turning to the two officers that brought Roberto into the prison.

"A little rum later would be nice," yelled Roberto over his shoulder as the two guards led him from the warden's office.

"You need to learn when to keep your mouth shut Ramos," said one of the guards.

The guards led Roberto down a long, dark hallway at the end of which was a heavy rusty steel door with only a single six-inch square window at shoulder height containing three vertical steel bars. A guard on the other side of the door motioned to the two men with Roberto that it was safe to open the door. Pressing a button on the wall to the left of the door, it began to slide slowly into a pocket in the stone wall to the right.

Passing through the doorway and turning to the right, Roberto and the two guards came to a narrow set of stone stairs, only wide enough for two men at a time. The bigger of the two guards took Roberto by the arm and began leading him down the steps while the other guard unholstered his handgun and followed just behind.

Because of the leg shackles Roberto had to move slowly, placing both feet one at a time on each step as they made their way down. He counted each step as they went, which when reaching the bottom totaled twenty-four. He realized judging by the number of steps and the much cooler air, they were well below ground level. Looking around Roberto could see the lower half of the stone walls covered in a thick layer of mildew. It was damp and there was a strong smell of urine. The only light came from a single, naked, yellow bulb hanging from a frayed, cloth-covered cord half-way down the hall. Roberto counted eight cell doors down the hall in front of him, four on either side.

"Last door on the left Ramos. Let's go," said the guard, motioning with his pistol for Roberto to keep moving.

Stepping in front of the door, Roberto paused and looked up at the number chiseled in the stone above the doorway.

"*Numero ocho*. My new lucky number," said Roberto with a rueful smile.

"Shut up Ramos. You'll be lucky to get out of here alive. Turn around, and don't even think about doing anything stupid," said the bigger of the two guards as he pulled open the door to the cell.

Roberto stepped just inside the doorway and into the cell where he waited for the guards to remove his handcuffs. After removing the handcuffs, they then removed the leg shackles and shut the door behind Roberto. The metallic sound of the door closing echoed loudly in the stone hallway and then quickly faded.

"Enjoy the rest of your day, Ramos."

Roberto could hear them laughing as they walked back down the hallway to the stairs. With the light from a tiny window in the door and a one-foot by two-inch opening at the bottom of the door along the floor, Roberto's eyes slowly adjusted to the darkness. The cell was only six feet long and five feet wide, with the two-foot-wide stone bench running along the length of the longer wall. Roberto could stand fully upright, but only just, the ceiling being no more than six feet in height. In one corner on the floor was a four-inch-wide hole, which judging by the smell coming from it, was the toilet.

He sat down on the stone bench and carefully felt the swollen areas around his mouth and eyes, checking to see if anything might be broken. With the adrenaline in his body having worn off, the pain in his face was beginning to increase rapidly, making it difficult for him to recall in detail the events of the morning. He assumed the other seven cells were unoccupied because there were no sounds coming from any of them. He heard no other sounds except the faint sound of water dripping, coming from above his cell.

Surprisingly, he felt rather calm. Surely assaulting a superior office would not be a capital offense, he thought. He would serve some time perhaps, and maybe Antonio Castro would be able to aid in his release. After all, Antonio had told Roberto Charon was trouble.

Just then Roberto heard two guards coming down the steps and into the hallway toward his cell.

"Ramos," said one of the guards. "Take off your clothes and when we open the door you place them on the floor in front of the cell. Do not step out of the cell. Understand?"

Roberto took off his military uniform and when the door opened, he handed it to one of the guards who then handed Roberto the prison-issued shirt and pants he was required to wear. As the guard started to shut the door Roberto peered through the slight opening and asked," What about some water?"

"You get water twice a day and food once a day in the evening. You'll get water this evening along with your food."

Turning around as the guards closed the door to the cell, Roberto sat on the stone bench, which was very cold, and began putting on the uniform. It was difficult. He was stiff and his entire body now ached from effects of the fight on the parade grounds. He managed to first put on the pants and then slowly he lifted his arms to a point high enough that allowed him to slip the shirt on over his head. He sat back on the bench and leaning against one of the end walls he slowly pulled his knees up to his chest for warmth and tried to sleep.

He hadn't been asleep long when he was awakened by the muffled, rumbling sound of heavy, tropical thunder coming from above. He could feel a slight vibration in the stone walls of his cell each time a new clap of thunder broke. The little bit of sleep he'd had seemed only to make his body ache even more. Slowly he lowered his feet onto the floor and stood up, stretching his shoulders one at a time and then bending at the waist he stretched his hamstrings which eased the tightness in his back. The cold damp stones and air accentuated every pain he now felt.

Sitting back down, his mind began to race back and forth between anger and fear. He had heard stories about this place and knew the odds of making it out alive, sane and in one piece, were poor. He had not been arrested however, on any political charges he thought, so that was in his favor. The political prisoners were the ones that rarely made it out. Everyone else just went crazy or died from disease. Someone who has gone mad is much easier to control than someone who is passionately motivated by an ideal, like freedom, he thought.

Thinking he'd heard footsteps coming down the steps at the end of the hall, Roberto stood up and looked through the tiny opening in the door. The opening was only four inches wide and no more than six inches tall. Due to the thickness of the door and the narrow width of the window he could only get a clear view of the door of the cell on the opposite side of the hallway.

Then he heard two voices and recognized them as those of the guards who had taken his military uniform and had given him his prison uniform.

Roberto stepped back and up onto the stone bench. Not knowing why the guards had returned, he was cautious.

"Ramos," one of the guards yelled, just as they reached the door to Roberto's cell. "You hungry?"

Roberto stepped down from the bench and looked through the window. One of the guards was holding a small steel plate of what looked like pasta noodles.

"Here's your water," said one of the guards who then proceeded to pass a glass bottle full of water, bottom first, in through the window.

The other guard then slid the plate of noodles in under the narrow slot in the bottom of the door.

"You have 10 minutes," said one of the guards.

"10 minutes for what?"

"To eat. That's it."

Roberto, not trusting the men, held the plate up to the light coming through the window from the hallway. The plate felt cold, but the noodles looked clean enough to eat. Without hesitating, he proceeded to eat everything in less than four handfuls, quickly washing the starchy lump of noodles down with the bottle of warm water.

When he was finished eating Roberto slid the empty plate underneath the door and back out into the hallway. "Here's your bottle," said Roberto. "How about next time you mix in a little rum," he said with a laugh.

"See you in twenty-four hours," said the guard, ignoring Roberto's request for rum.

The sound of the guards' footsteps as they made their way back up the stairs faded quickly into silence. The thunderstorm had passed, and the only thing Roberto could hear now was the faint rhythmic pumping sound of his heart.

Four days had passed since Roberto had been arrested and put into solitary confinement. He knew it had been four days because he had been given four plates of noodles and eight bottles of water. He was losing weight and it was impossible to sleep for more than a few hours at a time on the stone bench due to the fact that the cell was underground and never warmed, even during the day.

On the morning of the fifth day, the two guards whom he had seen twice a day for four days, came to his cell several hours after Roberto had been given his morning water and well before the time he thought they would return with his once a day meal.

"Ramos, the warden wants to see you," said one of the guards. "I want you to kneel down on the floor with your back to the door and put both hands behind your back."

"Social visit?" Roberto asked sarcastically as he turned around and knelt down on the floor.

"Colonel Torres doesn't do social visits," said the second guard as he cautiously opened the cell door.

After placing a set of handcuffs around Roberto's wrists the first guard then quickly shackled both legs.

Roberto, upon hearing the clicking noise from the shackles locking around his ankles, immediately stood up with no assistance or instruction from either guard, surprising both men.

"What the hell are you doing Ramos? You don't move until you are told to," said the guard angrily.

"My apologies," said Roberto slowly, pretending to be sincere.

"Alright smart ass, let's go," said the guard.

As the guards led Roberto back up the stairs to the warden's office, Roberto tried to imagine why the warden wanted to see him. After all, he thought, he had only spent four days in solitary confinement.

Upon entering the office one of the attending guards motioned for Roberto to sit down on a wooden stool several feet away and directly in front of the warden's desk.

"Ramos," said Colonel Torres. "I spoke with your good friend Antonio Castro yesterday. He spoke very highly of you. Said you were a loyal friend and that whatever you had done to Charon was probably justified. He said it was wrong, but justified. He can say that because he has privilege."

"What do you want from me, Colonel?" asked Roberto confidently, sensing that Antonio Castro had not revealed any of his true feelings toward Fidel.

"I want to know why you assaulted your superior officer," said the warden.

"I told you, he's a shit head," said Roberto.

"You seem to have issues with aggression Ramos," said the warden.

"I am turned into a fighting machine, a killing machine by the military and you are surprised when I defend myself," said Roberto. "What do you expect?" asked

"Apparently you need a little more time to come up with the right answer. Take him back to his cell," said the warden.

Again, at night Roberto found it nearly impossible to sleep. There was water seeping in through several cracks in the wall above the bench making it difficult to stay dry. It must be raining hard he thought for the water to penetrate this far underground. The additional moisture only added to the cold, and he began to shake uncontrollably as his body temperature dropped.

Eventually succumbing to exhaustion, Roberto fell asleep. That night he dreamed he was fishing in the Gulf Stream with Maykel and his brother. In his dream, the sun, not yet above the horizon, had turned the sky to the east a pastel lemon color and the full moon, magnified half again as large by the earth's atmosphere, was simultaneously beginning to set on the horizon to the west.

"Look boys," said Maykel, pointing to the west. "See the moon? She is kissing the ocean. That means we'll have luck today."

"How do you know, Maykel?" asked Roberto.

"You always want to know why, Roberto," said Carlos.

"It's okay, Carlitos," said Maykel, placing his hand upon Carlos's shoulder. "There is a good explanation, Roberto. You see the tides become stronger when the sun, the earth and the moon are aligned during new and full moons. The stronger tides make all the life in the sea more active. It's not luck really, the fishing is simply better when the tide runs stronger."

"It would make a beautiful painting Maykel, don't you think?" said Roberto. "I would call it, *Beso de La Luna.*"

"Kiss of the Moon," repeated Maykel. "I like that."

Maykel turned the wheel slightly starboard, heading the boat down sea and to the north.

Awakened again by the inescapable cold and dampness in his cell, Roberto noticed the water had stopped coming through the walls onto the stone bench, the surface of which was beginning to dry out.

Standing, he slowly brushed the pools of water off the bench onto the floor. After shaking the excess water off his hands and rubbing them together for warmth he sat back down on the bench. With little food and no exercise, he thought, it would be impossible to maintain his strength. Fortunately for Roberto, a part of basic training for all military personnel in Cuba dealt with survival strategies should you become a prisoner of war. Being a prisoner in his own country, however, was not something he had imagined.

Roberto knew he was strong physically and even stronger mentally, so a basic routine of exercise would help maintain a portion of his fitness level he thought, and also help to pass the time.

Every morning, or what he thought might be morning, as it was impossible to know the time of day, he went through a routine of ten different body weight exercises, careful not to overdo it and begin sweating. He knew that if he were to begin sweating, even lightly, he would run the risk of hypothermia.

On the ninth day of his imprisonment, at a time he thought might have been some time around midday, the same two guards he saw every day came to his cell and ordered him to kneel on the floor, back to the door and with his hands behind his back—the same procedure as the first time they had taken Roberto to see the warden five days earlier.

One of the guards then opened the door, threw Roberto's uniform he had been wearing the day he was arrested, onto the bench, and closed the door.

"Put them on," said the guard.

"I assume the Colonel would like to chat?"

"He thinks you're a bit *alocado*, Ramos," said one of the guards.

Roberto changed into his uniform, on which the blood stains were now hard and dry and beginning to crack. He turned around and knelt down on the floor with his back toward the cell door, waiting for the guard to shackle his ankles.

The guard then ordered him to stand. Roberto turned around and shuffled out of his cell and into the hallway, pausing briefly to make eye contact with the guards.

"Crazy? Maybe a little," said Roberto.

"Ramos," said Colonel Torres, as Roberto shuffled into the Colonel's office. "My favorite prisoner in solitary."

"You must not be remembering, Colonel. I am the only one down there," said Roberto.

"Ramos, I'm not in the mood," said the Colonel. "I met with Doctor Hernandez from the psychiatric clinic at Censam Marin Hospital. It's his opinion you would benefit from a little time there."

"Because of my anger and aggression issues, I suppose," said Roberto.

Roberto could tell by the look on the Colonel's face he didn't appreciate sarcasm.

"You're lucky to be alive, Ramos," said the Colonel, raising his voice slightly.

"I don't believe in luck," said Roberto.

"We're done here," said Colonel Torres. "Take him to the clinic."

The words from the Colonel came as an enormous relief to Roberto. Now, he thought, he would at least be able to see the sun, feel its warmth, breathe the clean, tropical air of Havana, and have three meals a day. He wondered also if he would be permitted visitors.

V

Roberto knew little about the Censam Marin Hospital Prison on the outskirts of Havana. The prison held high-level military personnel who had been charged by the regime mostly with political subversion, many of whom had been close to Fidel. Presumably they were sent there in an effort to rehabilitate them politically.

Aside from the numerous guards stationed throughout the hospital grounds, many carrying Kalashnikovs and looking bored, there was little evidence of security other than the double razor wire fencing surrounding the complex.

After arriving at the hospital Roberto was registered, again stripped of his military uniform, given a dull grey hospital-issued uniform, and then sent for psychological evaluation by the military doctors.

The evaluation lasted nearly two hours and seemed to Roberto little more than an attempt at forcing him to reveal his true feelings about the communist regime. He was intentionally vague with his answers and careful not to say anything that could potentially make life at the hospital more difficult. At the end of the evaluation he was given no indication by any of the military doctors how long he would be incarcerated.

Compared to solitary confinement, the living conditions at the hospital prison were infinitely more humane. The buildings were clean and even the guards seemed more relaxed. The sleeping ward Roberto was assigned to contained only a dozen beds, with less than half appearing to be unoccupied. There were several inmates in the ward, most of whom looked older and appeared to be asleep.

One of the men was sitting by an open window at the far end of the room. Roberto approached the old man and introduced himself.

"*Hola, senor.* My name is Roberto, Roberto Ramos," he said politely.

"*Mucho gusto*, Roberto. I am Tiburcio," said the old man, who turned and continued staring out the window.

"May I sit down, *senor*?"

"If you'd like."

"How long have you been here, Tiburcio?"

"I don't remember exactly. Ten years, maybe longer, and before that 10 years in DTI."

"I was in solitary there the last eight days."

"You're lucky to be here son. Lucky to be alive."

"Why are you in prison, Tiburcio?"

"The government was not happy with my professional work."

"What did you do?"

"Well, before I entered the military I was a professional painter, an artist. I had many wealthy clients here in Cuba and in Spain. After I entered the military, they wanted me to paint images glorifying communism, Fidel, Che, you know, but I refused. For some time they left me alone, and when I was on leave, I continued painting. It wasn't until after I was discharged that someone informed on me, and the military police came and arrested me one day at my studio.

"Why do they keep you here?"

"Because I don't tell them what they want to hear," answered the old man. "If you want to leave here some day, you should remember that. Never reveal your true feelings to the communists, and when you have the chance, I recommend living somewhere else."

"You mean to flee Cuba?"

"Yes. You have only one life, Roberto and it's not a dress rehearsal."

"Tiburcio, my brother and I have a painting done by Carlos Sobrino. Did you know him?"

"Of course I knew him. He was one of greatest artists from Cuba in the 20th century. He was one of the fortunate ones. He was able to escape to Spain and continue painting. I think he is dead now."

"Yes, I know that he died in 1971. I am acquainted with his daughter, Anabela. I have been to her house. She has many wonderful paintings from her father."

"Did you know, when Castro took over the palace in Havana in 1959, he ordered every painting in the palace that he didn't like, for any reason, taken down and destroyed," said the old man. "Many great works. Important works for the people of Cuba. There was a painting that for many years hung in the entrance hall of the Presidential Palace in Havana, done by Esteban Valderrama. The painting was entitled, *Finlay's Triumph*. In the painting, the Cuban doctor, Dr Finlay, is presenting the evidence from his research to the U.S. Yellow Fever commission, which included the most famous American doctor of the time, Dr. Walter Reed. Finlay had discovered how yellow fever was transmitted from person to person. It was one of the most important discoveries in the history of medicine. A great source of pride for the Cuban people. It took Valderrama more than two years to complete! Two years of his life, destroyed, and now the painting is lost forever."

"Why would Castro want it destroyed?" asked Roberto.

"Because there were Americans depicted in the painting. He came to hate the Americans."

"What about your paintings? Does your family have them?"

"My family lives in Spain. The communists destroyed my studio and confiscated all my work. They are nothing more than common criminals."

"I'm sorry, Tiburcio. Do you know how much longer before you are released?"

"I doubt they will ever release me."

"Why not? You have been here many years."

"Like I told you before, Roberto, I will never compromise my principles. And besides, my health is failing and I am tired, so I don't think about getting out anymore. They feed me here and I have a warm place to sleep and it's safe. If I am set free, I have nowhere to go and no money."

The old man turned once more toward the open window, as the last bit of light from the setting sun filtered through the coconut palms outside the window briefly illuminating his face. Roberto continued staring at him until the light had faded and the old man closed his eyes and fell asleep.

Shortly after sunrise Roberto was awakened by two men in hospital uniforms, one of whom was holding a small container filled with what looked like a pink milkshake.

"*Senor* Ramos, here is your medication," said one of the attendants. "You need to drink this before eating."

"Medication, for what?" asked Roberto, sitting up on his elbows.

"It's part of your treatment program."

"I'm not drinking anything."

"You have no choice. You drink it or we call security."

Roberto slowly pulled back the sheet he was sleeping under and swung his legs over the side of the bed placing his feet on the floor. He took the container from the attendant, unscrewed the lid, and pretended to smell the bottle as though it was a glass of rum, then handed it back to the attendant.

"What is the medication?" he inquired.

"I don't know. It's prescribed by the doctor. You are required to drink one of these every morning."

"Will it kill me?" asked Roberto, not yet fully awake.

"Only if you drink too much."

Roberto took the glass jar from the attendant and drank the entire contents, stopping once to catch his breath. The liquid was thick and sweet and reminded Roberto of a strawberry milkshake.

"I guarantee tomorrow you will be asking for another one," said the attendant, laughing as he turned and walked away.

Within minutes, Roberto began to feel the effects of the drugs contained in the pink liquid. At first he simply felt a little light-headed and very relaxed, but quickly his vision began to sharpen, colors intensified, and his hearing even seemed more acute. It was not unpleasant he thought, and he enjoyed the enhanced sensory state. Roberto had no experience with any sort of mind-altering drug up to this point in his life and so the effects of the medication were likely more intense. He felt very calm and very alert.

Looking around the room he noticed the other men were now awake, dressed and walking toward the door leading out of the ward. All except Tiburcio, who was again sitting by the window where Roberto had left him the night before.

Roberto walked over to the old man wanting to make sure he was alright.

"*Buenos dias*, Tiburcio. You're not going to have something to eat with the other men?"

"I don't think so, Roberto. I'm not particularly hungry and I prefer to be alone."

"Are you sure?"

"Yes, I am sure."

"I will come back later," said Roberto.

Roberto left Tiburcio alone and followed the other men from the ward to the cafeteria for the morning meal, which consisted of a single piece of bread, some avocado, and several slices of mango. The food was surprisingly fresh he thought and a welcome relief after a week of nothing but pasta. After the meal he was taken by the two attendants who had earlier given him the drug concoction, to see two of the hospital doctors.

"Ramos," said one of the doctors as Roberto entered the room. "Sit down, please. I am Dr. Perez, the head of the hospital and this is Dr. Diaz, the head of psychiatry. I assume you received your morning medications?"

"Yes, but why do I need drugs?"

"It's part of your treatment. It says here in your paperwork you have difficulty controlling your temper, and according to this report assaulted and seriously injured your commanding officer. Is that true?"

"It is true. He deserved it."

"Ramos, you seem like an intelligent young man. I think we can help you but you need to be aware of some rules. Violence of any kind is not tolerated. You will have regular opportunities to exercise and are allowed family visits once a month. Only family, no friends. Also, I'm putting you in group therapy once a week."

"Group therapy? What the hell for? I don't need therapy."

"Everyone here is required to attend therapy once a week. You'll be placed in a group with inmates who have similar issues."

"What do you want from me?"

"Compliance, Ramos. Best not to forget that."

"What about my family? When can I see them?"

"We will notify them this week. If they are interested to come, visitors are allowed the last weekend of every month. Two family members at a time for two hours."

"What about books?"

"We have a full library here in the hospital."

"Let me guess, everything ever written by Fidel and Che," said Roberto with a laugh.

"Your family is allowed to bring books, but they need to be checked and approved by security before they can be brought into the prison."

"Are we done here?"

"We're done. Ramos. If you're smart, you'll remember what I've told you."

Realizing it was better to say nothing than to say what he wanted to and run the risk of a provocation, Roberto nodded to the doctors and quickly left the room.

The attendants escorted Roberto back to the ward, locking the door to the outside behind him. The other men were playing dominoes at the far end of the room. Tiburcio was still sitting by the window where Roberto had left him earlier that morning.

Roberto wasn't in the mood for dominoes even though he loved playing, but rather wanted to continue his conversation with the old man from the previous evening.

"Tiburcio," said Roberto quietly, careful not to surprise the old man who appeared to be sleeping. "May I sit down?"

"Certainly. I could use a little company. How are you enjoying your milkshake?" said Tiburcio, smiling.

"Maybe ask me when it wears off."

"By the time it does they'll be giving you another one. I've come to enjoy the high. Helps to pass the time and it keeps me out of trouble."

"Tiburcio, I've been doing a lot of thinking lately."

"About what?"

"Art, from my country. I want to learn everything there is to know."

"Why?"

"Because I see it as my future, my path to freedom," said Roberto.

"There will never be freedom in Cuba, Roberto. Not as long as the Castros remain in power."

"All I know, Tiburcio, is how art makes me feel, and I want that feeling to somehow last forever."

"Do you want to become a painter?"

"No, I want to learn the history."

"The true history of Cuban art, the government has made that impossible."

"I understand what you're saying but I've already managed to learn many things the communists don't want me to know."

"And if you become educated, what then? What will you do with this knowledge?"

"I don't know. That's the problem. My brother tells me that knowledge is the ultimate true power."

"Your brother is a wise man."

"If he comes to see me here in prison, you will meet him."

"It will be my pleasure, Roberto. You know, there are many older people still living here in Havana that have paintings from the time before the revolution. They are very knowledgeable. You can learn from them as well."

"Like Anabela Sobrino."

"Yes, like Sobrino's daughter."

"She offered to sell me paintings from her father's collection. I would have bought them, but I couldn't afford the price."

"There are many Cubans living in Spain that still collect old works. Though if you're caught smuggling art-work out of Cuba, you'll spend many years in prison," Tiburcio cautioned.

"I'm already in prison," said Roberto with a laugh.

"And why are you here?"

"I assaulted my commanding officer."

"That's a serious offense. But not a political one. Remember what I told you yesterday. You tell them what they want to hear," said the old man with a wry smile.

"I'll remember, Tiburcio."

Roberto, thinking the old man looked tired, decided to leave him alone. The initial effects of the drugs Roberto had been given earlier that day were beginning to wear off, leaving him feeling tired as well. Returning to his bunk at the far end of the ward he laid down on his bed and immediately fell into a deep sleep. Several hours later he awoke to the occasional slapping sound coming from four of the other men from his ward who were playing dominoes at a small table in the middle of the room.

Roberto walked over to the men and sat down on a nearby chair. He, like all Cuban men, grew up playing dominoes or watching the older men in his neighborhood play, and he knew how to play, but had never taken the time to learn the strategy required to be a good player.

"*Tu juega?*" one of the men said, looking at Roberto.

"*Solo un poquito.*"

"Would you like to sit in? I could use a little break."

"Sure."

After brief introductions Roberto sat down at the table. Saying little as he played, he preferred instead to watch the older men closely in an effort to figure out why he kept losing.

After his eighth consecutive loss he'd had enough. The men were too good, he thought.

"How long have you been playing?" asked Roberto, directing his question to the other three men at the table.

"Longer than any of us can remember," said one of the men. "It takes time to become really good at this game, and you need to have a good memory."

"What is your name?" asked one of the other men.

"Roberto, Roberto Ramos," he said.

"I remember you. You're a national Taekwondo champion if I'm not mistaken," said one of the men.

" 'Was' is more like it."

"Once a champion, always a champion Roberto."

"What about the old man, Tiburcio? Does he play dominos?" asked Roberto.

"Not anymore," said one of the men. "He used to play with us all the time, but lately all he does is sit by the window," said the man, pointing toward Tiburcio. "He stopped eating maybe a week ago. Just before you arrived."

"Stopped eating?" asked Roberto, surprised by the comment.

"Yes, says he's tired and doesn't feel well," said another one of the men.

"Excuse me gentlemen, I need to talk with Tiburcio," said Roberto.

Roberto stood up, thanked the men for their company and the invitation to play dominos. Carefully pushing his chair under the table, he placed both hands on the top of the rear chair legs and leaned over the table slightly.

"Next time, the outcome will be different. Remember, I'm a champion," said Roberto, trying not to laugh.

"I don't think so. We went easy on you today. Tomorrow, you'll see."

Roberto turned and walked toward Tiburcio, who appeared to be asleep in his chair by the window.

"Tiburcio," Roberto whispered. "Tiburcio," Roberto said again, a little louder.

Roberto stood directly in front of the old man and put his hand on the old man's shoulder, shaking it gently.

"Tiburcio," he said again.

The old man's chin was resting on his chest and there was no response. Roberto put his right hand under the old man's chin and slowly lifted his head. Tiburcio's face was an ashen yellow color, his skin was cold to the touch, and he wasn't breathing. With his left hand, Roberto checked for a pulse in the old man's neck. Roberto felt nothing. The old man was dead.

VI

It had been two weeks since the death of Tiburcio, and Roberto could not stop thinking about the old man. His death only increased Roberto's feeling of bitterness toward the communists, and Fidel in particular. The old man had been robbed of his dignity, his purpose in life, and most importantly, his passion for living. Roberto knew deep inside, the heavy residue of negativity he was feeling was useless if he was ever going to somehow create a meaningful life for himself. A life he thought, where he was free to learn, to engage completely with whomever he chose, and to unleash fully the power of his intentions. He realized now more than ever, none of these things would ever be possible in Cuba.

Roberto's tolerance for his incarceration and for his captors was helped immeasurably by the drugs he was forced to take on a daily basis. Realizing the beneficial effect the drugs had in helping to moderate his anger, and with plenty of time on his hands, Roberto developed a tolerable daily routine spending time alternately exercising and reading from the works of Marti, Guillen, Ortiz, and others, doing his best to remember the advice of his brother Carlos about the power of knowledge.

Remembering that in two days' time he would have a visit from his brother Carlos, and perhaps his mother, the thought began to lift his spirits. He couldn't be sure his mother would make the nearly fifteen-kilometer trip to the hospital prison unless she could find someone with an available car, the time, and enough gas to get them there and back from Santos Suarez. Carlos could manage such a long walk, but it was too much to expect of his aging mother, especially during the heat of the day.

Roberto awoke early the morning of the expected visit from his brother Carlos, and with any luck, his mother Rosa. Inmates were only allowed two family members at each visit and if either of his parents would make the trip to the hospital prison, it would likely be his mother. Roberto knew it was Guillermo's memory of being tortured when imprisoned under the Batista regime, and the brutality he witnessed while in prison that would prevent him from visiting his son in prison.

The sun was not yet up, and he wanted to spend the time with a clear head before the attendants arrived with his daily concoction of drugs. He sat down in the chair in front of the window where Tiburcio had died several weeks earlier and stared out into the darkness.

The window faced northwest toward the sea, less than 800 hundred meters distant on a direct line, and even though the trees blocked any view of the ocean, with the aid of a light north wind, Roberto could smell the salt air and hear the faint noise of the diesel motors coming from the power yachts as they began leaving Marina Hemingway for a day of marlin fishing, carefully navigating the narrow channel bordered on either side by shallow coral reef, leading out into the blue water of the Gulf Stream.

Sitting in the old man's chair Roberto began to think about Tiburcio and how different the old man's life might have been had he found a way to flee Cuba in the early days of the revolution. Once free to continue his work as an artist, he no doubt would have gone on to create many more great works. How many more artists, writers, poets, musicians, and film makers, he wondered, must there be living in Cuba, whose professional lives had been destroyed by a senseless and cruel dictator whose political ideology had been an utter failure.

Having fallen asleep, Roberto awoke, stirred suddenly by the sharp metallic clap made by the morning attendant opening the cast iron lever lock on the door leading into the ward.

The attendant slowly wound his way through the ward with his metal cart that contained the mandatory dose of drugs, handing one to each of the men, finishing with Roberto, who remained seated by the window at the far end of the room.

Slowly, Roberto drank the mixture. He had become accustomed to the physical effects the drugs had on his body but not the psychological ones. The drugs slowed the process of comprehension while reading and affected Roberto's ability to remember much of what he had read from the day before.

"*Senor*," said Roberto, addressing the attendant. "What time are visiting hours?"

"From ten o'clock until noon."

"How will I know if my family is coming?"

"You won't. Some of these men will be lucky to have a visitor once a year."

"I am certain my brother will come to see me today," said Roberto, looking down at the jar the attendant had given him, still half full of liquid.

"Finish drinking the medication, Ramos," ordered the attendant, who was becoming impatient.

Roberto finished the remaining liquid in the jar and handed it back to the attendant, saying nothing. He continued sitting by the window until just before ten o'clock, standing up when one of the hospital attendants entered the ward and called the name of one of the other men, instructing the man to follow him to the visitor area where his wife was waiting to see him.

Roberto felt apprehensive and knew it would be difficult for his brother Carlos, because of his autism, to overcome the anxiety he would feel simply contemplating such a trip to the prison, especially if he was to come alone.

Twenty minutes had passed since the first man left the room and Roberto was beginning to think that Carlos, who was never late for anything, wasn't coming to the prison to see him. Surely something must have prevented Carlos from coming, thought Roberto. Feeling disappointed, he returned to the chair by the window and sat down.

It was then Roberto heard the door to the ward swing open and one of the attendants shout his name. "Ramos, your family is here."

Standing in the hallway just outside the door holding two large books was Carlos, and behind him next to the hospital attendant stood his mother Rosa, carrying a small canvas bag. Roberto could see that his brother was struggling. Carlos was fearful by nature and had clearly reached the limit of his ability to deal with the situation.

"You have until 12:00. You're not to leave this room under any circumstances until I come back to get you," said the man, looking in the direction of Rosa.

Roberto quickly gathered two chairs from beside the domino table and placed them beside the chair he had been sitting in by the window.

"Carlitos, *Madre, por favor*," said Roberto as he motioned for them to sit down.

"Roberto, what have you done?" asked Rosa.

"I had a conversation with my commanding officer and it didn't end well for him," said Roberto with a slight grin.

"But why are you here, do they think you're crazy? asked Rosa.

"I suppose," said Roberto. "Look, I don't want to talk about any of this. What about you? How are you? And the family—how is everyone?"

"Roberto, I brought these for you to look at," said Carlos. "One is the Leopoldo Romanach book. Remember when I showed it to you the night you went to see Anabela Sobrino at La Bodeguita del Medio?"

"I remember. I remember also, you told me they call him the father of Cuban painting. Let me see,"

"The other one is a collection of old Cuban masters."

"Roberto," said Rosa sternly. "I wish you would learn to control your anger. Do you have any idea how hard this is on your father and I, and Carlitos?"

"How is *Padre*, Mother?" asked Roberto.

"He's tired and I think he's depressed. He doesn't talk much. He's worried about you."

"When I get out of here, I'll finish my military service and he won't have to worry about me anymore. I have a plan."

"A plan, to do what?" asked Carlos.

"To buy and sell art, in Spain," said Roberto.

"Can I help you?" asked Carlos. "I have been studying everything I can find about the *viejos maestros*."

"We would make a good team, Carlitos," said Roberto. "But remember what Anabela said—it's risky. We'll talk about it when I'm out of here."

"I don't know why I waste my time with you, Roberto," said Rosa. Here, I brought this for you." Reaching into her bag she took out a small metal can, wrapped in newspaper and handed it to Roberto.

"What is this, *Madre*?" asked Roberto, as he carefully unwrapped the package. "How did you manage to get this past Security?"

"Do you remember Rafael, from the neighborhood? He is one of the security guards. I think he felt sorry for me," said Rosa. "Anyway, it is some *fanquito*. I haven't made that for you since you went to the tobacco fields as a schoolboy. You always loved it, remember?"

"Of course I remember. It's my favorite."

"I've been wanting something sweet to eat lately. Would you like one, Carlitos?"

"No, they're both for you," said Carlos.

"Roberto, I am not allowed to leave these books with you," said Carlos. "We don't have much time. Please, they're for you. I don't mind if you look at them while I'm here."

Roberto spent the remainder of his time with Carlos and Rosa carefully looking through both of the books his brother had brought to the prison. Page by page he became increasingly immersed in the contents of the books while at the same time his awareness of his surroundings began to fade, and he felt happy.

A little past 12:00, at the end of the visitation hours, the attending guard returned and led Carlos and Rosa from Roberto's ward. Carlos promised to bring more books when they returned the following month, and Rosa said she would try and convince Roberto's father to visit his son in the hospital. The time spent together was far too brief and left Roberto with a feeling of emptiness.

VII

The weeks and months of incarceration passed slowly and uneventfully for Roberto at the Censam Marin Hospital. Even though he made every effort possible to stay busy, the frustration and boredom he felt from having so little to do, though tempered somewhat by the narcotics he was given daily, was at times overwhelming, even for someone as disciplined as Roberto. The monthly visits from his family, and in particular his brother Carlos, always came as an enormous mental relief and comfort.

In particular, it was the numerous, out-of-print art books his brother somehow managed to locate through elderly friends in Old Havana, and always remembered to bring for Roberto to read during those hospital visits, that inspired him the most and gave him the added strength to endure. The feeling of transcendence he felt while examining closely every painting on every page in every one of the old books became an emotional refuge for Roberto, where he felt completely free, and where no one could control how he thought.

Exactly one year had passed since Roberto had been transferred from the old Spanish prison where he had been held in solitary confinement to the Censam Marin Hospital prison for the criminally insane on the outskirts of Havana. During his incarceration he had never been given any indication how long he would be held, and so it came as a surprise, early one Saturday morning, when the two military doctors who regularly interviewed Roberto, and who conducted the weekly group therapy, came to his ward and notified him of his immediate release and reassignment to his former special forces unit at the Presidential Palace.

Roberto was stunned, and at first thought perhaps he must be dreaming. It was true he had always tried to remember the words of Tiburcio, the old man he met the first day he'd been sent to Censam Marin, never to reveal his true thoughts or feelings to the communists if he had any hope of one day getting out, but he'd not been given any indication his release was coming.

"Ramos, these are your discharge papers. Read them carefully. You have one week to report back to your unit," said one of the doctors.

"What about my former commanding officer, Colonel Charon? Will I be serving under him?"

"No. You've been assigned to another unit. Ramos, you should be grateful for the opportunity to return to service."

"And my training, will I be able to resume training and competition?" asked Roberto.

"That is up to your superior officer. Unless you have any further questions you may change into your uniform and leave immediately," said the doctor, who then handed Roberto his uniform and the shoes he was wearing the day he had been arrested. Surprisingly, Roberto could see the uniform had been cleaned and folded neatly, and the blood stains were now gone.

After changing into his uniform and saying a few goodbyes to several of the inmates from his ward, Roberto was taken by the doctors to the hospital security headquarters where he was required to sign release papers. After signing the papers Roberto was escorted by several armed security personnel to the main entrance and released.

Standing for a moment on Calle 236 A, the main road running north and south in front of Censam Marin Hospital, and realizing, at least for the next week until he had to return to military duty, that every decision he made was going to be his own. It should always be this way, he thought to himself.

The hospital was located very near to Punto Cero, one of Fidel's so-called secret residences, and a place Roberto knew well, having been assigned regular duty there many times before being arrested. Considered now to be somewhat of a security risk, Roberto doubted he would be reassigned to the residence.

It was still early in the day and even though he knew it would take him most of the day to walk the 15 kilometers to the home of his parents, he was in no particular hurry to get there. Wondering how he would be received by his father, whom he hadn't seen in over a year, and whom he suspected would not be happy with him, Roberto decided it might be best to arrive late, at a time when the whole family would be home, and when his mother, the only one in the family his father ever really listened to, could prevent him from becoming angry with his son for having caused her so much grief and worry while he'd been in prison.

Before being released from the hospital he'd had nothing to eat and only a little water to drink. He was feeling hungry, and without any money he realized he would need to ask a friend for some food if he was going to have something to eat.

He remembered his good friend Maykel lived on the way to his parents, but with the weather conditions being perfect that day for fishing the Gulf Stream, and if the fishing had been good, Maykel would not return home until late.

It suddenly occurred to him, because it was a Saturday, perhaps Anabela Sobrino would not be working and might be home and would gladly give him something to eat. It was true he didn't know Anabela very well, but he'd always felt from the first time they met, that she trusted him and that she wouldn't mind if he stopped by to see her.

El Barrio de La Rampa, where Anabela lived, was at least a three hour walk from the hospital, and if he went by way of La Quinta Avenida, he would arrive at her house on Calle 15, just before noon.

It wasn't a particularly hot day and there was a light ocean breeze coming from the northeast, so he decided to head to a small in-home, unauthorized, and therefore illegal restaurant he knew of nearby, called, La Pescadaria. The restaurant was an informal collection of small buildings piecemealed together, overlooking the Rio Jaimanitas, where it flowed into the sea, and where he would sometimes go alone to relax after an athletic training session with Antonio Castro, to drink fresh coconut water straight from the young coconuts that had been chilled in a small, rusty, upright freezer after they had been picked by the owner's son from the tall coconut palms that grew along the banks of the river. Even though it had been more than a year since Roberto had been to the restaurant, he knew Luiz, the elderly owner well, and was confident he would happily give him some fresh bread and hot coffee.

Roberto remembered too, the numerous types of fruit trees that lined the edges of the gravel road leading down to the river to the restaurant that Luiz had planted many years ago in order to have fresh fruit year-round for his customers, who were mostly all family and friends. Among the different types of fruit growing there, and now in season, were sugar apples and small, sweet mangos. Roberto was particularly fond of both and decided he would ask Luiz's permission to pick a handful of each to take home with him. He could give some to Anabela he thought, as a gift, and save the rest for his family.

Walking around to the back of the oldest building, which looked more like an organized debris pile left after a hurricane rather than any sort of public establishment, Roberto found Luiz alone in the kitchen, beginning preparations for the daily meal, which he always served at midday.

"*Hola, amigo,*" said Roberto, surprising the old man who had his back turned toward the door. "How have you been, my friend?"

Roberto could see that he had startled Luiz and immediately apologized. "*Lo siento* Luiz. I didn't mean to frighten you."

"Roberto!" said Luiz loudly. "I heard you were in prison in Havana."

"I was, they released me this morning. I was being held for the last year at Censam Marin. You know, the hospital nearby."

"Censam Marin? I thought that was for crazy people from the military. You haven't gone crazy, have you?" said the old man laughing.

"No, they thought I had an anger management problem, but I was able to convince them it was only temporary."

"What did you do?"

"I sent my superior officer on a little vacation, to the emergency room."

"I know you, Roberto, and I'm sure he deserved it."

"A little. Luiz, could I ask you for something to eat? I don't have any money and I have a long walk today to my parents' house in Santos Suarez. I've been reassigned to my old post, and when I get paid, I'll be sure to pay you back."

"Anything you want, you know that. Here, sit down. I have some fried *dorado* I can fix for you, with some sweet plantains. Have some coffee, I just made it. And I have fresh fruit. How's that?" asked the old man as he poured the coffee.

"I would love that, thank you."

"So what now Roberto? You need to find a job?"

"No, I have been reassigned to another unit. I have another three years before I am discharged. What about your son, Barbaro, is he still playing baseball?" asked Roberto.

"Roberto, I have to tell you something. Barbaro fled Cuba maybe two months ago, by boat. Him and two other guys from the team, in the middle of the night. After that, the authorities came here many times to question me. I thought they were going to shut me down. I told them I didn't even know he was planning to escape."

"How did you know what happened?"

"One of his teammates came and told me. He said they left from Bacunayagua, a little village to the east. I don't know it. He couldn't take it anymore Roberto."

"Have you heard anything?"

"No, we don't even know if he is alive, or if he made it across the straits to the U.S. Nothing. It's been really hard on his mother."

"I'm sorry Luiz."

The old man stopped what he was doing and looked over at Roberto. "He's my only son Roberto. I was so proud of him. I never expected this to happen," said Luiz as he turned around and continued to prepare the food for Roberto.

"Maybe I can help, Luiz," offered Roberto, intentionally trying to sound positive.

"How?" asked Luiz. Again, stopping to turn around and face Roberto.

"You remember my friend, Antonio, the son of Fidel I was training at Punto Cero?

"Of course, but I don't want you to get in trouble for my sake, Roberto."

"Antonio is a loyal friend. I trust him. He would do it for me, I know he would. Let me ask him."

"Only if you feel comfortable doing it. I tell you what, you find out what happened to Barbaro, good or bad, I don't care, I just need to know, and you eat here for free, for life."

Roberto took the last sip of coffee and set the cup back down on its saucer on the table. "It's a deal then Luiz."

"You're a good man Roberto. I won't tell his mother until I hear something from you. I don't want to get her hopes up. Here's your food. Be careful, the fish is very hot. I just took it out of the fryer. What about some *jugo de maracuya*? It's fresh squeezed."

"It's my favorite. My mother claims the juice is where my passion comes from."

Roberto finished the meal Luiz had prepared for him and after a little small talk about each other's families, he said good-bye, promising again to try and find out something for Luiz about the fate of his son, Barbaro.

After asking permission, Roberto stopped along the road leading up the hill from La Pescadaria, to pick a small bag of fruit, still intending to stop and see Anabela Sobrino. He hoped that she was home and wanted to ask her if she remembered the old man from the hospital prison, Tiburcio, who told Roberto he had known her father and remembered him fondly as a great man and someone who played an important part in the history of Cuban art in the 20th century.

It was early afternoon by the time Roberto turned the corner onto Calle 15 where Anabela lived. Roberto couldn't help but notice several people from the neighborhood eyeing him suspiciously as he walked past the half dozen houses from the corner to number 1465. Remembering he was in uniform, Roberto began to feel a bit self-conscious, realizing the neighbors knew there would be no good reason why anyone wearing a special forces uniform would be walking in La Rampa neighborhood, especially on a Saturday afternoon.

He quickly knocked on the door and waited for what seemed like several minutes for Anabela to come to the door. No one answered. Just as he raised his hand to knock once more he heard Anabela's voice coming from the room overlooking the street on the second floor.

"Who is it?" she said, not bothering to step out onto the balcony.

"Anabela, it is Roberto Ramos. I am sorry to bother you, but I . . . ."

Anabela had just washed her hair and was drying it with a towel when she stepped out onto the balcony and looked down at Roberto.

"Roberto!" said Anabela excitedly, and clearly surprised, not letting Roberto finish what he was saying. "Just a minute, I'll be right down."

When Anabela opened the door she was smiling and seemed genuinely excited to see Roberto. Holding the handle to the door with her left hand she motioned for Roberto to come in.

"*Por favor*, Roberto, come in," she said.

"Thank you, Anabela," he replied, taking off his military hat and setting the bag of fruit on the floor by the door. "You know, your neighbors are not very friendly."

"I know, I know. Believe me, the rumors will be flying tonight. I don't have any patience for it. Please, sit down," said Anabela. "What are you doing in La Rampa?"

"I was just released from the Censam Marin Hospital and I'm on my way to my parents' home." Becoming increasingly nervous, he was beginning to second guess his decision to stop and see Anabela. "Sorry for stopping by unannounced."

Anabela paused and sat back in her chair. "Well," she said with a smile, waving her finger at Roberto while she spoke. "I always suspected you were crazy, Roberto, I mean, you love art. What the hell happened?"

"Oh, I'm so glad you're not upset with me."

"Upset? Listen, you're always welcome here Roberto. So what happened?"

"I assaulted my commanding officer who was threatening me. I'd had enough and one day I just exploded. He hit me and, well, let's just say he didn't have the skills to match his physical strength or the size of his ego. Anyway, I was arrested and sent to Censam Marin for one year. They told me I had issues with aggression."

"I can't believe they only held you for one year."

"Let's just say, I know a few people. And I was careful not to do or say anything that would prolong my visit."

"So what now? I see you still have your uniform so you must be reassigned."

"I've been reassigned to my old unit, under a different commanding officer of course, and I will continue my martial arts training."

"I didn't know you were an athlete, Roberto."

"Yes, national champion in Taekwondo, several times. Anabela, could I trouble you for something to drink?"

"I'm sorry, what would you like? You must be thirsty. The hospital is a long way from here, no?"

"I would really love a little coconut water if you have any."

"Wait here."

While Roberto waited for Anabela to return, he began looking around at the many paintings hanging in the small living room, covering almost every inch of available wall space. One in particular caught his eye. Roberto stood up and walked over to get a better look at the small painting done in the same style as *El Saxofonista* and thought perhaps it had been painted by Anabela's father. A close examination of the signature in the lower right-hand corner confirmed his suspicion.

"You like that one, Roberto? It's a portrait of my mother as a young woman."

"She's very beautiful."

"Yes, she was."

"Does she live here in Havana?"

"No, she died in Spain, not long after my father," said Anabela.

"I'm sorry, Anabela," said Roberto.

"Here, have some coconut water. In the painting my mother is wearing a scarf to protect her from the sun while she's picking flowers from her garden. She's just finished and has the flowers in a vase which she's holding from underneath with both hands. She loved to garden. Back then, in the 30's, when my father did the painting, everyone in the neighborhood had a garden."

"The colors are fantastic. It reminds me of a stained-glass window. You know, from a church."

"You're welcome to look around if you'd like. Most of the works I have were done by my father, before he left the country. I have many pieces from his collection as you may remember. Unfortunately, he was unable to take much of it with him when he fled Cuba."

"I would love to, but only if you have the time," said Roberto. "When I was in prison, my brother Carlitos—you remember him—when he came to visit, he would bring books for me to study on the works of many old *maestros Cubanos.*

"Here, we'll start with this one," said Anabela, pointing to another portrait, done by her father. "This is the earliest work I have of my father's."

One by one, Anabela went through each piece in her collection, explaining carefully to Roberto who the artist was for every painting, what the artist was trying to convey in their work, and the historical significance of each piece.

Nearly three hours had passed by the time they came to the last painting. The work depicted a woman, dancing alone. It had been done by her father and was the last one he completed on Cuban soil before fleeing to Spain. They stood together for a moment in silence, looking at the painting. The late afternoon light was beginning to filter in through the window, at the end of the long hallway where the painting hung, near the back of the house, illuminating the painting as though a spotlight had been shone directly on the painting and nothing else around it.

"I think this is the most important one, Anabela," said Roberto, continuing to stare at the painting.

Anabela turned and looked at Roberto. "The Cuban people have forgotten why these paintings are so important," said Anabela.

Roberto understood innately that what Anabela had said was a complex commentary on post-revolutionary, Cuban societal values determined now solely by political priorities. But he couldn't find the words to respond.

"The right of the individual to freely express oneself in Cuba and the right of the average person in Cuba to celebrate that expression through the arts, has been taken away forever. I hate them for it," Anabela continued.

It was then Roberto remembered the old man Tiburcio, from the prison hospital, whom he wanted to ask Anabela if she remembered.

"Anabela, I met an old man when I was first sent to the hospital prison, whom I think you may have known. His name was Tiburcio. I never knew his last name. He said he was an artist, a painter, and a friend of your father's. Do you remember him?" asked Roberto.

"Tiburcio, of course, Tiburcio Valdez. He was well known in Cuba and Spain. He was an exceptional portrait painter. I remember he painted the portraits of many wealthy Cubans before the revolution. He got into trouble with the communists after Fidel took over. I don't think he was particularly political in any way. He simply enjoyed portrait painting, and the people with the money, you know, they could afford to hire him. It paid the bills. What he really loved was painting scenes that depicted ordinary people from the countryside. But after the revolution the people with money were leaving or their businesses had been put under government control and so no one could afford to hire him. I believe he's been in prison a long time, no?"

"He is no longer in prison."

"Really, I can't believe that he was finally released."

"He wasn't. He died in Censam Marin, right after I met him. From what I could tell he went on a hunger strike and died in his sleep. I was the one that found him."

"You're learning first-hand how unhappy our country is, Roberto. The Cuban people have a great history. I suppose that's why we're so unhappy."

"I should be going, Anabela."

"You are very kind for stopping to see me, Roberto. I enjoy your company. If you have time this week, before you return to service, perhaps we can meet at La Bodeguita for a mojito."

"Maybe another time. Remember, I haven't worked in a year. I have no money," said Roberto, with a laugh.

"My treat then. I insist."

"I'll let you know. I still have your number. Oh, I forgot. I brought you some fruit from my friend's restaurant. Here, take what you like." Roberto held open the cloth bag full of mangos, sugar apples, and large avocado, or alligator pears as they were known locally.

"I love sugar apples, thank you. You know, I had an uncle I never knew, who died when he was a young boy, when he choked on a seed from one of these. His mother, my grandmother, would never allow anyone to bring another sugar apple into her home after her son died."

"*Ten cuidado entonces,* Anabela," Roberto remarked affectionately.

"I'll be careful," said Anabela opening the door for Roberto. "Stay out of trouble kid."

"I'll try," he promised. Stepping back out onto the sidewalk he noticed many of Anabela's neighbors were still sitting on their stoops and leaning from their balconies, seeming not to have moved since he entered Anabela's house more than three hours earlier. It was almost as though they had been waiting for him to emerge, and so he couldn't help himself, and stopped to wave goodbye.

"Anabela, I will always remember this afternoon," he said with a smile, thinking he would give the neighbors a little something to talk about.

"Yes. Me as well," she shouted. In the fading light of the cool and clear Havana evening, she waved one last time to Roberto from her doorstep, before turning to go back inside the house, ignoring the prying eyes of her neighbors.

It was just after sunset when Roberto arrived at the home of his parents in Santos Suarez. After entering through the front door he quietly closed the door behind him and stood for a moment inside the entrance at the front of the hallway.

VIII

One year had passed since he'd been home. It seemed much longer he thought to himself, and the house felt unfamiliar. The light from a single kerosene lamp with the flame set low, burning in the living room, provided only enough light to see to the end of the hallway leading to the back of the house, and he could hear the faint sound of voices coming from the kitchen. A slight haze, produced by the smoke from something cooking on the stove, combined with the fresh-smelling smoke from someone's cigar, hung in the hallway.

Carrying his bag with the remaining fruit from Luiz, Roberto walked to the end of the hall, turned the corner to the left and stood in the half light of the doorway to the kitchen.

Seated at the kitchen table with his back toward Roberto, was his younger brother Lazaro, along with his brother Carlos, and his sister Rosalena. Sitting around the large wooden table on the terrace outside the kitchen, all three enjoying a cigar and a small glass of rum, was the rest of the family: his father Guillermo, and the two older brothers, Pedro and Guillermo junior. There were three empty rum bottles on the terrace table, one at either end, and one in the middle. Each held a lighted white candle, and the table was set for seven. His mother Rosa, who always refused any help in the kitchen, was finishing the last few preparations for the evening meal.

No one heard Roberto when he entered the house. Nor had they noticed him standing just outside the doorway leading into the kitchen.

"What," said Roberto. "I'm no longer invited to the Saturday family supper?"

Roberto's mother Rosa, surprised by the sound of Roberto's voice, and turning around quickly nearly dropped the large bowl of peas and rice she was holding.

"It's not enough I have to visit you in prison and now you want to scare me half to death," said Rosa, looking over her shoulder as she placed the bowl on the table.

"Roberto! When did they release you?" cried Carlos.

Roberto walked into the kitchen from the hallway and placed the bag of fruit he was carrying on the kitchen table. "Just this morning, Carlitos. They never told me I was going to be released. The doctors came to my ward early, handed me my old uniform and told me I was free to go. I couldn't believe it."

Roberto, stopping first to kiss his sister Rosalena on the top of her head and slap Carlos and Lazaro each on the shoulder, quickly followed his mother outside to the terrace.

Rosa was standing next to Roberto's father Guillermo, who was still seated at the table. Her head was down and she was bent over slightly with her hands on the table.

"I'm sorry, Mother," said Roberto, as he put his arms around her. "I found out early today I would be freed only minutes before I was to be released. I should have called."

Rosa turned around and held Roberto and began crying. "I had convinced myself you would end up like the old man," said Rosa, now sobbing uncontrollably.

"You mean, Tiburcio?" asked Roberto.

"I don't remember his name. It doesn't matter. Here sit down with your father," said Rosa.

Rosa took a small, peach-colored handkerchief from a pocket in her cooking apron, carefully dried her eyes and returned to the kitchen to finish preparing the meal.

Roberto had not seen his father in over a year. He was nervous, and he was unsure what to say to him.

"How is the cigar, Father?" asked Roberto. In an effort to ease the tension, unable to think of anything else to say.

"It is a very fine cigar. Vicente rolled these yesterday. He received a small shipment of leaves from Vuelta Abajo," said Guillermo. His father placed his cigar in the glass ash tray and looked directly at his son. "Roberto, I want you to know I am very proud of you. Believe me, I know what you did to Charon was dangerous, and maybe you shouldn't have reacted the way you did, but you did the right thing. We don't need to talk about what happened any more than that."

"Understood," said Roberto.

"I see you are wearing your uniform," said Guillermo.

"Yes, I have been reassigned to my old unit."

"What about your training? Are you going to continue?"

Roberto was about to answer his father when his mother, along with the rest of the family who were in the kitchen, returned to the terrace with the remainder of the evening meal, which consisted of land crab and cornmeal stew with fried sweet plantains.

"Talk later, I cooked all afternoon," said Rosa.

"Can you believe we were never given any *cangrejo de tierra* in prison," said Roberto, sarcastically.

"Well then, you should be particularly grateful for this evening," said Rosa softly.

"I am always grateful, *Madre*. You know that."

"Well, maybe you would like to show your gratitude then and say the blessing," said Rosa.

"It's been awhile, *Madre*, but I'll do my best."

Roberto realized how long it had been since the entire family had been together and wanted to find just the right words to express his feelings of gratitude, not just for the occasion, but more importantly for the unconditional love and support from each of them, and so he began.

"I am only able to tell you how I feel at this moment, and what I know to be true. I want you to know there is nothing more important to me than the love and loyalty I receive from you, my family. Moments such as these are becoming less frequent for us and so, more important than ever. I am grateful, and I will cherish this moment forever. I know also there is not a lot of hope today in Cuba, but there is a lot of love, and it is powerful. I love you all, and promise you, one day, with this power, I will bring you hope. God bless this food and God bless my family, amen."

No one spoke. Rosa was holding back tears, and everyone else but Carlos was unable to look at Roberto.

"I believe you, Roberto," said Carlos, breaking the silence. "I don't know how it will happen, but I know one day you will find hope."

"Not only for me, Carlitos, but for all of us."

"You are still young, Roberto," said Roberto's father. "You think you can't be broken. What I know is eventually they break us all. We are powerless against them."

"I respect you, Father, but you are wrong. I will not be broken. I would rather die than live without freedom. It is the most precious of all human rights," proclaimed Roberto.

"Enough foolishness, all of you," said Rosa. "I would like to enjoy the meal which I worked very hard to prepare and to enjoy in the company of my family."

"*Lo siento, Madre*," said Roberto.

It would be many years before Roberto and his family would be together once more. His brothers and sister, with the exception of Carlos, had one by one left home and were all busy with their own lives.

IX

Roberto's return to military service with his former special forces unit was surprisingly uneventful. Due to the large number of new recruits assigned to his unit his return went virtually unnoticed. It was a different situation, however, when he returned to the athletic center where he and Antonio Castro had trained regularly. All but a handful of his former teammates would acknowledge him publicly and were reluctant to interact with Roberto, even in private.

Roberto understood the situation and wasn't bothered by it. With a renewed sense of purpose his immediate goal was to try and regain his position on the national Taekwondo team. No easy task, as he had lost a full year of training, along with the sharp edge of athletic perfection that can only be acquired through repeated high-level competition with athletes of similar abilities.

After four months of intense training, Roberto, continuing to gain confidence in his level of fitness, and with the national championships only a month away, knew his chances of making the team were high. He was fit, focused, and relaxed. Once again, he was beginning to dominate the informal competitions in his weight class and in so doing had slowly regained the respect and trust of the other athletes, eventually getting to a point of acceptance where he and the other athletes felt comfortable spending time together socially.

Roberto understood intuitively it was in his best interest to keep a low profile while in the presence of all but a few of the ranking officers in his unit. He could sense a level of suspicion among a number of his immediate superiors and carefully avoided any unnecessary interactions with them, especially those officers who still had connections to Colonel Charon. The only constant in the Cuban military hierarchy more prevalent than paranoia was revenge, and the two typically went hand in hand.

Fortunately for Roberto, the officer in charge of his unit, Captain

Rafael Perez, had no connection to his former commanding officer, Colonel Charon, and knew little about the incident which led to Roberto's arrest and imprisonment. Roberto had a good relationship with Perez, and while mostly professional in nature, it was without problems. Roberto liked and trusted Perez and felt he had gained the respect of his commander.

Late one afternoon at the end of a particularly long and uncomfortably hot time on duty at Punto Cero, Perez invited Roberto and several other men from his unit for a beer at the officers' club. He had not been in the club at the Havana Biltmore since returning to service, but remembered clearly the last time he was there and his conversation with Antonio Castro. He was somewhat surprised by the invitation from Captain Perez, but thought little of it and happily accepted.

Captain Perez could not have been more different than Colonel Charon. Small in stature, Perez was unassuming and selfless. He regularly showed interest in and respect for his men, and with a propensity for compliance, he had all the qualities the military required of a loyal midlevel military officer. Men like Perez were a mystery to Roberto, and he never understood what motivated them.

The Captain chose to sit with his men at a table on an outdoor terrace overlooking Castro's private football pitch, known only to elite military personnel and recognized as the finest in the country. Roberto remembered it well as he had played there many times with Antonio Castro when they were training together before his arrest.

"Have you been here before, Ramos?" asked Captain Perez.

"Only once to the club, sir, but I competed many times on this field with Antonio Castro. We used to train together."

"It's the finest in the country."

"What about you, Captain, have you ever had any athletic training?"

"Some baseball, but that was a long time ago. I was a good fielder but had trouble hitting, so my career was a short one."

"You need to have both to make it as a player. I think baseball is the most competitive sport in Cuba today."

"What about you, Ramos?"

"What do you mean?"

"When you leave the military, what do you plan on doing?"

"I have no plans. I would like to find a nice woman, maybe settle down. I only have experience in athletic training, so my career options are limited. Without any university training a professional job is out of the question, and the time I spent in Censam Marin has become a liability, especially when it comes to women," said Roberto.

"I can imagine."

"I remember once, several years ago, before I entered the military, I was interested in this girl in my neighborhood. She said she wouldn't go out with me unless I wore a pair of American blue jeans."

"Did you ever get the blue jeans?"

"No," said Roberto. "Not the blue jeans or the girl. I didn't have the money at the time. I'd still like a pair of jeans though," Roberto laughed.

"You ever decide you want the jeans Ramos, let me know. I have a friend who has connections in Florida. I can get almost anything I want from him."

I think it would be a little risky for me, given my record."

"There's no risk to you, Ramos, trust me. I do it all the time for these guys," said Perez, pointing to some of the other officers sitting nearby.

"Yeah, and none of these guys were ever in prison, as far as I know," Roberto countered.

"Suit yourself, but I'm telling you I'm the one taking the risk."

"How much?"

"The last time I was able to bring in a pair of American blue jeans it was $150, American dollars."

"But Captain, you know it's illegal to possess American dollars, and, you know I have a record. Where the hell am I going to find one hundred and fifty American dollars? That's a lot of money for an enlisted man."

"The dollars are no problem. I have a good friend who can exchange the money for you. You want his address? He can give you the money tomorrow. You let me know and in one week you'll have your jeans. The rate right now is 5 1/2 to 1. It's up to you. You want the girl or not, Ramos?" said Perez, now smiling.

"I don't know Captain. Let me think about it."

"Here is the name of my friend. Just tell him I sent you. Just don't tell anyone where you got his name."

The Captain wrote down the name and address on a small card, and slid it across the table next to the beer in front of Roberto.

Roberto picked up the card and looked at it closely. "You do this all the time?" asked Roberto, looking for additional reassurance.

"All the time," said Perez, confidently.

Although Roberto had no reason to believe the Captain was being untruthful about his ability to deliver on his promise of a pair of American jeans, there was something about the way the Captain had casually answered all of Roberto's questions that left him feeling uneasy and suspicious.

It was after questioning some of the other men who had been with Roberto and the Captain at the Havana Biltmore Club, what they thought of the Captain's offer, that Roberto became sufficiently convinced he was not personally at risk, and so decided to make arrangements to exchange the money and to pay the Captain for the jeans.

Due to go on leave in several weeks, Roberto was increasingly excited about the prospect of wearing the blue jeans in his old neighborhood while on leave. But after two weeks had passed with no word from Captain Perez about the jeans, Roberto began to wonder if his Captain would follow through on his promise. Not wanting to wait until his scheduled leave, he felt he had no choice but to ask his commanding officer when he could expect to see the jeans. After all, he thought, he had promised to pay Perez almost his entire savings and couldn't afford to lose the money.

Late one afternoon at the end of his time on duty, Roberto was preparing to return to his barracks when he noticed Captain Perez entering the security headquarters at Punto Cero, along with several other officers. He decided to follow the Captain to his office and ask Perez if he intended to follow through on his promise.

Roberto didn't have security clearance credentials to enter the headquarters, and had never even been inside the building, but thought perhaps he could bluff his way past the guards in the lobby by simply showing them his Secret Service badge.

Upon entering the building, Roberto confidently walked up to the security desk, pulled out his SS badge and showed it to one of the guards standing beside an additional set of doors leading to the interior.

"I am here for a meeting with Captain Perez," he announced.

"Wait over there," said the guard pointing to a wooden bench at the end of the lobby. "I'll let the Captain know you're here."

Roberto had been waiting nearly thirty minutes, and was beginning to second-guess his decision to confront the Captain when the security guard reappeared in the lobby and motioned for Roberto to follow him into the building.

"Follow the hallway around to the right and the Captain's office is the last door on the left. He's waiting for you," said the guard.

When Roberto reached the office the door was open slightly and he could hear Perez talking on the phone. He knocked lightly several times and then pushed the door open slowly. Standing in the doorway he waited for permission to enter.

Captain Perez was seated at his desk with his back toward the door still talking on the phone.

"Then it's agreed, we'll take care of it tomorrow," said the Captain, as he hung up the phone and turned around to face Roberto. "Ramos, have a seat. I assume you're here about the American jeans."

"Yes. You said you would have them a week ago. I went to see your friend so I have the money."

"I'm sorry Ramos, it's taking a little longer than I expected. My friend had a few issues in Florida which delayed the shipment. I will have them here in three days, I promise. I tell you what, you know La Pescadaria, down by the river? You can meet me there tomorrow, after you are off duty. I prefer to meet there. Bring the money with you. It's $150 American dollars."

"I know La Pescadaria. My friend Luiz is the owner. What time?"

"I'll meet you there at 5:30. Best to come alone. The fewer people with us the better."

"I'll be there with the money," said Roberto as he turned to leave.

Knowing if he was caught with American dollars in his possession he would unquestionably be sent back to jail, he was becoming increasingly nervous and wanted to back out of the deal, but realized that after exchanging Cuban pesos for dollars, he had no other options for getting rid of the American money, other than to buy the American blue jeans from the Captain.

After Roberto's shift ended at 4:30, he decided to leave early for La Pescadaria, which was only a ten-minute walk from Punto Cero. He would have something to eat and a cold beer, he thought, and have a little time to speak with his friend, Luiz. Roberto wanted to know if Luiz had received word from his son, Barbaro, since his defection.

When Roberto arrived at the restaurant, he noticed there were few customers and thought it strange, especially for a Friday evening. Luiz was speaking to two men seated at one of the tables and hadn't seen Roberto enter the restaurant.

Walking over to Luiz, Roberto tapped him on the shoulder, apologized to the two men for interrupting, said hello to Luiz and told him he wanted to sit outside on the veranda, overlooking the river. Neither of the men said anything to Roberto, and Luiz, who hadn't seen Roberto in several months, seemed oddly subdued.

When Luiz had finished taking the men's order, rather than coming out on the veranda to speak with Roberto, he went straight to the kitchen. While Roberto continued to wait for Luiz to return, he noticed one of the men had left the restaurant and had been gone for some time before returning.

Roberto was becoming impatient waiting for Luiz and decided to go to the kitchen and ask Luiz for a beer and to order some food. It was then he saw Captain Perez enter the restaurant, dressed in civilian clothing.

After greeting the Captain, Roberto told him he had a table on the veranda and was just on his way to the kitchen to order something to eat, and would he like to sit outside where they could talk alone.

"I'm sitting at the first table along the railing. Would you like a cold beer?" asked Roberto.

"Sure, and Ramos, did you bring the money?" asked the Captain.

"Of course. And what about the jeans?"

"I have them outside in the jeep. I can give them to you just as we are leaving. Safer that way. Why don't you give me the money now."

"I'll give it to you when I come back with the beer."

When Roberto entered the kitchen Luiz was busy preparing the food for the two other men in the restaurant.

"Luiz," said Roberto.

"Oh, Roberto. Sorry I was a bit rude earlier. I was nervous about those two men. I've never seen them before and I thought maybe they were here to shut me down. I'm a little paranoid about that."

"No problem, Luiz. You doing okay?"

"Yes, of course. What can I get for you?"

"A couple beers for now and maybe some food later."

"Okay, I'll bring them to your table when I finish here."

As Roberto was leaving the kitchen he noticed the Captain had come back inside the restaurant and was talking with the two men he had seen when he first arrived at La Pescadaria. It seemed strange to Roberto that Perez was acquainted with the men but thought little more about it.

The Captain's conversation with the two men was brief and when he returned to the table and sat down Roberto noticed he was sweating heavily.

"You have the money?" asked the Captain.

Roberto, not answering, reached into his pocket and pulled out the clip containing the $150 dollars in American bills and handed it to Perez. Perez quickly counted the money, making sure it was the correct amount and put it in his pocket.

"You seem a little nervous Captain."

It was at that point that the two men from inside whom the Captain had been talking with appeared in the doorway leading out onto the veranda, each holding what Roberto immediately recognized as Russian made Makarov handguns.

Roberto, realizing what was happening, instantly stood up from the table, holding his chair as though he was about to hit the Captain with it.

"You set me up," said Roberto realizing what had happened. "I trusted you, you prick."

"If I were you Ramos, I would go peacefully," said Perez.

"If they weren't armed, you'd all be dead," threatened Roberto angrily.

"Turn around and lie face down on the floor. Now!" said one of the men.

Although barely able to contain his anger, Roberto knew he had no choice other than to obey the man's order. He paused briefly and then threw the chair he was still holding to the side, the noise attracting the attention of Luiz who was coming out of the kitchen holding the two beers Roberto had ordered.

"Get back in the kitchen old man," said Perez.

"You hurt my friend and I'll kill you, Perez!" yelled Roberto.

"You do as I say and no one gets hurt," said the Captain.

Luiz began to back up slowly in the direction of the kitchen but stumbled over a chair and fell to the floor, dropping the beer bottles he was holding in an attempt to break his fall.

Roberto waited until Luiz had gotten up and was out of sight in the kitchen before he turned around and laid face down on the floor, where he was quickly placed in handcuffs.

"Put him in the jeep," yelled Perez. "Colonel Torrez will be happy to see you, Ramos."

"Torrez, Colonel Torrez at DTI?" said Roberto. "You send me to DTI because I have American dollars?"

"You should be more careful, Ramos," said the Captain, with a laugh.

It was raining heavily when the jeep Roberto was riding in passed through the wooden gates leading into the DTI prison compound where he had been held in solitary confinement a little more than a year ago.

There was no wind and the unrelenting, heavy tropical rain was now coming straight down, quickly filling the courtyard in front of the prison entrance ankle deep, turning the red limestone grassless soil to a muddy soup.

"Alright Ramos, let's go," said one of the men, as he opened the rear side door of the jeep and motioned for Roberto to step out.

By the time the two men had escorted Roberto the thirty feet to the doors leading into the prison headquarters, his uniform was soaked through from the rain and he was covered in mud from the knees down.

Once inside Roberto was taken to the warden's office where he was again met by Colonel Torres, the prison warden.

"Ramos, I remember you," said Torres. "What have we done now?"

"I was set up by another one of the Comandante's stooges," said Roberto.

"Captain Perez is a loyal and honorable Communist," said the Colonel.

"There are many loyal dogs who suffer at the hands of their owners, and there is no such thing as an honorable Communist," replied Roberto.

"Ramos, unless we come to an agreement you will never see the light of day. We'll continue our discussion later. Put him in solitary," said the Colonel.

"I need some dry clothes, Colonel," said Roberto.

"You don't need anything. Take him to solitary immediately."

As Roberto descended the stone stairs leading down to the prison's solitary confinement, flanked in front and behind by the two men who had arrested him, he could hear voices coming from two of the cells.

Upon reaching the bottom, Roberto recognized the hallway and the eight cell doors as the same location he had been held after he was arrested for assaulting Colonel Charon.

Walking by the first cell on his right, Roberto could just make out in the low light of the hallway, the yellowed, bloodshot eyes of one of the men he had heard talking, peering through the small head-height window in the steel door. The man's eyes were wide and unblinking and looked like the eyes of a dog that had been living in a cage for a long time rather than those of a human being.

"*Hola*," said Roberto. The man said nothing and continued staring at Roberto through the window as he walked past the cell.

"Keep moving, Ramos," said one of the men escorting Roberto to his cell. "*Numero ocho*, on the left."

"Know it well," murmured Roberto.

The guard unlocked the door to the cell and ordered Roberto inside and to stand with his back toward the opening while he removed the handcuffs from Roberto's wrists.

As the guards shut the door to Roberto's cell, the remaining light coming through the door opening from the hallway quickly faded to near total darkness. It was cold and Roberto remembered how difficult it had been to stay warm in the cell, especially at night. The uniform he was wearing was still wet from the rain, only adding to his discomfort, and unless he was issued dry prison clothes it would be a long night, thought Roberto.

"Ramos," said the other of the two men he had heard talking.

Roberto looked out through the small window in his cell door but could only see the door to the cell on the opposite side of the hallway, which was unoccupied.

"Ramos," the man said again. "What's your first name?"

"It's Roberto. And what about you, what is your name?"

"My name is Barbaro, Barbaro Perez. It is my pleasure, Roberto."

"Barbaro?" said Roberto. "Are you the son of Luiz Perez, the owner of La Pescadaria?"

"Yes, you know my father, Roberto?"

"Yes. As a matter of fact I was arrested there today. Your father is a good friend," said Roberto.

"Is my father alright? They didn't harm him, did they?"

"Your father is okay. A little frightened, but fine. He's very worried about you. He told me you attempted to escape by boat several months ago. What happened?"

"The boat was old and in disrepair. We didn't make it very far before it began to take on water and we had to abandon it for a small raft we had on board for emergencies. We floated for two days before the Cuban Coast Guard picked us up. They roughed us up pretty good."

"What about the other two guys? Your father said there were three of you. What happened to them?"

"I don't know what happened to them. I was a little more outspoken, shall we say, when they hauled us on-board and I ended up in this rat-infested shit hole. I should have had a better plan. I didn't know anything about boats. I just knew I had to get the hell out of Cuba. And what about you, why were you arrested?"

"I was arrested for possessing American dollars. I'd been in prison at Censam Marin for about a year when they released me. After that I returned to duty. I was special forces at Punto Cero. They were constantly watching me after I was released. I got set up by my commanding officer," said Roberto.

"Roberto," said the other man. "I am Enrique."

"*Encantado*, Enrique. And why are you here?" asked Roberto.

"It is my pleasure also, Roberto. Well, you see I write; well, I used to; mostly poetry, and it is not very flattering to the revolution. Why did they send you to Censam Marin Roberto? I thought that place was for the mentally ill."

Roberto, hearing footsteps coming from the stone stairway, did not answer Enrique.

Two guards had come down the steps into the hallway and were now standing in front of Roberto's cell.

"Ramos, take off your uniform. When I open the door you place it on the floor in the hallway in front of the cell," said one of the guards.

Thinking that they had arrived with a clean, dry prison uniform, Roberto quickly took off his soggy military uniform, and when the guard opened the door to his cell, placed it on the floor in front of the cell.

"Enjoy your evening, Ramos," said one of the guards taking the wet uniform and closing the cell door.

"What about some dry clothes?" yelled Roberto.

There was no response from either of the guards as they made their way back up the stairs. Roberto heard only the sound of their footsteps scraping against the stone steps followed by the metallic muffled sound of a steel security door opening and closing.

"Barbaro, have the guards brought the food this evening?" asked Roberto.

"Yes, maybe an hour ago. I don't think they're coming back tonight. I'm sorry Roberto."

"I'll manage, thanks," said Roberto.

Roberto sat down on the stone bench and leaned back against the wall. The stone was cold and damp and there would be no way to keep warm he thought. He remembered from the first time he had been held in solitary confinement how difficult it had been to keep warm, especially at night, and always when it rained heavily the rainwater would seep down from above, the water cooling as it passed down through the stone making it feel colder in the cell.

"Roberto," said Enrique. "What do you do in the military?"

Roberto stood up in order to be a little closer to the small window opening in the cell door and to answer Enrique.

"I am in the special forces unit assigned to Punto Cero. I also compete on the national Taekwondo and Karate teams."

"What is Punto Cero, a military base? I've never heard of it."

"No, it's not a military base. It's one of Fidel's private houses. If you could see how he lives you wouldn't believe it. He has many houses all around the country."

"But he says his house is a fisherman's cottage. I've heard him say as much, many times in his speeches."

"Fidel is a liar and a paranoid con artist, Enrique, and if you challenge him in any way, no matter who you are, you're liable to end up dead or in prison. Hell, look what he did to the people that fought with him to liberate Cuba from Batista in the Sierra Maestra. People like Cienfuegos and Huber Matos. Especially Matos. They tortured Matos in this very prison, for many years. Matos was a patriotic Cuban and always anti-communist. Hell, he probably spent years in one of these cells. Imagine Enrique."

"I don't have to imagine, Roberto, nor do you," said Enrique, his voice drifting off.

Roberto sat back down on the bench. The conversation with Enrique had been a distraction from the cold and he was grateful to have someone to talk with. I can deal with the cold he thought, but it was the near total darkness and isolation that Roberto feared most.

His thoughts eventually turned to his mother and father, and to his brother Carlos. They were expecting him to be home on leave from the military next month, and if his imprisonment were to last more than a few weeks they would begin to worry. The crime of possessing American dollars he was certain was not a capital offense in the eyes of the government. The government was simply trying to teach him a lesson, he thought, and would release him within a few days.

Roberto again stood and looked out the small window in the door. He wondered how long Enrique had been imprisoned. The look in

Enrique's eyes, he thought, was a combination of terror and helplessness, and he could sense that Enrique was nearing the limit of his ability to control his sanity. Roberto felt sorry for him because he knew the heart of a poet is fragile and not easily repaired once broken.

"Enrique," said Roberto, waiting for a reply before continuing to speak.

"Yes, Roberto," said Enrique.

"How long have you been here?"

"I am not sure. It's impossible to keep track of time because you never see any daylight and they don't allow anyone in from outside. At first I would count the number of meals I received, two for each day, but after several months I began to forget. I've lost track of time."

"They can't hold you forever. It's illegal. Did you have a trial and were you sentenced?"

"They can do whatever they want. True they can't hold you forever, but they can hold you until you are dead."

"But did you have a trial?"

"Sure, I had a trial, but political trials in Cuba are a farce. They're intended to instill fear in the masses, not to determine justice. The psychology of the tyrant is the same everywhere. Funny how dictators always seem to find just enough support among the ordinary people to retain power."

"What do you mean when you say the ordinary people?" questioned Roberto.

"Ordinary people who lack the ability for critical thought and so easily fall victim to the charms of someone like Fidel. Tyrants are always charismatic, make a lot of promises, and easily convince the plain folk that the current leadership is the reason their lives are a failure, like Fidel did in 1959. I write about it in my poetry, or at least I used to."

"What will you do when you are released, Enrique?"

"I don't think about it, not anymore."

"I've thought about leaving Cuba for the U.S., especially recently."

Barbaro had been listening to the conversation between Roberto and Enrique. "If you want my advice, Roberto, find someone who knows something about boats," said Barbaro. "And you need to study the weather and the Gulf Stream currents. The ocean is always changing, and conditions need to be perfect to make the crossing. It is not so easy."

"You have a bigger problem now, Roberto."

"You mean how the hell do I get out of here?"

"Yes, and if you are lucky enough to get out alive they will always be watching you."

"I understand that now. Barbaro, how much for a good boat? A safe one that can make the crossing," said Roberto.

"At least twenty-five thousand pesos. You need something that can make 15 knots or more. It is difficult to find a boat like that."

"So is finding twenty-five thousand pesos," replied Roberto.

"I know but I'm telling you, if you buy some old leaky piece of junk you'll never make it. It's nearly 160 kilometers and with the strong Gulf Stream current pushing you on a diagonal to the east, the distance is even greater. There have been thousands of people who have attempted to make it across and were unprepared. Many paid the ultimate price, Roberto. I was lucky in some ways. I'm still alive."

"And what about your future, Barbaro?" asked Roberto.

When Barbaro didn't respond Roberto regretted having made the comment.

"I'm sorry. I shouldn't have asked you that. It's not as though I have a lot of options either," said Roberto.

"No, it's okay. You're just being honest. I'm still young and—who knows—someday if I manage to get out of here I will try again. I have no choice. I'll never be happy here in Cuba. Not unless and until the Castros are gone and we have a government that is capable of providing some sort of hope for the average Cuban." "That could be many years from now," Roberto replied. "I'm not prepared to wait."

"Roberto, I feel a little weak and need to rest. We will talk again tomorrow. I hope you don't suffer too much from the cold," said Barbaro.

"Thanks, but I'll manage. I've suffered worse."

Roberto sat down and leaned against the wall on one end of the stone bench. The rough surface of the sandstone had been worn down from countless men leaning against it, and it felt smooth to the touch. Rubbing his arms with his hands to create warmth he pulled his legs up to his chest and tried to think about anything but the cold. Sleep was impossible and Roberto knew it would be a long night.

The hours passed slowly, and the damp cold was taking its toll physically and psychologically on Roberto. At times during the night when his body temperature dropped too low, he would begin to shake uncontrollably. The cell was small, barely five-feet long, and only allowed for limited movement, but it was just enough to help raise his body temperature to the point where he could then sit for a few minutes without shaking.

By the time the guards arrived the next morning with water and a prison issued uniform Roberto was exhausted from trying to keep warm. He felt miserable and was beginning to panic, but sensing the guards were expecting to find him in a state of desperation, he was determined to reveal nothing.

"Ramos!" shouted the guard as he looked through the small window in the cell door. Before we open the door, you turn around and kneel on the floor. Don't move until you hear the cell door close. Understood?"

"I could use some water."

"Just do as you're told."

With his back toward the door, Roberto knelt down and waited for the guards to open the door. When the door opened, the light coming from the hallway cast a shadow of the two men on the wall on the back of the cell. Roberto could tell from the shadow that one of the men was holding something that appeared to be made of cloth.

"Here is some water and a uniform," said the guard. The guard placed both on the stone bench in front and slightly to the side of where

Roberto was kneeling.

Upon hearing the metallic clicking sound made when the guard turned the key, locking the door to the cell, he immediately stood up and felt around in the dark for the uniform, being careful not to tip over the water bottles which he remembered were open on top.

After allowing his eyes to readjust to the darkness and before he put on the uniform, he placed the two bottles of water in a small depression in the stone in the corner on top of the bench against the wall in such a way that they would be less likely to fall over.

He picked up what he thought was the top of the uniform, felt around for the metal clasps on the front of the shirt and quickly slipped it over his head. The shirt was long sleeve and made from a heavy coarse cloth that when in contact with his skin began to stimulate the flow of blood, gradually leading to a feeling of warmth. After closing the last clasp on the shirt, he turned up the collar to keep the cold off his neck and without taking his boots off, pulled the pants on, one leg at a time, leaned back against the stone wall, and fell asleep.

Hours later, Roberto was awakened by voices coming from the hallway. He had no idea how long he had been asleep but was feeling better after having slept and was no longer cold. Looking out the small window he saw no one but recognized the voices of Barbaro and Enrique.

"Buenos dias, amigos," said Roberto.

"I believe you may have missed the morning, Roberto," said Barbaro.

"How are you feeling now, Roberto?" Enrique asked.

"Better now with some dry clothing. I'm a little hungry."

"You missed the morning meal, I'm afraid. They feed us what they call the main meal sometime in the early morning, and then breakfast in the afternoon," explained Barbaro.

"When I was here before I received only one meal. Why do you have breakfast late in the day?"

"They do it sometimes simply to mess with us. To make us think it's morning when it's not and evening when it's actually morning. It makes it a little harder to keep track of the days. But what does it matter?"

"Roberto, when you were here before, did they torture you?" asked Enrique.

"No, and what about you?"

"Sometimes, yes. Nothing brutal, only what they call white torture. The kind that doesn't leave any marks. I survived."

"And you, Barbaro? Have they tortured you?"

"No, not yet anyway. The warden is a big fan of my team, Occidentales, so maybe he has a soft spot for me, who knows."

"Do you think you are good enough to make it in the American Big Leagues, Barbaro?" asked Enrique.

"Honestly, I feel I am a better player than my name sake, Barbaro Garbey, and he made it in the Big Leagues and even won a World Series Championship with the Tigers of Detroit. I know I could make it in the Big Leagues."

"Then you should never give up your dream," encouraged Roberto.

"What is your dream, Roberto?" asked Barbaro.

"Promise you will not laugh?"

"Freedom is not something to laugh about," said Enrique.

"I want to become a scholar of Cuban fine art, and collect works from the time before the Revolution," replied Roberto.

"What would you do with your collection?" asked Enrique.

"I could be an art dealer, or maybe have a museum, or maybe both. All I know is that art is the only thing that gives me a feeling of freedom. For me, there's nothing like it."

"I believe it is illegal to deal in antiquities in Cuba," said Enrique.

"It is illegal, but it is not impossible," said Roberto.

"Where would this gallery or museum be?" asked Barbaro.

"In the U.S.," said Roberto. "It's hard for us to imagine the kind of money people must have there and the extent of the opportunities. But I believe it is great."

"I can tell from the tone of your voice that you are sincere and that your dream is real," said Enrique. "Who knows, maybe someday, if I make it out of here alive, I will visit you in your gallery."

"We're going to make it Enrique, and you too, Barbaro. Once you know what it feels like to be free, nothing less will do."

"How do you know when the feeling is true?" asked Barbaro.

"Well, for you, Barbaro, surely you remember stepping up to the plate when you felt completely relaxed and you were full of confidence and the ball that day looked as big as a football when it left the pitcher's hand. Your balance was perfect and when you swung the bat, every movement seemed effortless, and at the point of contact with the ball, the feeling was like none other. The sound of the bat cleanly striking the ball was sharp but thick and fat sounding, and you felt the baseball compress slightly. Your hands were relaxed, so the feeling was somewhat soft but solid, and even though you had felt the feeling many times before, it still felt new and wonderful. That fleeting moment of perfection that you and you alone had created, was all you ever wanted, and for an instant you felt free, truly free," said Roberto.

"Yes, it is all I ever wanted, and they've stolen my dream to make it happen," said Barbaro in a low voice.

"What about you, Roberto. Have you ever felt truly free?" asked Enrique.

"Yes, I remember clearly the first time I had the feeling, Enrique. I began to develop a sense of it shortly after my brother and I acquired a very important painting from a family friend, as payment for moving his belongings. It was quite unexpected actually. I had never been exposed to any sort of fine art and at the time it meant nothing to me. During the time I was being held at Censam Marin, my brother Carlitos would visit me once a month, always bringing with him art books containing the works of old Cuban masters from the time before the revolution. As soon as I opened one of those books—I don't know how to describe the feeling—it was as though I stepped into another world. A world where I was free to imagine a life of unlimited possibilities. Art for me has become a refuge from the oppression we are forced to endure every day here in Cuba. I'm not a writer, Enrique, but surely that is how you must feel when you are writing, and when the writing is going well," said Roberto.

"That is exactly how I feel. Totally free. Of course there are days when the words do not come easily and the writing is hard: more like work. But then there are the days when your mind is sharp and clear and you are able to effortlessly express your thoughts and feelings. I live for those moments. You know, the end result is not that dissimilar from your description of how Barbaro must feel when he is hitting a baseball. We just have a slightly different pathway to the same place," said Enrique.

"I never thought of it that way," said Roberto, with a laugh. "Now I feel compelled to read poetry."

"I must tell you, Roberto. For someone who has no formal training in the arts, you are surprisingly aware. That is a rare quality; it is a gift," said Enrique.

"Maybe it is the key to my future," said Roberto.

"They've stolen our futures," said Barbaro quietly.

"Not yet, Barbaro," replied Roberto.

"Maybe, but if we can't find a way out of here, we have no future."

"This situation is temporary."

"I worry about going crazy, Roberto."

"As long as you are able to prevent the regime from inhabiting your mind, you will remain unbroken, Barbaro," said Enrique.

"Easier said than done Enrique," Barbaro answered.

"Don't give up your dream, Barbaro. You're too young. Imagine how you would feel if you one day made it to the Big Leagues, and the feeling of pride your father would have for his son," said Roberto.

Barbaro did not answer Roberto and the conversation among the three men ended. Roberto wanted Barbaro to understand that because of his status as a professional athlete, Barbaro had some leverage, but Roberto could sense that Barbaro was in a dark place mentally. Now was not the time to pressure him further or examine the degree of his commitment to a more hopeful future.

Roberto sat down on the stone bench with his back toward the side wall. Stretching his legs out along the top of the bench he leaned against the back wall of the cell, rolled his hands under his shirttail for warmth, crossed his outstretched legs, and fell asleep.

X

Several months had passed, or so it seemed to Roberto, since he had been arrested and sent back to DTI. It was impossible to keep track of time in solitary confinement, and ultimately, unimportant. Barbaro was no longer in the cell block with Roberto and Enrique. Perhaps he had been taken to another area of the prison, or possibly sent to another prison. It was impossible to know what happened to Barbaro, and Roberto could only hope for the best.

Roberto was losing weight and could feel his body weakening from the lack of food. He was determined to maintain some level of fitness, employing a modest, but regular routine of stretching and body weight exercises.

One day not long after what he thought may have been the morning meal, Roberto heard voices and the sound of footsteps coming from the stairway at the end of the cell block.

Roberto knew a visit from the guards so soon after a meal was not routine and he immediately became suspicious. Unable to see the guards through the small window in the cell door, Roberto waited until they reached the bottom of the stairs and then began to count their footsteps. Remembering that Enrique's cell was no more than three paces from the bottom of the stairs, Roberto quickly realized they hadn't stopped in front of Enrique's cell and were coming for him.

"Ramos," said one of the guards loudly. "The warden is requesting the pleasure of your company."

"Delightful. What if I told you I'm not in the mood," Roberto shot back.

Roberto knew antagonizing the guards was not a good idea, but he had little respect for them and couldn't help himself.

"I would tell you to reconsider," replied the guard.

"Well then, *vamos*," said Roberto.

It was an enormous physical and psychological relief for Roberto, simply to be out of the tiny cell and to feel the sensation of his muscles contracting under his weight as he climbed the stairs to the main level of the prison.

Upon entering the warden's office Roberto was confronted by two other guards who, like the others, were armed only with batons. He was told to sit in a chair directly in front of the warden's desk and to wait for Colonel Torres.

The guards did not take their eyes off him, in a not-so-subtle but predictable effort to intimidate him.

"Ramos, thank you for coming," said Colonel Torres as he entered the room, walked around to the back of his desk and sat down. "Sorry to keep you waiting. One of the other guests here at the hotel was in need of a rules clarification."

"I'm sure you were very helpful," said Roberto.

"Ramos, I have an offer, a proposition for you," said the Colonel.

"And what might that be, Colonel?"

"You have a release review in several weeks," said the Colonel.

"I was not informed of that."

There was no way for Roberto to know for sure if Torres was telling the truth and Roberto thought it best to say as little as possible.

The Colonel reached into the top right hand drawer of his desk, and pulled out a single piece of paper, placing it right side up on the table in front of Roberto.

"What is this?" asked Roberto.

"It is your confession and pledge of loyalty, to the Comandante."

"I was set up by Perez and you know that, Colonel."

"A minor detail, Ramos. It's of no consequence to you. Your commitment to the revolution is the important part."

"The revolution is a failure, sir."

"I think maybe you are confused," said Torres. The Colonel was beginning to lose his patience.

Roberto, refusing to back down, continued. "Give me the name of one ordinary Cuban who is motivated to work hard and who is free to pursue the dream of a better life here in Cuba. Just one."

"Am I to understand that you refuse to sign the paper?" demanded the Colonel.

"Colonel, I want to pursue my dreams, not the dreams of El Comandante," said Roberto.

"Take him back to his cell," the Colonel shouted. "You're going to regret this Ramos."

Back in his cell, Roberto sat down on the stone bench and held his face in his hands. He could feel himself slipping into a dark place emotionally and he began to think of the old man, Tiburcio, from the Censam Marin hospital, and how, once broken mentally, he had lost the will to live, and how he had chosen death over the surrender of his dignity.

"Roberto," said Enrique.

Roberto stood up and leaned against the cell door with his head next to the small window in order to hear Enrique better.

"Yes, Enrique."

"What happened with the warden?"

"He wanted to cut a deal."

"What kind of a deal?"

"They asked me to sign a pledge of loyalty to El Comandante."

"What did you tell them?"

"I told them my dreams and the dreams of El Comandante, were not compatible. Obviously they were not happy with my response."

"You know, Roberto, they will not give up, and they will probably resort to violence at some point. When tyrants become frustrated they always choose violence. Violence is the only way they are able to maintain control of the people."

"Why do you think that is?"

"Because they're incapable of feeling compassion or empathy. That's why it is so easy for them to justify their cruelty. Tyrants never have trouble sleeping Roberto."

"You're a wise man, Enrique."

"I've had the benefit of a few more years than you. And besides, it's my job, so to speak."

"What do you mean?"

"Well, I write. To be a good writer one must have the ability to observe the world around you in a very detailed way, and to objectively interpret those observations."

"There's not a lot of objectivity right now in Cuba. Plenty of lies, yes, but not much truth."

"A life well lived is all about the revelation of truth. In the end, what else really matters Roberto?"

"Enrique, you give me strength."

"We gain strength from each other."

"I'm not afraid of them, Enrique. I don't care what they do to me. I just wish they would get on with it."

"Pressuring you to sign that paper makes me think they have become impatient with you. They don't give up easily."

"They obviously have the advantage in many ways physically, but I have the advantage of them not knowing who they're dealing with and what I'm capable of."

"You know, Roberto, the more I get to know you the more impressed I am."

"I may be young, Enrique, but one thing I've learned in the last few years is the importance of remaining true to oneself. If they want to steal my dreams they'll have to kill me. I'm telling you; I will not give up easily."

"I have no doubt you will not give up Roberto," replied Enrique.

XI

Over the following weeks and months Roberto and Enrique had regular daily conversations—sharing information and stories about each other's families, along with details of their professional lives. Even though they rarely spoke about their developing friendship, each man realized the importance of the bond they had made, and were grateful.

The cumulative effect of Roberto's confinement however, continued to take a toll on him physically and he began to have doubts about his ability to remain resolute. He knew his imprisonment would eventually end, but it was the uncertainty he felt from not knowing when or how it would end that he found most difficult to deal with.

For months now, Roberto and Enrique had been the only ones held in the crumbling old stone basement cell block, and neither man had had any interaction with another person with the exception of the prison guards and each other. So it came as a surprise, when one day they heard voices coming from the stairwell, from two men whom they did not recognize.

"No, not this one, cell number eight," said one of the men, as they walked past Enrique's cell.

"Ramos," said one of the men. "The warden is moving you to another cell block. When I open the door, turn around and put your hands behind your back."

Looking through the window in his cell door, Roberto could clearly see the two men. The uniforms the men were wearing looked unfamiliar to Roberto and were not the ones normally worn by the prison guards.

"What for?" asked Roberto.

"A little reward from the warden for good behavior. Now let's go," said the guard.

"*Cuidado*, Roberto," warned Enrique.

"Shut up, Garcia," said the other guard closest to Enrique's cell.

"It's okay, Enrique," said Roberto.

When the guard opened the door Roberto turned around slowly and placed his hands behind his back as he had been instructed to do.

"I believe you are going to enjoy your new accommodations Ramos," quipped one of the guards as they led Roberto up the stone stairs from the basement cell block where he had spent the last ten months.

As the two men led Roberto up the stairs to the main level of the prison, he felt weak. The farther he walked the more he could feel the stiffness in the joints of his lower body. The months of inactivity had been devastating physically on his body and he was surprised at how much his level of fitness had dropped.

Once on the main level Roberto was led into a large cell block housing a total of perhaps thirty prisoners. There he was assigned a new cell with a small cot and something that resembled a toilet in the back corner of the cell opposite the cot.

Upon entering the cell the guards immediately removed Roberto's handcuffs. They then locked the door behind them as they left the cell, giving Roberto no real explanation for his transfer out of solitary confinement.

Each cell had a small window, in the back of the cell that let light in from outside of the building, and unlike the heavy solid metal door in Roberto's basement cell, the door to each cell here was barred, making it possible to see into or out of the cell at any time.

Walking to the back of the cell and looking through the window to the outside, Roberto could see a small courtyard surrounded by very high, thick stone walls, topped with several rows of razor wire. He could tell from the angle of the shadows cast by the sun on the courtyard walls, that it must be late afternoon or evening. It had been many months since Roberto had seen the sun, and his eyes were having trouble adjusting to the light. Despite the fact that it was late in the day the light from the sun was still too intense for him to look through the window for long.

Turning away from the window Roberto laid down on the canvas cot which had become stained with mildew from the tropical climate, and stared up at the ceiling. He was becoming increasingly suspicious of his captor's intentions, and knew the explanation he had been given by the guards about his transfer was untrue. There was no reason why they had moved him out of solitary into what was, comparatively speaking, a fairly tolerable living situation, unless, he thought, they had something else in mind. He knew he had to remain vigilant and not let his guard down.

Less than an hour had passed since Roberto had been removed from his old cell, when the two prison officials who had escorted him to the new cell, appeared in front of his cell door.

"Hey Ramos," said one of the men. "Time for dinner. You'll be handcuffed until you get to the mess hall."

Saying nothing, Roberto stood up, walked over to the cell door, turned around and put his hands behind his back.

After being led through a maze of dimly lit, stone hallways, Roberto and the two guards came to a large iron door with a window in the wall to the right of the door. Looking through the window, Roberto could see another guard with a Russian made Kalashnikov draped over his shoulder. Upon seeing Roberto and the two guards, the man unlocked the door, pushing it open and stepping aside, letting the three men enter.

As soon as the door opened, the other men in the room immediately turned and stared in the direction of Roberto. Quickly looking around, Roberto counted maybe twenty other men in the room. From the look of their clothing, all appeared to be fellow prisoners. At the far end of the hall he could see an open double window with several prisoners lined up to the left of the opening, each holding a steel tray they had taken from a wooden table in the corner of the room.

"Ramos. You have half an hour to finish eating. No more," said one of the guards, as he removed the handcuffs from Roberto's wrists. "Pick up a tray and wait in line by the window."

As the other prisoners continued staring at Roberto, he slowly made his way among the dining tables to the side of the room, preferring to walk along the wall to the other end of the room where the food was being served.

"Roberto," he heard a familiar voice say. "Over here. It's Barbaro."

"Barbaro!" said Roberto, excitedly. Roberto walked over to the table where Barbaro was sitting, eating his evening meal. "I was so worried something bad had happened to you."

"No, I've been here ever since they took me out of solitary. And what about you? Why did they move you here?"

"They told me I was being rewarded for good behavior."

"The only people who are rewarded for good behavior are the prison goons," said Barbaro.

"What do you mean?"

"You see those two guys over there? They're not political prisoners, they're criminals. Really hard core. The one guy—the bigger one—he's in for murder. And the other one I'm not sure—attempted murder, I think. When the prison needs a favor, that's who they call. If they carry out the favor, their reward is a reduced sentence."

"What kind of favor?"

"Well, if you're being held for political reasons, which everyone here is, and you're unwilling to adjust your political philosophy, shall we say, to accommodate our beloved Comandante, the warden hires these guys to persuade you to change your mind."

"And if you don't?"

"Then you wind up dead."

"Barbaro, let me get some food. I'll be right back."

Roberto walked over to the stack of metal food trays in the far corner of the room, picked one off the top of the pile and took his place in line, waiting to be served.

When he reached the window, the man serving the food looked at Roberto, pausing briefly before handing him a plate.

"Ramos, right? Roberto Ramos," said the man.

"Yes. Who are you?" asked Roberto.

"Camilo. Remember? We worked together at Punto Cero. Here, a little extra. You could use a few more calories," said the man.

"Yeah, Camilo, the musician," said Roberto.

"Not so much these days. Better keep moving Roberto. We'll talk some other time. *Cuidado*."

"Thank you, my brother. We'll talk later."

Roberto returned to the table where Barbaro was sitting and sat down to eat his food—the first substantial meal he'd had in nearly ten months. The food, for the most part, was unrecognizable he thought, but at least it was warm, and Camilo had given him a little extra.

"So, Barbaro, do they allow visitors in this part of the prison?" asked Roberto.

"Sometimes. But you never know when. Depends on their mood it seems."

"What about your father? Does he know you're here?"

"Yes, fortunately. The last time I saw him was a month ago. He looks so much older. He's really worried."

"I worry about my family also, Barbaro. Especially my mother."

"Look out, Roberto!" shouted Barbaro, as he ducked out of the way of a waxed cardboard milk carton, thrown in the direction of Roberto by the bigger of the two men Barbaro had warned him about, striking Roberto in the right side of his head. The force of the impact caused the milk carton to break apart spraying the full liter of milk on Roberto, soaking his prison uniform and turning his meal into a cold soupy mess.

Roberto remained perfectly still as the last few drops of milk dripped from his chin onto the table in front of him. He could feel the adrenaline in his body beginning to surge. His military and martial arts training told him he needed to assess the situation quickly in order to calculate a response.

"Who threw the carton, Barbaro?" asked Roberto.

"The big guy I told you about. These guys are killers, Roberto. You tell me what you want me to do," said Barbaro, in a low voice.

"Stay here. I can handle this myself. I don't want you to get hurt."

"But there are two of them, Roberto. I'm telling you they're dangerous."

Roberto slowly got up from the table and picked up the empty milk carton from the floor at the end of the table. As he began walking in the direction of the two men, the normally noisy prison canteen room fell silent. Everyone was now staring at Roberto. No one moved.

When Roberto reached the end of the table where the two men were sitting, one on either side, he pushed the bigger man's food plate to one side and placed the milk carton on the table directly in front of him.

"I believe you dropped something, *senor*," said Roberto.

"I believe you may be mistaken," the man replied.

"Hey, what is your problem?" asked Roberto, who was beginning to lose his patience. "I have no problem with you."

"No problem," said the man without looking directly at Roberto. "Maybe you should go back and sit down with your baseball friend."

"And I would advise you to be careful."

The man slowly rotated his position on the bench in front of the table where he was sitting, so that his legs were no longer underneath the table, and leaned back against the edge of the table, placing his elbows on top of the table.

"Listen little man, I don't need any advice from you," said the man, now staring directly at Roberto.

It was clear to Roberto the two men were deliberately trying to provoke him, and that if he was the one to start a fight it could mean additional time in prison. He decided instead to return to the table where he had been sitting with Barbaro.

Turning slowly to his right, Roberto took a step in the direction of the table where he and Barbaro had been sitting. He instantly realized he'd made a crucial mistake—but it was too late.

Leaping at him from behind, the larger man quickly had Roberto in a choke hold. With his left arm around Roberto's throat and his right hand holding tight to the wrist of his left arm, he attempted to swing Roberto across his left leg in an effort to throw him on the ground, where his superior size would make it easier to increase the pressure on Roberto's neck.

Roberto could tell from the simple nature of the attack that the man had no martial arts training, and instinctively moved first to relieve the pressure on his windpipe by pressing the side of his face, hard, against the man's left forearm. While simultaneously neutralizing the effect of the choke hold, Roberto was able to grab the upper portion of the man's left arm and pull with both hands toward the ground in front of him while bending slightly at the waist, allowing him to gain the critical advantage necessary to redirect the initial momentum of the attack in his favor.

As the man's feet came off the ground, and in an effort to break his fall, he was forced to abandon his choke hold on Roberto. This allowed Roberto to slide his right hand down the man's forearm, grabbing onto the man's wrist and straightening his arm. With his attacker airborne, Roberto was now free to use both hands, enabling him to increase the leverage, more than doubling the amount of pressure he was able to apply to the man's arm, redirecting it in a direction opposite that of the man's fall.

The tearing sound made by the rupturing rotator cuff tendons at the moment the man's body impacted the ground, combined with the loud popping noise made by the ball of the humerus dislocating from the scapula, was easily and clearly heard by the other inmates in the room.

Suddenly Roberto felt a searing pain in the side of his body above his left hip just below the bottom of his ribcage. The attack from the first man, and the chaotic several seconds it took to subdue him, had given his knife-wielding accomplice enough time to rush Roberto from behind, plunging the six-centimeter blade into Roberto's side up to the handle, narrowly missing several vital organs.

Wheeling quickly around, Roberto moved into a slightly more open area between two tables, where it would be easier to defend himself, and faced the man with the knife head-on.

Roberto's shirt was beginning to dampen as the blood oozed slowly from the wound, collecting along the top edge of his belt as it ran down his side. He realized the more blood he lost the more difficult it would be to defend himself, and the greater the likelihood he could pass out. He had to initiate a counterattack.

With the knife in his left hand the man began to circle slowly to his right. He held the knife in such a way that the short, blood-stained blade protruded from the side of his fist closest to his thumb, which in order to stab Roberto a second time, would require a flexing motion rather than an extending motion. Roberto knew this would be to his advantage, as would the fact that the man, holding the knife with his left hand, was apparently left-handed.

Moving to his left, Roberto cut off the man's effort to circle around him, bluffing the man into thinking he was attacking. Now, clearly panicked, the man realized the fight was on a level he knew nothing about. He lunged at Roberto, in a desperate attempt to stab him in the upper right side of his torso. This was the precise response Roberto was looking for, and he wasted no time. Side stepping quickly to his right, he was able to create the space necessary to unleash a powerful kick with his right foot to the back side of the man's arm, just above the elbow, resulting in an immediate and excruciatingly painful dislocation of the joint. Roberto's attacker, having lost the use of his left arm, was unable to hold onto the knife. Screaming in pain as he bent over, the man had all he could do to hold the badly injured, limp, and now useless arm in his right hand, giving Roberto the split second he needed to land a second blow to the left side of the man's neck, rendering him unconscious.

While Roberto had been engaged with the second man, the first man, in a frantic attempt to get away from Roberto had stumbled over one of the table benches and was now lying motionless on the floor, after hitting his head against the edge of the table as he fell, severely injuring his neck.

Breathing heavily, Roberto could feel the adrenaline beginning to drain from his body as he stood looking down at his two attackers, both of whom were lying barely conscious, face up on the floor, laboring to breathe.

The entire fight had lasted no more than a minute and easily could have gone either way. Roberto was badly injured and lucky to be alive.

He carefully loosened his belt and pulled his blood-soaked shirttail out of his pants and examined the knife wound.

"Roberto!" yelled Barbaro, as he came to the aid of his friend. "Let me help you. Here, sit down. Lean over a little."

Barbaro slowly lifted Roberto's shirt-tail and examined the wound. "It's bleeding badly Roberto. You've lost a lot of blood. I'm going to get a clean towel from Camilo."

Barbaro ran over to the kitchen window and yelled for Camilo to bring him a towel, and to soak it in warm water.

The lone guard stationed at the entrance of the canteen, who witnessed the assault on Roberto, and who must have known of the warden's planned attack, had already called for more guards, even before the fight had ended, having realized it was not going according to plan.

Roberto was lying on his side on one of the benches, being attended to by Barbaro, when eight armed guards, guns drawn, followed by three medics and the prison warden, Colonel Torres, burst into the room.

"Ramos!" yelled the warden, who was clearly alarmed by his plan's failure.

"Sorry to disappoint you, Colonel," said Roberto. "Perhaps you should send me two more."

"I'm charging you with assault. Get him out of here," said the

Colonel, motioning to the guards.

"Everyone in this room saw what happened, Colonel. You know it was self- defense."

"Shut up!" yelled the Colonel.

"He needs to go to the hospital," said one of the medics who was attending to Roberto. "His wound is too deep for me to treat here."

"Then take him to the hospital," said the Colonel, motioning once more to two of the guards. "Put him in cuffs. When you bring him back, he goes back in solitary."

The sun was coming up by the time the doctors had finished attending to Roberto's wound, which after a less than careful cleaning and examination, was determined to be non-life-threatening. The lack of sleep, combined with the powerful pain medication he'd been given, and the lingering effects from the physical effort that had been required to defend himself had left him exhausted, drained.

Upon arriving back at the prison, Roberto was returned to the basement cell block where he had spent the better part of the last year.

Looking through the window in his cell door, Enrique, still the only one being held in solitary, could see that Roberto was struggling physically as the guards led him back to his old cell.

Enrique waited until the guards were out of earshot before speaking to Roberto.

"Roberto," said Enrique, just loud enough for Roberto to hear him. "What happened? Are you okay?"

"You were right, Enrique, about the warden not giving up trying to change my mind. Two of his goons tried to kill me."

"How do you know he was behind it?"

"Barbaro told me."

"You saw Barbaro?"

"He is the one that warned me about these guys and told me how the warden hired them specifically to intimidate prisoners who refused to fall in line, shall we say."

"You look like you are in pain. Did they hurt you?"

"One of them had a knife."

"Jesus, Roberto, did he cut you?"

"Yes. But it's not that bad. The wound is deep, but the knife just missed puncturing my spleen. I was lucky. The other two guys were not so lucky. I hurt them pretty bad I think."

"What happened to them?"

"I don't know. They were only semi-conscious when they were taken to the hospital. That is only the second time I ever had to use my training outside of athletic competitions."

"All of that training finally paid off."

"I know, but believe me, I take no pleasure in hurting anyone. There is nothing satisfying about it."

"What happens now, do you think?"

"The warden says I will be charged with assault."

"Maybe you will have a sympathetic judge. Not all judges in Cuba are corrupt."

"I'm not expecting much. Enrique, if you don't mind, I need some rest. We'll talk more later." With that, Roberto sat down, pulled his legs up onto the bench in front of him and leaned with his right side against the cold stone wall, not wanting to put pressure on his wound, and fell asleep.

He had not been asleep for long when he was suddenly awakened by the sound of Enrique calling his name.

"Roberto, Roberto!" said Enrique in a loud whisper. "Someone is coming."

Awakened by the sound of Enrique's voice, Roberto realized he was in the same position as when he had fallen asleep. Rotating his body on the bench, he placed both feet on the floor, careful not to make any sudden movements that would exacerbate the pain he was feeling. The pain medication he had been given had worn off and his body ached from the after effects of the fight from the day before.

As the men came closer, Roberto recognized one of the voices as that of Colonel Torres, the warden. He knew then they were coming for him.

"Ramos," barked the warden. "Let's go."

"I need more pain medication."

"You'll need more than that after the judge is finished with you."

"Where are we going?"

"Municipal court. You're being charged with assault, Ramos."

Roberto was nearing the limit of his ability to resist emotionally and was happy to be leaving the prison, even if it was only temporarily. I am unbroken, he thought to himself. If I am given the chance to explain my side of the story, there is always the possibility something good will happen.

The thirty-minute drive to the Tribunal Municipal, located on the south side of Havana, gave Roberto time to gather his thoughts and consider what he would say in his defense, given the opportunity.

Arriving at the courthouse, the military police van Roberto was riding in was directed to an entrance at the rear of the building where he was turned over to several non-military officers of the court, and placed in a holding cell with two other prisoners.

"My name is Santiago," said one of the men. "This is my friend Mateo."

"*Mucho gusto*, Santiago. I am Roberto."

"What are you charged with?" asked Mateo.

"Assault. A couple of prison goons tried to kill me."

"Who won?" asked Santiago, smiling. "I'm guessing not the goons."

"No, I think I hurt them badly. I don't know what happened after they were taken to the hospital," said Roberto. "Another inmate friend of mine told me they were hired by the warden to change my mind about a few things."

"Did you change your mind? Maybe not if you're here," said Mateo.

"No, not yet anyway. What about you guys? What are you charged with?" asked Roberto.

"Officially, I guess we're being charged with *jineterismo*. We had a little black market business. We sold just about anything we could to make a little money. You know how it is; everyone here is poor. We're just trying to make it from one day to the next. The economy is a failure," scoffed Santiago.

"Yeah, everyone is poor except Fidel and his family. I know, I worked in special forces at Punto Cero," said Roberto.

"What is Punto Cero?" asked Santiago.

"One of his private estates. He has many throughout the country," replied Roberto.

"Cuba has so much potential, Roberto," Mateo responded.

"Nothing will ever change. Not as long as Castro is alive," said Roberto.

Just then, the door at the end of the hallway leading into the courtroom opened and the two court officers who had taken custody of Roberto when he arrived at the courthouse walked over to the holding cell, unlocked the door, and motioned for Roberto to come with them.

"*Buenas suerte*, Roberto," said Santiago.

"*Gracias*, Santiago. You as well, Mateo," said Roberto, stopping to address the two men directly before walking down the hallway and into the courtroom.

The courtroom was small, and the judge had not yet arrived when Roberto was led into the room by the officers. Seated on the opposite side of the room at a long table facing the judge's bench, was Colonel Torres, the two prison guards who had taken Roberto to the hospital, and a government attorney. None of the men made eye contact with Roberto as he entered. Sitting alone at a table on the left side of the room was a sheepish-looking young man who upon seeing Roberto, stood up and motioned for him to sit down at the table next to him.

"Good morning, Mister Ramos. My name is Orlando Diaz. I am a public defender, and I will be helping to represent you today.

"*Encantado*, Orlando. Excuse me, I don't mean to be rude, but you know nothing about my case or why I was in jail to begin with."

"I know a little bit about your case, but only the warden's version of events. Maybe you can tell me about why you are in prison. Anything will be helpful Roberto," said Mr. Diaz.

"It's simple, really. I was serving in the military, special forces, working at Punto Cero. My commanding officer had it out for me and set me up. I wanted to buy a pair of American blue jeans and he offered to help me. I had no reason to think it was a set-up. He connected me with a friend of his—or someone he claimed was a friend—who got me the American dollars I was to use as payment for the jeans. When I met with him to make the payment, I was arrested for possessing foreign currency," explained Roberto.

"Okay, that is no longer considered a serious offense. That law was changed several months ago."

"Are you fucking kidding me?"

"One thing at a time, please. What happened at your trial?"

"Trial? There was no trial," said Roberto, clearly surprised by the question.

"In accordance with Cuban civil law, this is classified as a misdemeanor. Incarceration, according to the law, is limited to those who have committed crimes that cause public fear—for example, murder, rape, robbery, etc. So your case was never submitted to an investigator? Is that correct?"

"Mr. Diaz, I have been in jail for almost a year. You can't imagine what it's like in DTI. It's a cold, dark, wet, rat infested shit-hole. I was in solitary the entire time—well except for when they tried to kill me—but I'm one of the lucky ones."

"Why do you say you're lucky?"

"Because I'm alive and I haven't gone mad," said Roberto, feigning a laugh and staring directly into the eyes of the young attorney.

"I'm sorry for your suffering, truly, Roberto. What else can you tell me about the fight in the prison?"

"Two days ago, I was removed from solitary and into the general prison population with no explanation. The first time I went to the prison canteen to eat I was having a conversation with a man I knew when I was hit in the head with a full carton of milk. My friend had warned me, just minutes before, about the two guys that ended up attacking me, one of whom was the guy that hit me with the milk carton. It is well known that the warden hires these thugs to, shall we say, change the minds of certain prisoners. If they're successful the warden reduces their original prison sentence."

"Why do you think they targeted you?"

"Because I wouldn't sign their confession."

"Cuban law prohibits the use of violence or force to obtain a confession, and also requires that no one is required to testify against themselves. What did you do in response?"

"I picked up the empty carton and took it over to the table where these two guys were sitting and set it down on the table. I asked the guy what his problem was. He told me he didn't have a problem. I made the decision to walk away. It was at that point the guy put me in a choke hold from behind. You need to understand, Mr. Diaz, I competed on the national team at the highest levels in Taekwondo and Karate. I was trained by the government to kill."

"What happened next, exactly?"

"Well, you probably don't need all the details."

"No, just the important parts."

"The first guy—I was able to dislocate his shoulder, basically destroying his rotator cuff. It's an excruciating injury, trust me. So he was finished. Although in an effort to get away from me he ended up falling and knocking himself out when he hit his head on the edge of a table. The second guy, however, had a knife and before I was able to turn around and confront him, he stabbed me. Here," said Roberto, pointing to his side. "It was deep, about six centimeters. Neither of them knew what they were doing. In the process of getting the knife from the second guy, after dislocating his elbow, I knocked him out, and that was it. There were maybe, oh I don't know, twenty other inmates in the room when it happened."

"Roberto, we're pleading not guilty to everything, and I am asking for all charges to be dropped. I know this judge. He's by the book and he will not be happy with the way you have been treated. You need to trust me."

"I have to trust you Mr. Diaz. You're my only option at this point."

"All rise," announced the court clerk as the judge entered the courtroom.

"Your honor, the first case is that of the government versus Roberto Ramos. Mr. Ramos is charged with the unprovoked assault of two other inmates at *DTI*," said the clerk.

"How do you plead Mr. Ramos?" asked the judge.

Diaz motioned for Roberto to stand before answering the judge. "Not guilty, your honor," said Roberto, who remained standing.

"Mr. Ramos, what are you serving time for?" asked the judge.

"For the possession of foreign currency."

"How long have you been incarcerated?"

"I have been in solitary confinement Your Honor, so it is difficult for me to know for sure, but I think a little more than eleven months."

"What happened at your trial, Mr. Ramos?"

"I never had a trial Your Honor."

"Can you repeat that, Mr. Ramos?"

"Yes. I was never tried, Your Honor."

"What did you intend to do with the money?" the judge asked.

"My intention was to buy a pair of American jeans from my commanding officer. It was a set-up."

"My understanding, Mr. Ramos, is that you were a member of the Secret Service at the time of your arrest. Is that correct?"

"Yes sir. Your Honor, if I may."

"You're free to speak, Mr. Ramos."

"The charges against me are false. The same day I was moved out of solitary into the general prison area I was attacked by two men in the prison canteen who had been hired by the warden . . ."

"Objection, Your Honor. The . . ." said the government's attorney loudly.

"Overruled," said the judge, not letting the prosecuting attorney finish speaking. "You may continue, Mr. Ramos."

"I had been taken that evening to the canteen and had just sat down to eat when one of the men threw a full carton of milk at me, which basically exploded when it hit me in the side of the face. I picked up the empty carton and set it on the table in front of the man and asked him what his problem was. All he said was, 'I have no problem,' and I turned to walk away. That's when he put me in a choke hold. Your Honor, you should know, I have many years of martial arts training, and I am capable of killing someone. I mean without a weapon."

"I understand. Continue."

"I had nothing against either of these men. Had never seen them before. I had no reason to pick a fight with them."

"You're telling me then this was entirely self-defense. Is that correct?"

"Yes. I had to defend myself. They were trying to kill me, and in fact the second guy had a knife. He stabbed me once from behind before I was able to subdue him."

"Warden, were you in the room at the time of the attack?" asked the judge.

"No sir, Your Honor," replied the warden.

"Does the prosecution have anything to add?" asked the judge without looking in the direction of the warden.

"Your Honor, we feel the defendant is a danger to the general public and should remain in prison," asserted the government attorney.

"Counselor?" said the judge, addressing Roberto's attorney.

"No sir, Your Honor. The defense rests," said Mr. Diaz, standing to address the judge.

"Mr. Ramos, you'll have my decision in thirty minutes. Court is adjourned until one o'clock."

After the judge had left the courtroom, Roberto's attorney turned to him and said, "He's not happy. I know this judge well and I can tell he's upset."

"Upset with me?" asked Roberto in disbelief.

"Absolutely not. Like I told you, he's by the book and doesn't tolerate this kind of low-level corruption. He views it as a disgrace to the ideals of the revolution," said Diaz.

"What now?"

"We wait."

At precisely one o'clock the door to the judge's chamber opened. Without speaking to one another, Roberto and his attorney stood up and waited for the judge to take his seat behind the bench. Colonel Torres, the prison guards, and the government prosecutor stood on the other side of the courtroom.

Out of the corner of his eye, Roberto thought he could see Torres looking in his direction. The colonel's eyes appeared to be squinting slightly and Roberto detected a slight grin. He knew the look. It was the confident look of a cruel person, one who is certain of victory, thought Roberto.

"You may be seated," instructed the court clerk.

After taking his seat, the judge folded his hands and looked briefly in the direction of Torres before turning to address Roberto.

"Mr. Ramos, it is clear to me that you bear no responsibility for the situation you have found yourself in, or for the suffering you have been forced to endure while being incarcerated," said the judge, pausing briefly before continuing. "Furthermore, Colonel Torres, I have no tolerance for your intentionally corrupt interpretation of Revolutionary Constitutional Law. Therefore, I find the defendant, Roberto Ramos, not guilty of all charges. Mr. Ramos, you are free to go. This court is adjourned."

With that, the judge returned to his chamber, leaving everyone in the courtroom slightly stunned and in disbelief, especially Roberto, who was suddenly overcome by exhaustion, struggling to process what had just happened.

"Roberto, hey, Roberto" Diaz, with a smile. "We need to find you some nicer clothes."

"That's it?" Roberto said in disbelief. "I am free?"

"Yes, for the most part."

"What do you mean, for the most part?" asked Roberto, nervously.

"We can talk about it outside. First you need some clothes. Do you have some place to go? I mean to spend the night. Family, or a friend?"

"I have family in Havana, yes, but I haven't spoken to them in nearly a year. They don't even know I'm alive. I need to see them."

"*Vamos entonces.*"

"Where are we going?" inquired Roberto, as the two men walked out of the courthouse.

"I told you. You need some clothes. Let me see," said Diaz stepping back slightly to look at Roberto. "You and I are about the same size, more or less. Besides, I live not far from here. I'll lend you some clothes and then I can take you to see your family. I live outside of the city, near Finca Vigia, you know, the old Hemingway farm. And, I am the proud owner of a Buick Super Sedan. A blue one. We ride in style. I'm parked right behind the courthouse," said Diaz proudly.

"Mr. Diaz," began Roberto.

"Orlando. Please."

"Orlando, why are you doing this for me? You don't owe me anything. I'm the one that owes you."

"Every day, when I was a little boy, when I would leave for school, my mother used to say to me, 'Don't forget Orlando, kindness will open more doors for you than cruelty.' I always find that something good happens to me when I'm positive. Eventually, anyway."

As Roberto and Orlando made their way around to the back of the building, Roberto happened to notice Colonel Torres, and the prosecuting attorney sitting in a car parked across the street from the courthouse.

"Orlando, look."

"Yeah, I see them."

"You think they'll follow us?"

"They may try, but the guy who's driving, the attorney, he's from Santa Clara and has only been in Havana a few months. He doesn't know the city like I do. Besides, I know a little back alley we can take out onto D Street. The only way they can follow us is if they wait for us at the other end of the alley. From there I take the Linea to the Malecon, and then to the Tunel de La Habana, to the Via Monumental."

"I'm sure you can understand why I am a little paranoid at this point. I mean the guy just tried to kill me."

"Did you forget what the judge said? You are free to go. *Mantente positivo* man," said Orlando.

"Here she is," said Orlando, as they approached the car.

"Impressive. What year is she?"

"1950. As you can see, she needs a little body work but the engine is original. 4.3 L Fireball 18. 112 horsepower. She'll do 140 when she's tuned."

Orlando walked around to the driver's side, opened the door, and sat down behind the wheel. "Look, when we get to the end of the alley, you get down on the floor, just in case they're waiting for us. It will look like I'm alone."

He started up the car and slowly drove the length of the alley way, stopping briefly at the end to check for the warden's car, before turning right, and heading north.

"I think we're good, Roberto. I don't see them."

Roberto lifted himself back up onto the seat with both arms, wincing slightly from the pain caused by the muscles in his ribcage contracting from the effort, applying pressure to his wound.

Leaning against the seat back, he put his arm out the window, trying to relax.

"You need to have that looked at, Roberto. It could easily become infected," said Orlando, glancing down at Roberto's side.

"I know this neighborhood, Orlando. I have a good friend who lives nearby. I think this is her street. Yeah, Calle 15. She lives one block that way," said Roberto.

"Girlfriend?"

"No, no. She's a bit older than me, although she is rather attractive," said Roberto, looking down the street in the direction of Anabela Sobrino's house.

"I think women are most beautiful when they are past the age of forty," said Orlando.

"Her father was a famous artist. Before the revolution anyway. My brother and I own one of his paintings."

"How did you come to own the painting?"

"We received it as payment for work we had done for a friend."

"You took the painting as payment? Why didn't he pay you with money?"

"He's poor, like everyone," said Roberto, staring out the car window as they merged onto the Malecon.

Always at this time of year after a strong norther, the wind would come around to the northeast and blow for days, flooding the streets of Old Havana with a blend of fresh, cool, salt air mixed with the smell of sea life. Roberto had always loved the winter in Cuba, more than any other season.

As they rode along the Malecon, he wondered about his friend Maykel, and the old fisherman from Cojimar, Gregorio, whom he had met at the dock one afternoon years earlier when he had first entered the military. He remembered, Gregorio giving him a bag of fish steaks cut fresh from the enormous blue marlin the two men had caught that day and the plan they made to one day fish together. I need to take Carlitos fishing, he thought to himself.

When they arrived at the hilltop home of Orlando, the sun was beginning to set over Havana. The air was dry and clear and because it was the time of year when there was no Sahara dust blowing in from the east, you could see all the way to the ocean. The last rays of the sun washed over the city, reflecting yellow off the aging neoclassical facades of the city's buildings, giving them the appearance of tarnished brass.

Orlando's home was a modest, one-bedroom clapboard, shotgun-style house with a terracotta tile roof, surrounded on three sides by a porch and framed in front by two large ceiba trees, often thought of as the "holy tree" of Cuba and considered by Cubans to be a source of abundance, life, and energy.

Stepping out of the car, the two men stopped long enough to watch the sun setting over the ocean to the west, in the direction of Mariel, before walking up the handful of wooden steps onto the porch and into the house.

"Orlando, would it be possible to shower before changing into some clean clothes?" asked Roberto.

"*Claro, absolutamente*, Roberto."

"You're rather tidy for a bachelor," commented Roberto, looking around once inside the house.

"It helps me to keep a clear head. Here, take these," said Orlando, as he handed Roberto a pair of tan linen pants and a long sleeve white *guayabera*. "You need to look good for your mother."

"I hope her heart doesn't give out when she sees me."

"Take this also and put it on your wound after you clean it."

"What is it?"

"It's an ointment a local woman makes from prickly pear. It will help it to heal faster."

The shower was fed by an old wooden cistern made of Spanish cedar, mounted on the back of the house, kept full by a simple system of pipes that redirected rainwater into the cistern as it drained from the roof. Roberto didn't care that the water was cold as it was his first decent shower in many months. The rainwater was clean and felt soft and had a faint smell of cedar that came from the wood and reminded him of his grandfather's cigar boxes.

Before he finished showering he carefully cleaned the knife wound with soap and water as best he could. Drying off, he checked his wound to see that the stitches were holding and then carefully applied a small amount of the ointment he'd been given by Orlando.

Not wanting to keep Orlando waiting, he dressed quickly, stopping for a moment to look at himself in the mirror. He looked pale and thin, and wondered if his mother would even recognize him.

"*Estoy listo*, Orlando," said Roberto as he walked onto the front porch where Orlando was waiting for him.

"I'll say you're ready. You look good, my brother. *Vamos!*"

Not hesitating, the two men walked back to the car, got in and headed back down the hill toward Havana.

When Orlando turned the corner onto the street where Roberto had grown up, and where his parents lived, Roberto could just make out in the dim light from the car headlamps someone sitting on the steps in front of the house.

"I think that is my brother, Carlitos, Orlando," said Roberto, pointing in the direction of the figure sitting on the steps.

"I will drop you off and then I can get going. I'm sure it will be emotional for your family."

"No, no, I want you to meet them. For sure. Without your help this wouldn't be happening."

The car slowly came to a stop in front of the house. Roberto sat for a moment in the car, looking up at his brother Carlos sitting on the steps. Carlos didn't recognize or know the car and it was too dark for him to see his brother clearly.

Roberto could tell immediately that Carlos didn't recognize him and was having difficulty processing what was happening. He spoke his name before opening the door and stepping out onto the sidewalk.

"Carlitos, *hermano, como tu ta?*"

"Roberto?" said Carlos, still a little unsure of the situation.

"Yes, it is me, Carlitos."

Carlos looked at Roberto and then toward Orlando who was standing in the street on the driver's side of the car with his arms crossed, leaning on the roof of the car.

"*Madre!*" yelled Carlos, turning toward the house as he stood up, calling once more for his mother through the open doorway.

"What is the problem, Carlitos?" Roberto heard his mother say from inside the house.

"*Es* Roberto!" said Carlos loudly. Not waiting to see if his mother was coming, he threw his arms around his brother, causing Roberto to recoil slightly in pain from the pressure of Carlos's right arm across his wound.

"What, what's the matter, Roberto?" asked Carlos.

"I had a little accident in prison. I'm okay. Carlitos, this is my friend Orlando. Orlando, my brother."

"Carlitos, *mucho gusto,*" said Orlando, reaching out to shake hands with Carlos.

"It's okay, Orlando is a good guy."

Carlos paused briefly and then reluctantly shook hands with Orlando, nodding slightly as he did, but did not speak.

Roberto's mother had come to the door and was standing at the top of the steps, holding a cloth handkerchief over her mouth.

"*Madre,* this is my friend, Orlando. Can we come in?"

"Yes, yes of course. Come. I don't know what to say," said Rosa, still crying. "Your father is out back, on the terrace."

"Mrs. Ramos, it is my pleasure," said Orlando.

"You are a friend of my son's?"

"Yes, but only recently. Roberto will explain."

"Roberto you are so thin. Nothing but bones. Where did you get these clothes? They look expensive."

"Orlando lent them to me. I just got out of prison. Today in fact."

"Oh, my God. Come. I hope your father doesn't have a heart attack when he sees you," said Rosa. The realization of Roberto's sudden arrival was beginning to sink in and she was nervous about her husband's reaction upon seeing his son.

Guillermo was alone on the terrace enjoying a small, neat glass of rum and had not heard any of the conversation outside at the other end of the house.

Rosa went ahead of the others, drying her eyes with the handkerchief, trying to compose herself, not wanting to alarm Guillermo.

"Guillermo," she said, nervously, calling to her husband as she stood in the doorway leading from the kitchen to the terrace.

"Hola, padre," said Roberto as he slipped past his mother, stopping to kiss her on the cheek before walking outside to greet his father.

Roberto's father looked up from the table but did not stand up or speak.

Roberto wanting to ease the tension as quickly as possible, turned toward the doorway and called for Orlando. "Orlando, I'd like you to meet my father."

Orlando walked through the doorway out onto the terrace and stood next to Roberto.

"Father, this is my friend, Orlando Diaz. He defended me in court today."

"You are a friend of my son?"

"Yes sir. I was assigned his case in municipal court today."

"So you must be a member of the Cuban Law Association."

"I am. I defend people who have been charged with penal and civil crimes."

"And what was my son charged with?"

"Roberto was falsely accused of assaulting two inmates, Mr. Ramos, they were hired by the prison warden to kill your son. He was simply defending himself."

"Please sit down," said Guillermo, motioning to Roberto and Orlando. "Rosa, could we have three more glasses please? Thank you. Carlitos, come sit down."

Rosa brought the three rum glasses from the kitchen and placed one in front of each of the men.

"I am grateful for your services on behalf of my son. I sincerely hope you do not suffer any repercussions from the government. They have long memories," said Guillermo.

"This particular judge is always very fair. The warden at DTI is notoriously corrupt and had broken several laws relative to Roberto's incarceration. It was a simple case," Orlando explained.

"Roberto," said Guillermo, pausing slightly before continuing. "Your mother and I, along with your brothers and sister, have suffered greatly over the last year, not knowing if you were alive or dead. I'm not blaming you, but you need to understand how difficult it has been for us. I assume you have been discharged from the military?" asked Guillermo.

"Yes, but not officially."

"What are you going to do now? There is no demand in Cuba for someone with martial arts skills and you have no university training. You can live here temporarily, but we have little money and cannot support you for long."

"I understand. I'll find something. I just need some time to think."

"What about Maykel? Maybe you could work with him as a fisherman," said Carlos enthusiastically.

"Fishing is unpredictable and there are many days when you cannot work due to the weather," said Rosa, listening to the conversation from the kitchen doorway.

"Whatever you do, Roberto, make sure it is legal. The government will be watching you now. They have informants in every neighborhood," Orlando warned. "I should be going, Roberto. I am working tomorrow.

Senor Ramos, it was a pleasure, and thank you for the rum. We'll keep in touch, Roberto, no?"

After saying good evening to Roberto's parents and his brother Carlos, the two men walked back through the house and out onto the sidewalk, stopping for a moment to talk.

"Orlando, I owe you man. We'll keep in touch for sure," said Roberto.

The two men shook hands, embracing briefly before Orlando got back in his car and started up the old Buick, waving his hand above the roof on the driver's side as he drove off, heading south out of the city.

Roberto watched Orlando drive away, waiting until the car was out of sight before turning to walk back inside the house. Out of the corner of his eye, halfway down the block, he noticed someone sitting on the steps in front of an old house that Roberto had always known to be abandoned. Remembering what Orlando had said earlier in the evening about neighborhood informants, he decided not to stop and get a better look at the man.

He rejoined his parents and Carlos on the terrace behind the house, sitting down at the table alongside his mother. It was the first time since before he had been sent back to prison that he felt relaxed, he thought to himself, and despite the fact the future was so uncertain, he felt optimistic.

"May I have a little more rum?" Roberto asked his father.

"Of course."

"I'm sorry this keeps happening," Roberto said to his parents. "I want you both to know, and you, Carlitos, as well, that one day, I will make you proud. I don't know how exactly, but I am determined. I refuse to lead a life of subjugation and poverty. I prefer to see the world as infinitely abundant, where possibilities are limited only by your imagination, and not as a place of scarcity and desperation. I don't think it is possible to have that life in Cuba. Not now."

"And where did you learn such big words?" asked Rosa.

"From my friend, Enrique, in prison. He is a poet," said Roberto.

"I was in the same cell block with him. The government doesn't like his poetry, so they keep him locked up. They are afraid of his words, apparently."

"They're afraid of the truth. If they spoke truth themselves the threat of violence would be unnecessary. Everything is backwards with *El Cangrejo*," said Guillermo.

"Can we change the subject please? I haven't seen my son in almost a year and this conversation is upsetting to me," said Rosa, looking in the direction of Guillermo.

"Whatever you like, Rosa," said Guillermo. "So Roberto, where do you intend to look for work?"

"*Padre*, I only just got out of prison. I need a little time. I will find something."

"What about art?" asked Carlos.

"Art is not a career, Carlitos," said Rosa. "Besides, it is not legal. You want to see your brother back in jail?"

"No, you know I don't."

"Then stop talking foolishness."

"Have you heard from Anabela since I was in prison?" asked Roberto, directing his question to Carlos.

"Just once, a few months ago. She asked about you, of course. I didn't know what to tell her. She somehow knew you were in trouble."

"We should go to see her, Carlitos."

"How old is this woman?" asked Rosa.

"Why?" asked Roberto in response.

"Don't become involved with her," said Rosa.

"*Madre*, she's probably twice my age. She's a good friend. That's it. We understand each other, and besides, she is very knowledgeable about art and knows a lot of people."

"What do you mean she knows a lot of people?" asked Guillermo.

"She's connected with people in the art community, older people who used to collect art from the time before the revolution," said Roberto.

"There's no future for you in art. You need to think about doing something a little more practical," said Rosa.

"What about Maykel, Carlitos? Have you been to see him? Have you gone fishing?" Roberto asked Carlos, changing the direction of the conversation.

"No, I don't like going without you. You know how he is when he hooks up. Sometimes he gets too excited and starts yelling. I don't like it. But I did stop by the dock one day when I heard he had caught a big fish," said Carlos.

"A big blue one?" asked Roberto.

"No, it was a sword. It was too big to bring onboard. They had to tie it off fore and aft to bring it to the dock. He caught it right out in front. Maykel waited until the tide was all the way up and even with the dock, so it was easier to pull up out of the water onto the dock to clean. It still took six of us to haul the fish out of the water. He gave me some steaks," said Carlos.

"What did it weigh do you think?" asked Roberto.

"Maykel judged it for close to four hundred kilos," said Carlos. "You should have seen the tarpon in the harbor eating all the scraps they threw overboard as they were cleaning the fish. And when they cut open its stomach, they found a squid that was at least two meters long, and with the tentacles maybe four and a half meters. The fish must have eaten it just before it died because it was perfectly preserved."

"Did Maykel keep the squid?" asked Roberto.

"No. He said if you try and cook it the way you would calamari, it dissolves into nothing. He threw it overboard for the tarpon but they wouldn't eat it. The sharks must have eaten it overnight because it was gone the next day," said Carlos.

"Maykel is a hell of a fisherman. We need to ask him if we can go a day or two," said Roberto.

"Well, it is very late, and if all you are going to talk about is art and fishing I am going to bed," announced Rosa.

"Sorry, *Madre*, but this is the first normal conversation I've had in almost a year. We can catch up in the morning.

"I think I'll call it a night as well," said Guillermo. "We're grateful to have you home Roberto. We'll talk more tomorrow."

"Okay, until tomorrow. *Madre, Padre,* I love you."

Roberto's parents stopped and turned around to look back at their two sons sitting at the table on the terrace, before continuing into the house.

"They look older, Carlitos," said Roberto staring down at his half empty glass of rum.

"You can't imagine how worried they have been. They had almost given up hope, Roberto."

"We need to find a way into the art world, Carlitos," said Roberto.

"What do you mean, the art world?" asked Carlos.

"Buying and selling art," replied Roberto.

"But you heard what *Madre* said. You could wind up back in jail, and so could I. I wouldn't last two days in jail, Roberto. You know that."

"We're not going to jail, Carlitos, relax. I need to see Anabela. I need to figure out some way to connect with the people she knows in Spain who collect and have the ability to pay."

"But we have no money, Roberto. How do you expect to pay for even one painting?"

"I don't know. You see, in my mind I know how it could work. We need to find a way to make enough money for just one painting, Carlitos. Then if we can find a buyer in Spain, and get a good price, we can do more. The problem is making enough money for the first one. After that it will be easy."

"And how do you expect to find these paintings? I mean the ones you want to sell."

"Anabela knows a lot of people. Once you have a connection to that world the rest is easy."

"How do you know all this to be true?"

"Well, when you are in prison you have a lot of time to think. I've been thinking about many things, Carlitos," said Roberto, leaning back in his chair and staring up at the moonless night sky.

"Like what?"

"Like how to leave this country that is going nowhere," said Roberto, still staring up at the sky. "There is no future for us in Cuba, Carlitos, because the government has stolen it."

"What do you mean?"

"Here there is no incentive to work hard—you know—to build a life. Something to be proud of. The harder you work the wealthier the Castros become. It's all just one big con. Why should I work hard so they can grow fat?"

"But what about the family? We can't just abandon them."

"If we are successful, and make it to the U.S., we'll find a way to get them out of here. I know it would not be easy, but I've heard of people that have managed to do it."

"And so where do we find a boat? Have you considered the cost of a good boat? Something that is sea-worthy would not come cheap."

"That's the easy part, Carlitos. Maykel will help us. He knows everyone on the coast from Mariel to Mantanzas. And besides, I trust him more than anyone I know."

"I don't know, Roberto. Your plan sounds good but there are a lot of holes."

"I already have the vision, and it is very clear. Once you have the vision everything else will come. It's the intention that matters. It's powerful, more powerful than you know, brother," said Roberto, looking at his rum glass as he swirled the last few sips around in the bottom of the glass. "You think the Arechabala family had every detail of their rum business worked out when they decided to make one of the world's finest rums? Of course not. They just knew they had to try. We need to try too."

"I'm tired, Roberto. Maybe we can talk more tomorrow."

"You still have the painting, right?

"Of course," answered Carlos, somewhat surprised by his brother's question.

"I want to see it before we turn in," said Roberto, now slightly more animated from the effects of the rum.

"*Vamos*! I still have it hidden under the mattress, same as before."

"Promise you won't tell mother or father about our plan," said Roberto, raising his glass across the table in the direction of his brother as though to formalize the deal.

"Promise," said Carlos, pausing briefly before picking up his tumbler and touching it gently against the side of Roberto's glass.

Carlos leaned forward in his chair and slowly turned down the flame on the kerosene lantern on the table until it went out. Under a cool, cloudless, winter high pressure, and with only a few dim lights from the neighborhood to diminish its brilliance, the Milky Way shone unusually bright, stretching far to the northeast out over the ocean, fading only slightly where it met the horizon.

Roberto had slept little that night and was lying on his back looking up at the ceiling when he heard his brother stir in the bed next to him sometime just before sunrise. He had been thinking about Anabela Sobrino, and what she had told him about the wealthy Cuban she had known who lived in Spain, and who had continued collecting pre-revolution Cuban master art works even after leaving Cuba in the years following the revolution.

"Carlitos, are you awake?"

"Not yet, why?"

"We need to visit Anabela Sobrino, soon."

"What time is it?"

"I have a lot of questions for her," said Roberto, ignoring his brother's question about the time. "And another thing. I think I know where I can get a job. One that pays well, too."

"Nothing pays well in Cuba," said Carlos, yawning loudly.

"You remember when I got out of prison?"

"What do you mean, do I remember? It was yesterday."

"No, no—the first time, after I was released when I was on parole, and they were watching me all the time. I worked part time security for Colonel Antonio de la Guardia in his jewelry business. I'm going to ask him for the security job back."

"What makes you think he'll give you the job back? He probably knows you were in prison again."

"He trusted me, more than the other guys that worked there. They were always trying to figure out ways to steal from him and I refused to be a part of it. I know he was grateful for my loyalty. He always used to tell me how he had learned the hard way through his business how few honest people there were in the world—that integrity no longer existed because everyone in Cuba is poor and paranoid—only out for themselves."

"When do you want to see Anabela?"

"Today!" exclaimed Roberto. "I am going to see her today."

"I don't want to go, Roberto."

"Why not? I thought we were in this together."

"I'm not comfortable going. You can go, Roberto."

Roberto rolled onto his side and looked over at his brother. He remembered how nervous Carlos had been the first time they had gone to see Anabela. He stared quietly at his brother who was looking up at the ceiling, his arms folded behind and underneath his head, his eyes unblinking.

The seriousness of his brother's autism was becoming more apparent to Roberto, along with the realization that Carlos would probably never be able to function independently.

"Carlitos," said Roberto, waiting for Carlos to look in his direction. "Don't worry. Going to see Anabela will be part of my job. Yours will be to study and research. This will help us determine which pieces are important and have the most value. That's more important because we'll be dealing with a lot of money. We will need to be shrewd but also fair."

"What do you mean by shrewd?"

"I mean we need to have sound judgment. We'll probably deal with some people who will try and take advantage of us. So we need to be smarter and more knowledgeable than they are. That will require a lot of research. Like I said, that will be your job."

Carlos pulled back the sheet covering his body and turned his body toward Roberto, placing his feet on the floor and clasping his hands together with his elbows on his knees.

"I can do that. No one will know more than me. I read many books while you were in prison, and I forget nothing. You know that about me, Roberto."

Roberto was still lying on his side, staring at Carlos, somewhat surprised by his brother's unexpected and uncharacteristic display of confidence. "I do know that about you. Honestly, Carlitos, I don't know anyone with a memory like yours. I should be going. We have a lot to do. What day is it?" asked Roberto, moving slowly as he got out of bed, careful not to make any sudden movements that would exacerbate the pain he still felt from the stab wound in his left side.

"It's Saturday, why?"

"Good. Anabela will be home. Listen, I might be back late, so don't worry. I want to stop and see Colonel de la Guardia if I have time. Let's go. We'll have some coffee with mother and father before I go."

"*Hola, Madre*," said Roberto cheerfully, as the brothers entered the kitchen.

"*Buenos dias*, my prodigal son. What about a proper hug and kiss for your mother?" said Rosa, standing in front of the stove with her arms open to her side.

She was smiling and seemed genuinely happy and relaxed, thought Roberto. "I disagree with the prodigal part, but I will still give you a kiss," said Roberto, warmly embracing his mother and kissing her on the cheek. "Where is father?"

"He's outside. You having coffee?"

"Please."

"If you have a big day planned, which I'm sure you do, you need something to eat," said Rosa. "I can make you *pan tostado,* and there are still some avocado and mango," said Rosa.

"I'm planning on going to see Anabela Sobrino and later Colonel de la Guardia," said Roberto.

"De la Guardia," said Guillermo, who had overheard Roberto's conversation with his mother and had come inside from the terrace. "Why are you going to see him?"

"For a job. You said you can't support me for long, so I'm going to ask him for a job. You remember, I worked security for him a couple years ago in his jewelry business."

"You trust him?" asked Guillermo. "You know he is close to Fidel."

"I know. Anyway he was good to me when I worked for him. I have no reason not to trust him."

"Whatever happens, please promise me you'll stay out of prison," said Rosa. "Here's your coffee. Sit outside with your father and I will bring your *tostado.*"

The morning air was cool and pleasant. A heavy dew had formed overnight and still covered the table. The dew was heaviest in the tropics on nights when there was no wind. Roberto dried off the table and chairs with a towel that his mother Rosa kept hanging by the back door just for that purpose.

Rosa's coffee was always strong and sweet with a moist pungent aroma that only comes from freshly roasted beans. Guillermo insisted on buying beans that came from the Sierra de los Organos mountains in the Pinar del Rio province in western Cuba.

"When I was in prison, *Padre,* I would dream about this coffee," said Roberto, closing his eyes as he savored the first few sips.

"I wouldn't tell de la Guardia about your little art business plan. He's liable to steal your idea and do it himself."

"I don't plan on telling anyone," said Roberto, taking another sip of coffee.

"I hope you know what you're doing, Roberto," said his father.

"Not really, but I'll figure it out as I go. I'm going to do it, *Padre*, believe me. I just need the right connections," said Roberto.

"I'm sure you will succeed, or die trying. You're too much like your mother sometimes," said Guillermo.

"How so?"

"Persistent. Never taking no for an answer."

Roberto looked over at his father and smiled. "I need to be going," said Roberto.

"It's a long walk to Anabela's house."

Roberto went back inside the kitchen, placed his empty coffee cup in the sink, said goodbye to Rosa and Carlos and walked through to the front of the house, out onto the sidewalk and headed north toward Anabela's home in el barrio de La Rampa.

La Rampa was a little less than five kilometers from Roberto's neighborhood of Santos Suarez and would take about an hour to reach on foot without stopping.

It was still early in the day when Roberto left home, and even though he was anxious to speak with Anabela about his plan, he remembered she was a private person and might not appreciate him arriving unannounced at such an early hour. In order to arrive a little later, Roberto decided to kill some time along the way by stopping in Quinta de los Molinos Gardens. A lush, green oasis with many large trees in the middle of Havana, the gardens were free for locals and visited mostly by the elderly along with the occasional European tourists who come to Cuba during the winter months to enjoy the relative warmth of the Cuban winter.

Formerly the home of General Maximo Gomez, the gardens were a place where Roberto could gather his thoughts and perhaps think of some way to convince Anabela he was serious about his intention to buy and sell art. If she could connect him with someone in Spain who was looking for important works of art from Cuba, Roberto was certain he could find a way to make his plan work. And if she was still interested to sell some of her father's collection all he needed was enough money to buy the first painting.

Roberto had been sitting under the shade of a large strangler fig thinking about what he would say to Anabela, and hadn't noticed the emerald-colored hummingbird moving from flower to flower in the bed of flor de mariposa. The bird hovered closer to the bench he was sitting on, until he could almost touch it as it fed on one of the large white flowers.

He wondered how such a fragile little bird managed to thrive in a dangerous and unforgiving world, surviving only on the sweet nectar of flowering plants. The bird was free to go wherever it wanted and lived its entire life surrounded by beauty. What a joyous life. I should expect nothing less, he thought.

The hummingbird continued feeding in the flower bed next to where Roberto was sitting until finally flying off, but only after meticulously checking each flower for fresh nectar. Five minutes earlier or later, he thought and he wouldn't have seen the tiny bird.

Leaving the gardens, Roberto had less than fifteen blocks to go before reaching Anabela's home. He was excited to see her and hoped that she would feel the same way when he arrived.

Rounding the corner onto Calle 15, he walked the last few steps to Anabela's house in the middle of the block. The front door was open slightly and there was a cloth bag filled with fresh vegetables and several loaves of *pan Cubano*, sitting on the top step. Roberto walked to the top of the steps, picked up the bag and stood in the doorway, slowly pushing the door open the rest of the way, surprising Anabela who was walking back toward the front of the house from the kitchen to retrieve the bag of food she had left on the step.

"Oh, Dios mio. Roberto. What the hell," exclaimed Anabela.

"*Hola*, Anabela. Am I too early?"

"No, no, of course not. I've just been to market. Come in, come in," said Anabela, holding the door open and motioning for Roberto to enter. "Where the hell have you been? It's been almost a year. Did you forget about our date?"

"You mean the mojito you were going to buy me at La Bodeguita?" said Roberto. "Of course not. When are we going?" he said with a smile.

"We go tonight. That is unless you already have a date with another old woman."

"Anabela, I have been in jail again. For the past year. They tried to kill me."

"What! What happened?"

"They didn't like what I had to say in response to their request for my loyalty to El Comandante, so the warden hired a couple of his goons thinking maybe they could change my mind."

"They obviously didn't know who they were dealing with."

"No, and they paid for it. Although one of them managed to stab me before I could take the knife away from him," said Roberto.

"Jesus, Roberto. Are you okay?"

"Yes, fortunately. If you're going to be stabbed though, this is as good a spot as any," said Roberto, turning to his right slightly and pulling up his shirt to show Anabela where the knife had entered his side. "Looks like it's still bleeding a little."

"Let me get some warm water and some soap. It looks terrible."

"It looks bad, but I think it's beginning to heal. The infection is going down and it doesn't hurt anymore."

"Sit down in here," said Anabela, pointing to the parlor. "I'll be right back."

"I have something I need to talk to you about," said Roberto, raising his voice slightly to make sure Anabela heard him as she hurried down the hallway.

"I'll be right back."

Anabela returned with a bowl of warm water, some soap, and a clean towel. "Here, stand up. Let me know if this hurts. There's a lot of dried blood. My god Roberto, this looks terrible."

"It's fine. I'm telling you. The doctor told me I was lucky the knife didn't go any deeper. A couple more millimeters he said, and it would have punctured my spleen."

"Wait a minute, I'm not finished. I want to put some mercurochrome on it. There, that looks much better. So what is it you want to talk about?"

"I need to figure out a way to make some money. Real money."

"You're living in the wrong country then, Roberto."

"Remember you told me about some wealthy expats you knew who were living in Spain and collected Cuban art from the time before the revolution?"

"Sure, I remember. But it's almost impossible to contact them, and even if you could somehow get in touch with a collector, there is no way to send a painting to Spain. It would be very dangerous. Especially for you, Roberto, considering you've spent time in prison. They'll always be watching you now. You know that."

"I know, but this is what I want to do. I would pay you for helping me," said Roberto.

"You have a job or any money?"

"Not yet. But I plan on having a job very soon."

"My God, you're persistent."

"I know, my father tells me the same thing. He says I get it from my mother."

"I'm going to make some coffee. You want some?"

"With some pan tostado?" asked Roberto, knowing she would say yes.

"Come with me. We'll sit out back."

Anabela led Roberto though the house to the back and onto a small terrace. "This is my little sanctuary, where I dream."

"It's lovely."

"I'll start the coffee. *Con azucar?*"

"Please."

Anabela returned to the kitchen and took down the large Moka pot from above the stove that she used only when she had company. After rinsing the dust from the outside of the pot she carefully filled it with water up to the pressure valve, first adding the raw cane sugar to the filter before topping it off with finely-ground coffee and placing it over a low heat on the kerosene stove.

"Would you like some guava jam with the *tostado*?" said Anabela, raising her voice slightly in order for Roberto to hear her from the kitchen.

"Did you make it?"

"What do you think? Of course I made it. It's impossible to buy any."

"Then I'll have some."

Looking around the tangle of plants on the terrace, Roberto counted more than a dozen different types of fruit trees, some of which he had never seen before. How could someone go hungry in a country where food was so plentiful, he thought.

"*Una colada, con azucar*," said Anabela, emerging from the kitchen carrying a large tray of warm *tostados*, two *coladas* and some mango slices.

"Anabela, what is that tree?" asked Roberto.

"Which one?"

"That one there," said Roberto, pointing to the other end of the terrace.

"That is a ciruela tree. The fruit is like a plum. It's good for indigestion. You're too young to know anything about that," she said with a smile, holding the hot cup up to her lips and gently blowing across the top to cool the coffee as she looked at Roberto.

"The jam is fantastic, Anabela. How do you make it without all the seeds?"

"With great difficulty. It takes me all day to make a batch."

"Well, it's worth it. I can tell you," Roberto remarked as he took another bite of the toasted bread.

"Roberto, I have an idea," said Anabela, pausing to take another sip of coffee.

"About my plan?"

"Yes, about your plan. There is a very wealthy Spaniard. His name is Mariano and he comes to Cuba from time to time on vacation. My father knew him and always spoke very highly of him. He has some of my father's work. Anyway, it's my understanding that he's managed to maintain a good relationship with Fidel."

"The same Fidel, who is a man of the people, who lives in a fisherman's cottage," said Roberto, feigning sincerity.

"Yes, the very one. Can you believe it?" said Anabela, smiling. "When Fidel took control in '59, he created something called, The Office for the Recovery of State Assets. They confiscated billions of dollars in private assets from wealthy Cubans and foreigners who fled Cuba right after the revolution. There were hundreds of thousands of paintings, sculptures, rare books, jewelry, you name it, the government simply laid claim to. A bit like the Nazis during their European occupation in World War II."

"What did they do with all of it?"

"I know for a fact that, seventy percent of the collection in the Museo Nacional de Bellas Artes, was confiscated from these private collections. I mean that's something like thirty-five thousand pieces."

"But you said there were hundreds of thousands of works of art."

"There were. Fidel has been selling off the rest since the 60's."

"And keeping the money for himself."

"Of course."

"Antonio says he spends a lot on Chivas Regal."

"Who is Antonio?"

"His son, Antonio. I use to train him when I was working at Punto Cero," he said.

"Jesus, it's a wonder they didn't try to kill you sooner. You know too much."

"So what about this guy Mariano? You said he comes to Cuba from time to time."

"Yeah, he has a house in Barlovento, at Marina Hemingway. I think he likes to fish. It's near the hospital where you were being held. He comes in January and stays until June. Then he goes back to Spain for the summer."

"Yes, I know where it is. The security there is very tight. It's where Fidel keeps one of his fishing yachts."

"Well, I'm telling you what I know. Maybe you should try and get a job there."

"I was going to speak with a military friend of mine later today about a job, but I suppose I can always work two jobs."

"What's the job?"

"Security for Cimex. You know the place—where the government buys gold, silver, diamonds, things like that from the public."

"I've heard of it. It's where they pay you with some sort of worthless currency that you can only spend in the government's stores."

"Right. I know the Colonel who runs the business. Then the government turns around and makes a huge profit by selling everything overseas for what it's actually worth, which is plenty in most cases."

"So Fidel can buy more Chivas Regal."

"*Exactamente.* And fancy fishing boats."

"Who is the guy running the business?"

"Colonel Antonio de la Guardia. I worked security there part time a couple years ago as part of my probation when I was released from Censam Marin. He's a good guy."

"Well, I strongly recommend not telling him about your little plan."

"I'm not planning to. What I'd really like is to learn how to appraise jewelry, especially diamonds. Sounds crazy, doesn't it?"

Anabela smiled, took another sip of coffee, and sat back in her chair, smiling slightly. "Coming from you, not really."

"I should be going. It's a long walk to Cimex."

"You'll let me know what happens? You need to be careful Roberto, and smart. What about tonight? We're going to La Bodeguita?"

"I don't have any money. Remember, I just got out of prison."

"Yes, I know, and remember I said next time was my treat."

"Fair enough. What time?"

"Eight thirty, and don't be late. Women who drink alone always have a bad reputation," said Anabela, smiling warmly.

"Maybe I will have some news about a job," Roberto replied, standing up from the table and finishing the last of his *colada*.

Anabela led Roberto back into the house, stopping briefly in the kitchen. "Here, have some of these," she said, taking some bananas from a bowl on the kitchen table. "Take this, too," she said, as she handed Roberto a large Choquette avocado. "You have a long day ahead of you. We'll have something to eat tonight in La Bodeguita."

"Thank you. Someday I will pay you back for all your kindness," said Roberto, as he held open the cloth bag she had given him for the fruit.

"Maybe we'll sell some art together, *quien sabe*," she said. "See you tonight."

XII

The Cimex department store where Roberto had worked security part time while on probation, was near the Almendares River, on the southwest side of Old Havana, about an hour's walk from Anabela's house.

He remembered Colonel de la Guardia was often in the store on Saturdays, the day most Cubans were not working, and if they had anything important to sell, the day they would come to the store. The Colonel liked to personally oversee the jewelry purchases, especially the ones that, when resold, would make the government the most money.

Arriving at the store Roberto recognized the security guard stationed by the entrance. His name was Mateo and he had also been assigned security as a condition of his probation from prison about the same time

Roberto had been released from Censam Marin.

"*Hola*, Mateo!" said Roberto enthusiastically, as he approached the guard.

"Roberto. Man, where have you been?" asked Mateo, first securing his Kalashnikov over his shoulder with the strap and then giving Roberto a hug.

"Prison, where else," said Roberto, casually.

"What for this time?"

"It's a long story. I'll tell you sometime over a beer. How's that? Is the Colonel here today?"

"Yes, he's in his office. He'll be happy to see you, Roberto. The Colonel was complaining to me just the other day that he was looking for help but couldn't find anyone he knew to be trustworthy."

"Really? Maybe good timing then. I'm actually here to ask about a job."

"You received a discharge from special forces?"

"Yes, unofficially. My military career is over."

Mateo signaled to the guard inside the entrance that it was safe to unlock the door. Roberto remembered the Colonel's office was on the second floor and headed straight for the stairs, excited by Mateo's comment about the Colonel lamenting the current lack of reliable help.

"*Buenos dias, senorita*," said Roberto to the young woman behind the desk at the entrance to Colonel de la Guardia's office.

"*Buenos dias, senor.* What can I help you with?" she asked, somewhat tentatively.

"I'm here to see the Colonel."

"He's expecting you?"

"Uh, no, actually. I used to work here, and . . ." Roberto began to explain.

You are going to need an appointment then," she said, interrupting Roberto. "What is your name?"

"Roberto Ramos. Could you just let him know I'm here?"

The young woman paused, eyeing Roberto suspiciously, not responding to his question. "Just a minute. Have a seat over there," she said, pointing to several wooden chairs lined up along the wall by the entrance to the office.

When the woman returned her demeanor had changed dramatically. "The Colonel will see you," she said, smiling at Roberto as she moved to the side of the hallway, pointing in the direction of the colonel's office.

"*Gracias, senorita*," said Roberto, who had stood up when he saw the woman return to the front of the office.

"*De nada, senor*," replied the young woman.

Roberto had to turn his body somewhat as he walked past the woman in order to avoid touching her. Her decision to stand in the narrow hallway instead of out in the open, making it more difficult to pass, seemed deliberate to him. Roberto's attention quickly turned to Colonel de la Guardia and his reason for the visit.

"*Hola*, Colonel," said Roberto, leaning forward as he stood in the doorway to the Colonel's office, waiting for permission to enter.

"Roberto!"

"Sir," said Roberto, stepping into the office to greet the colonel who had by this time stood up from behind his desk to shake hands.

"How the hell are you? You don't look so good."

"I was back in prison sir, at DTI," said Roberto.

"What for?"

"Possessing foreign currency. I was set up by one of my superiors, Captain Rafael Perez. You know him, I'm sure."

"Yes, but not well. You know that's no longer a crime Roberto."

"I know now, sir."

"You've come here to see me. What for?"

"Colonel, I need a job. My military career is over, obviously, and I have no skills other than my security background. I thought perhaps you could use some help."

"Please, have a seat," said the colonel. "Well, I can always use help with security, but what I need more than anything is someone to work in purchasing. My duties with El Comandante are more complicated now and take up nearly all my time. To be honest, he's been a little edgy lately and I'm under a lot of pressure."

"From my time at Punto Cero, I remember El Comandante was always very demanding," said Roberto. "He likes to be informed."

"It's worse now than before, Roberto. Every day Jose Abrantes and I are required to meet with Fidel."

"What's changed?"

"It's because Cuba has lost nearly all of its financial support from the Soviet Union with the collapse of the Eastern Bloc and the government is running out of money. Fidel is desperate and trying to find ways to generate cash and doesn't care what it takes. He's always asking why Cimex doesn't make more money."

"Colonel, I know nothing about purchasing."

"I can help you, that's not a problem," said de la Guardia. "The most important purchases we make are gold, silver, and precious stones, mostly diamonds. The situation with the economy now is so bad, people are selling everything they can. Family jewelry is usually the last thing they sell because of the sentimental value. Fortunately for us, however, those pieces have the highest value. What do you say?"

"What about the pay?"

"Same as before, you know that. Everyone is paid equally."

"When do I start?"

"Come next Thursday and we'll work together. I'll teach you everything I know. Be here at eight in the morning."

"I will not disappoint you, sir," said Roberto, barely able to contain his excitement.

"My secretary will show you out."

Roberto stood up, shook hands with Colonel de la Guardia, and walked out of the office back to the front desk.

"*Buenos dias, senorita,*" said Roberto to the secretary as he passed by her desk.

"You're going to be working here, Roberto?" she asked.

"Yes," said Roberto, surprised to learn that she had been eavesdropping on his conversation with the colonel.

"I am Alina. *Mucho gusto*," she said.

It had been so long since Roberto had spoken to a woman his age, he had forgotten how to be natural. He had wanted to ask her name when he had first arrived, but she hadn't given him an opportunity and felt relieved that she had told him.

"*Encantado*, Alina. You have to forgive me, I'm a little nervous," replied Roberto.

"There is no reason to be nervous. You are a friend of the Colonel's, and now you know me," said the secretary. "*Tienes un buen dia.*"

"You as well, Alina."

Back outside Roberto stopped briefly to speak once more with his friend Mateo before heading in the direction of Barlovento and the Hemingway Marina, a two hour walk to the west from the Cimex department store, along La Quinta Avenida.

Roberto had been walking for a little more than an hour and was beginning to feel hungry when he remembered his friend Luiz, who owned the restaurant, La Pescadaria, along the Rio Jaimanitas, near the entrance to Hemingway Marina. He had been relieved to learn from Barbaro that his father finally knew of his son's fate and Luiz had been able to visit him in prison.

Roberto wished he was bringing Luiz good news about his son. He began to feel guilty that he was the one who had been freed from prison and not Barbaro.

It was almost exactly one year ago to the day that Roberto had been released from Censam Marin hospital, and he couldn't help feeling a sense of deja vu as he turned off La Quinta Avenida onto the gravel road leading down the hill to the restaurant.

Coming closer to the restaurant Roberto could hear live music coming from the side of the building that faced the river and could smell the heavy odor given off by the *pargo frito entero* boiling in the deep fryer Luiz kept in a separate room to the side of the kitchen.

He was beginning to feel nervous about seeing Luiz and decided not to go around to the kitchen as he had done before, choosing instead to use the front entrance.

"*Buenas tardes, senorita,*" said Roberto, upon entering.

"*Buenas tardes, senor.* Would you like to sit by the river?" asked the young woman.

"No, no. I would like to speak with Luiz if he is here. My name is Roberto Ramos. We are friends."

"I'll see if he is available. Please sit down," she said, disappearing into the kitchen.

The young woman had not been gone long when she reappeared from the kitchen with Luiz close behind her, waving his arms and shouting Roberto's name.

"*Hola,* Luiz. How are you, my friend?"

"Roberto!" said Luiz, hugging Roberto first, then stepping back still holding Roberto by his forearms. "Where have you been?"

"I was in prison again. Barbaro was in my cell block," said Roberto, lowering his head and glancing over at the young woman who had greeted him when he arrived at the restaurant who was now listening to their conversation.

"I know. We finally got word about six months ago. We've only been allowed to see him twice, and not until recently. He looks terrible. So thin."

"Any word on when he may be released?"

"No, but we're hopeful. He doesn't cause any trouble so maybe soon. His mother is not doing well. The stress is too much for her."

"Luiz, could I trouble you for something to eat? I don't have any money, but I just got a job at Cimex and can pay you back after my first paycheck."

"Of course," said Luiz. "Pilar," he called, turning to the young woman who had greeted Roberto upon entering the restaurant. "Give Roberto the small table at the end of the veranda. I have some fresh snapper frying Roberto. How is that? And some sweet plantains."

"That sounds wonderful. You are always so kind to me, Luiz."

"Pilar, bring Roberto a Cristal, and a cold glass."

Out on the veranda overlooking the river, a light north wind was blowing, coming in from the direction of the ocean toward the front of the old wooden building where Roberto sat, waiting for his meal. The veranda was shaded by four large mahogany trees fronting the restaurant, which helped to cool the persistent mid-day, sun fueled, winter breeze that almost always blew at this time of the year.

"Here you are, my friend," said Luiz, placing the meal of fish on the table in front of Roberto. The golden-brown colored snapper, scorched several times on both sides with a knife before deep frying, sat upright on the plate, the tail bent to one side as though it was swimming and kept balanced by the fish's pectoral fins, which had been spread apart underneath the body of the fish, made stiff by the cooking process.

"I'm always coming to you for food, Luiz."

"I made some *manjuas fritas* also. I know how you like them."

"I would be quite happy to live on these if I had to," said Roberto, as he took a small handful of fried glass minnows and squeezed some fresh lime over them. "With a cold beer, I can think of nothing better."

Luiz sat down at the table opposite Roberto and opened another beer. Taking the small chilled glass Pilar had given him, he tipped it sideways, and filled it halfway.

"*A tu salud y felicidad,* Roberto," he said, raising the glass.

"*Tu tambien,* Luiz."

"So what now, Roberto?"

"I want to have a business as an art dealer," said Roberto in a low voice. " And if I make enough money, I plan to buy a boat and leave Cuba for the U.S. Me and my brother, Carlitos."

"I didn't know you had a brother."

"Yes, I have four brothers and a sister. My brother, Carlitos, is brilliant, although he struggles with autism and suffers from anxiety and can't live on his own."

"Sounds like a pipe dream to me, Roberto. No one has money to buy art in Cuba. There are no customers."

"I don't plan on selling to Cubans. Not in Cuba anyway. A friend of mine told me recently about a wealthy Spaniard who collects Cuban art from before the time of the revolution who has a house in Barlovento. She said he spends the winter there, fishing, and returns to Spain in the summer," said Roberto.

"But security there is very tight. There's no way to get in. I hear some crazy stories from the head of security about that place. He comes here every Saturday, in the evening."

"What kind of stories?"

"Stories about all the famous people who come and go from there. Guests of Fidel."

"Like who?"

"People like Saddam Hussein. Oh, and Ted Turner, and that American guy, Robert Vesco. They say he's a fugitive from the FBI. A lot of rich people mostly."

"Fidel has no use for poor people," said Roberto. "So, who is the head of security there?"

"Pedro Ruiz. He's an older guy. I believe he used to be in special forces, like you," said Luiz.

"I know Pedro!" said Roberto excitedly, keeping his voice low so as not to attract the attention of the customers sitting nearby. "He's a good friend. We worked together at Punto Cero."

"You should speak with him. Maybe he can help you."

"Can you set up a meeting with him for me?"

"Sure, I guess. When do you want?"

"If he comes here this evening, set it up for next Saturday, around seven o'clock.

You can leave a message for me at my parents' house. Pedro is a good guy. I feel certain he'll help me contact this Spanish guy."

"Sounds risky to me. What if he doesn't? Or worse, he turns you in to the federal police."

Roberto poured the rest of his beer into his glass and slowly drank it. Placing the empty glass to the side he leaned forward, resting his elbows on the edge of the table, and crossing his arms, pausing slightly before continuing. "Luiz, I am out of options, and this is the only option I have. So at this moment, that makes it the best one. I have nothing to lose."

"What should I tell Pedro when I see him? You know he's going to ask why you want to meet with him."

"Tell him I'm out of the military and I'm looking for work."

"Alright. I'll do it."

"What time do you have, Luiz?" asked Roberto. "I am meeting a friend this evening in Old Havana at La Bodeguita del Medio."

"Half past five. You have a long walk then."

"I'll see you Saturday, Luiz, unless I hear from you."

The two men got up from the table and after a warm embrace, shook hands before Roberto made his way outside to the gravel road leading up the hill to La Quinta Avenida. It was an hour or so until sunset and the moon would be rising soon, thought Roberto. He was looking forward to the walk. Especially the last several kilometers where he planned to walk along the Malecon.

The Malecon was always filled with people on Saturday evenings, except when the winter northers blew, pushing the sea against the Morro, causing the ocean waves that had built far out in the Straits of Florida, to explode upward as they met the sea wall, spilling out onto the roadway. The towering plumes of salt water from the heavy sea would chase away the fisherman who would come for the evening bite, as well as the constant parade of young lovers, strolling endlessly along the seafront. Tonight though, the wind had fallen out. It was going to be a beautiful night.

By the time Roberto turned the corner onto Calle Empredado and walked the last few steps to La Bodeguita, it was nearly nine o'clock.

The front room of the bar, close to the street, was packed with tourists and locals drinking and listening to the live music. Roberto managed to push his way through the tightly packed crowd, being careful not to cause anyone to spill their drinks, to the back room where he found Anabela sitting with an elderly man he did not recognize.

"*Buenas noches*, Anabela. Sorry I'm late. I had a long walk from my friend's place near Barlovento," said Roberto, pulling a chair up to the table.

"Roberto, if you're going to be a big shot business-man, you need to be on time," said Anabela. She was smiling and he knew she wasn't serious. "This is my friend, *Senor* Carmen Pelaez. We were just talking about your career plan."

"Well at this point it's just an idea really," said Roberto. He looked at Anabela as if to say: can I trust this guy and why are you discussing my plan with him?

"Relax, Roberto. Carmen is an old friend. He was a patron of my father," said Anabela. "Carmen, *me gustaria presentar mi amigo*, Roberto. Roberto, Carmen."

"*Mucho gusto*, Roberto," said Carmen. "Anabela says you have quite the passion for the work of the old masters."

"Yes," replied Roberto. "Are you a painter?"

"No, I wanted to become a painter, but I didn't have the talent. I collected for many years. It's the next best thing in a way. Unfortunately, few people care about these things anymore, and of course no one has any money," said Carmen.

"Well I care, although I don't have any money either," laughed Roberto.

"What do you want to drink, Roberto? Remember, it's my treat this time," said Anabela.

"I would love a mojito," he said.

"I'll have Agustin make one for you. I prefer Agustin's over the other bartender's. Carmen, what about you?" asked Anabela, as she got up from her chair.

"We going to be here a while?" he asked.

"Of course. We just got here. Besides, we have a lot to talk about," said Anabela.

"*Senor* Carmen. You said you were a collector. Do you still have your collection?" asked Roberto.

"Yes, I have many wonderful pieces. For example some early Romanach, Antonio Araujo, Juana Pierra, of course Anabela's father, Carlos. Many great works," said Carmen.

"Do you still collect?" asked Roberto.

"No, it's impossible now. I have no money and besides, all of the great masters of the early 20th century have either fled the country or have passed away," said Carmen.

"What did you do before the revolution?" asked Roberto.

"I had a good job working for the Bacardi family in Santiago de Cuba. I traveled to Mexico, Puerto Rico, the U.S. . . . it was a good life. Then of course Fidel, heavily influenced by Che and the communists, confiscated all Bacardi facilities in Cuba in 1960, with no compensation. I lost my job because I refused to support the revolution. It was devastating. The world has no idea," said Carmen.

"How did you earn a living after that?" asked Roberto.

"Mostly automobile repair. I still have a small shop. I love the old American cars," said Carmen, staring down at his empty glass.

"Gentlemen, why so sad?" said Anabela, returning to the table with a mojito in each hand. "We're here to have a good time, so no more of this Carmen," she said, shaking her finger at her elderly friend, pretending to be angry.

"Roberto, Anabela tells me you are interested to have a little business buying and selling paintings."

"Yes, my brother and I actually. He's head of the research department," said Roberto with a smile. "He's brilliant but he suffers from autism, so I will be the one to actually make the deals. But I'm not in a position right now to buy anything. Although, just today I was hired by Cimex."

"That's fantastic, Roberto. Congratulations," said Anabela. "Doing what?"

"I will be working in the part of the company that buys jewelry, with Colonel de la Guardia."

"I know him. Not personally, but I have sold jewelry there. They don't pay much and the money they pay you with you have to spend in the company stores. It's hardly worth the effort," said Carmen.

"When do you start?" asked Anabela.

"Thursday. I have a lot of training I need to do first. I know virtually nothing about diamonds, or gold and silver for that matter, not to mention any other types of precious stones. But I will learn. I'm not worried. I have some other news, Anabela."

"What's that?"

"A good friend of mine is the head administrator with security at the marina. I am hoping to meet with him next Saturday to find out what he knows about the Spaniard, Mariano."

"Well, there you go. That's the connection you need," said Anabela, sitting back in her chair.

"You trust this guy?" asked Carmen. "I mean from what Anabela tells me, you've had a rough few years."

"Rough cannot describe it, Carmen. I need to feel him out first, but I believe I can trust him."

"Sounds like your plan is coming together," said Anabela.

"Little by little."

"I may be able to help you," said Carmen in a low voice.

Roberto glanced over at Anabela. "What do you think?" he asked.

"I think you should listen to his offer is what I think," she replied.

"What is your offer?"

"I have a very nice small painting that I think the gentleman from Spain would be interested in. It was done by Leopoldo Romanach in 1912 and is a portrait of an old lady sitting in a chair holding a fan."

"Like I said, I have no money, at least not until I begin working. How much do you want for it?"

"Five hundred pesos. It's a very fair price, and being a Romanach, I think he would be willing to pay good money for it."

"What is good money?" asked Roberto.

"I would recommend thirty-five hundred dollars," said Carmen.

Roberto could hardly believe what he had just heard. It was an unimaginably large sum of money and would be life changing if he could find a way to put the deal together. Slowly, he picked up his mojito and took a sip, purposely not looking at either Carmen or Anabela, in an effort to contain his excitement.

He put his drink back down on the table, looking now at Carmen. "What about Anabela?" asked Roberto. "Carmen, to be fair, I feel she deserves to be part of this also. After all, she and I had a conversation about several paintings she would like to sell."

"Yes, but I'm not willing to sell them at such a low price," she said. "Keep in mind, if you can make it happen, this will not be the only painting this guy is willing to buy. And, you can be sure he has many wealthy friends. There will be other opportunities, Roberto, don't worry about me."

"Listen, you start your job, you save some money, and in the meantime you find out what your friend at the marina has to say. I can wait," said Carmen. "One other thing, Roberto—if he says yes, he'll want a cut."

Roberto looked at Anabela, who was smiling and looking at Roberto. The look on her face was one that he had not seen before. It was one of genuine happiness, he thought. Looking directly into her eyes, he noticed for the first time their color, which had an electric blue-green quality and reminded him of the color of the shallow water sand banks he remembered seeing from Maykel's boat one day many years ago, while trolling outside the reef near Varadero. They were beautiful and hid well her many sorrows, he thought.

"I'll do it," said Roberto.

"This could change your life, Roberto. You realize that?" said Anabela. "And it's what you wanted. We should celebrate. Carmen, another mojito? What about you, Roberto? The music just started and it's Saturday night."

"I have nothing to do, and I can't think of anywhere else I'd rather be than La Bodeguita," said Carmen.

"Anabela, someday, many years from now, I hope we can have a proper celebration," said Roberto.

"What do you mean?"

"I mean a celebration where happiness has no conditions."

"I understand. But for now, this is all we have, and I plan on celebrating with the two of you," said Anabela.

"Fair enough, *Senorita* Sobrino. Tonight we will celebrate," said Roberto.

It was one in the morning when they left La Bodeguita and Carmen had agreed to escort Anabela to her home in La Rampa, leaving Roberto to walk the hour or so back to his parents house in Santos Suarez, on the south side of Havana. He had a lot to think about and the cool night air would help to clear his head, still a little foggy from the rum.

Upon arriving at the home of his parents' he was surprised to see light coming from the front room overlooking the street. The family was probably worried and would be waiting for him, he thought.

Looking through the window before going inside, Roberto could see that it was Carlos who had waited late for his return. He had fallen asleep in a chair, and a large book lay open across his lap.

"Carlitos," whispered Roberto. "Carlitos," whispering his name again.

Carlos slowly opened his eyes and looked at Roberto.

"I have a lot to tell you," said Roberto.

"I was worried. I thought something had happened to you."

"No, everything is fine. I was at La Bodeguita with Anabela. I'm sorry for making you wait up. Do you want to know what happened today?"

"Did you get the job?"

"Yes, that was the easy part actually. Before I met with the Colonel at Cimex I stopped to see Anabela. I wanted to ask her again about the Spanish guy she told me about who is the collector."

"What did she say?"

"She said he comes to Barlovento every winter and stays for several months. Apparently he is a fisherman. Anyway, after I got the job at Cimex, I planned to go to the marina and see if I could get a job there also. I mean we need all the money we can get if we plan on buying any paintings, right? On the way to the marina, I stopped to see my friend Luiz at La Pescadaria. I don't think you ever met him."

"What for?"

"I owed him a visit. Long story. In the course of our conversation he tells me he knows the head of security at the marina. He comes almost every Saturday for dinner at the restaurant. A guy I used to work with at Punto Cero, Pedro Ruiz."

"Forgive me but I'm having a little trouble following you."

"Pedro is a good friend."

"So?" said Carlos, not understanding.

"I am going to meet with him next week and see if he'll connect me with the Spaniard."

"Sounds very risky. What if the Spaniard isn't there, and how do you know you can trust your friend?"

"I don't know, but if I offer him half the money from the sale of the painting, I have a feeling he'll take it."

"What painting? How much did you have to drink?"

"Just enough to make a good plan," said Roberto, smiling confidently. "Here's the best part, Carlitos. Anabela introduced me to a friend who has a Romanach for sale."

"Leopoldo Romanach?" asked Carlos, surprised.

"Yes, for five hundred pesos."

"You don't have that kind of money."

"Not at the moment, but I will."

"Who is Anabela's friend?"

"An older guy. His name is Carmen Pelaez. He was good friends with her father and is a collector. Well, he has a collection. He used to be a collector. He is confident we can get thirty-five hundred dollars. Can you believe it?" exclaimed Roberto.

"Pesos?" asked Carlos, in disbelief.

"No, dollars. Even if I give half to Pedro we will easily be in a position to buy more. And I'm sure Carmen knows other collectors who need money."

"If I were you, I would not tell mother about the painting or your friend at the marina. She would not approve," cautioned Carlos.

"I don't plan on it. She'll be happy to hear about the job though."

"I can't process all this without some sleep."

"Alright, we'll talk more tomorrow."

Carlos closed the book he had been reading and showed the cover to Roberto before placing it on the table beside his chair.

Roberto picked up the book and read the title out loud. "*The Works of Leopoldo Romanach*," he said. "I wonder if the piece that *Senor* Pelaez is wanting to sell is in the book. I'll find out the title of the painting before we buy it so we can have as much information as possible to present to the Spaniard."

"First, you need to make sure it is authentic," said Carlos.

"I have Anabela's word. That's all I need. Let's go, Carlitos. The sun will be up in a few hours."

With that the brothers turned out the two kerosene lamps Carlos had been reading by and quietly made their way up the stairs in the dark, careful not to disturb their sleeping parents.

The three days prior to Roberto beginning his new job with Colonel de la Guardia at Cimex, he spent searching through the Biblioteca Nacional Jose Marti for anything he could find on the subject of how to grade diamonds, gold, and silver. Arriving on the first day of work with even a simple working knowledge, thought Roberto, would show the Colonel he was committed, and would help him to gain the colonel's trust.

Less than one week ago Roberto was alone in a jail cell, with no idea if he was going to live or die, much less be given back his freedom. Now his vision of a life shaped by his own determinants and based on personal choice, was not only a possibility . . . it was happening.

When Thursday morning arrived Roberto was up and out of his parents' house before sunrise. Walking the five kilometers to the facility would take a little more than an hour, and he remembered from his previous time spent working security for the colonel, that like everyone in the military, he wouldn't tolerate Roberto being late.

As he approached the Cimex building Roberto could see at a distance his friend Mateo was on duty working security at the entrance and a small line of customers had already formed waiting for the store to open.

"*Buenos dias*, Mateo. *Come estas?*" asked Roberto.

"I'm doing well, my friend. What about you, Roberto? First day at work?"

"*Si*, first day, and I'm a little nervous, Mateo. I don't want to disappoint the Colonel," said Roberto.

"The Colonel is a very reasonable man and a good guy, you know that. You'll be fine, and besides it's always so busy around here you're not going to have time to be nervous," said Mateo with a smile as he opened the door for Roberto and patted him on the shoulder.

Arriving at the Colonel's office on the second floor, Roberto found the door to the office open. The lights were on and Alina, the secretary, had not yet arrived. Assuming the Colonel was in his office Roberto let himself in, passing through the waiting area to the back where he had first spoken to Colonel de la Guardia.

"*Hola*, Colonel. *Buenos dias, senor*," said Roberto. He waited in the doorway for permission from the colonel to enter.

"Ramos. Come in please. You're on time. I like that," said de la Guardia. "Sit down."

"Thank you, sir."

"What I'd like to do this morning is go over the basics of evaluating diamond quality. Tomorrow we can work on gold and silver. It's a lot of information and it will take a little time for you to feel comfortable working by yourself."

"Sir, I've been researching for several days now and feel I have a fairly good understanding of what to look for in a quality diamond."

"You have to understand, reading and actually doing are two very different things. Suppose you tell me what you know and we'll go from there," instructed de la Guardia.

"Sure. The four primary considerations are, carat, which measures the mass of the diamond, and not to be confused with karat with a k, that is used to measure the purity of gold. Second is clarity, which is a fairly obvious quality. Any inclusions or blemishes seriously detract from the quality. Third is color. Colorless is best as it will not interfere with light refraction. The more of that the better. And fourth is cut, the most important quality. But like you say Colonel, I need the hands-on experience to feel comfortable, especially considering we are talking about potentially large sums of money when you resell them," said Roberto. He sat back in his chair and waited for the Colonel's response. He could tell by the look on the Colonel's face he was surprised by how much Roberto seemed to know.

"Ramos, I have to tell you, I was not expecting you to show up here today that prepared. I can see you are serious about this job," said the Colonel.

"I have to be, Colonel," replied Roberto.

"What do you mean?" asked the Colonel.

"My parents are poor sir. They can't support me any longer. Life is more difficult now in Cuba than it was when we were growing up. I'm sure you understand."

"I do, and life isn't going to get any easier Roberto, I can promise you. Without the support of the Soviet Union, the country will run out of money. El Comandante as you might imagine, is obsessed with the situation," said the Colonel. "We should be going downstairs. The shop will open in a few minutes and we've been busy lately. We'll work together for the next few weeks. I will teach you everything I know about the business."

"One more thing Colonel. When is payday? I told my mother and father I would do whatever I could to help them financially."

"At the end of every month. Shall we go?"

"I'm ready," said Roberto. "*Vamos.*"

At the close of business the following Saturday, Roberto was the last to leave except for Mateo and the Colonel's personal assistant, Andre, who Roberto reported to at the end of each day. Roberto could tell he was extremely loyal to the Colonel and appeared to be a genuinely kind man, but he had a nervousness about him and never stopped moving, which Roberto found troubling, and a little suspicious.

Roberto said goodbye to Mateo as he left the building and headed in the direction of La Pescadaria. He had received word the night before from Luiz, that he had successfully arranged a meeting with his friend Pedro, from the Marina Hemingway, and they were to meet at the restaurant at seven o'clock.

This was the final piece of the puzzle, thought Roberto. All that remained was for Pedro to agree to help him sell the painting to the Spaniard, and his plan would be complete.

Entering the restaurant, Roberto was greeted by Pilar, the young woman who worked for Luiz, whom he had met the week before.

"*Buenas noches,* Roberto. Your friend Pedro is waiting. He just arrived.

Follow me," said Pilar.

"*Gracias*, Pilar," replied Roberto.

Pilar led Roberto outside to the far end of the veranda where his friend Pedro, whom he had not seen since before being sent back to prison, was sitting, talking with Luiz.

"Pedro. How are you, my friend?" asked Roberto.

Pedro stood up to greet Roberto and the two men embraced warmly.

"*Estoy bien*. The question is, how are you? I heard you've had some problems recently," said Pedro.

"A few, but things are improving," said Roberto. "I just started working for de la Guardia."

"At Cimex?"

"Yes. I'm working with him in the jewelry department."

"I always liked Tony. He's a good guy. Sit down Roberto, please," said Pedro. "What is it you want to talk about?"

"I'll let you two guys talk," said Luiz. "Let Pilar know if you need anything."

"Luiz, I appreciate your help," said Roberto.

"No problem," said Luiz, returning to the kitchen.

"So Roberto, why did you want to see me?" asked Pedro.

"We have always been brothers, Pedro," said Roberto. "I always trusted you and you trusted me."

"Always," said Pedro.

"I have a business offer for you. Something that could be very good for both of us. It has a lot of potential," said Roberto.

"What do you want?"

"There is a guy who lives at the marina for the winter. A Spaniard, named Mariano. You know him?"

"Yeah, I know him. Not well, but we talk. He's extremely wealthy from what I understand. Anyway, I pretty much know everyone who comes there."

"Is he there now?"

arrived a couple weeks ago. I see him every few days."

"...e collects pre-revolution Cuban paintings. From the old masters," said Roberto.

"How do you know all this?"

"It's a long story, but through a good friend of mine. I have a painting I'm certain he'll be interested in buying."

"What do you want me to do?"

"Talk to him for me. Maybe we could all meet here. I'm willing to give you half of whatever we get."

"And how much is that?"

"Your half would be one thousand seven hundred and fifty dollars," said Roberto.

He leaned forward and folded his hands on the table without losing eye contact with Pedro.

Pedro was clearly surprised by what Roberto had said and did not immediately respond. Sitting back in his chair he readjusted the white fedora he was wearing and blew out through his mouth, buffing out his cheeks.

"You're serious?" asked Pedro, still not believing what he had heard.

"Dead serious, Pedro," responded Roberto.

"What do I tell him? I mean he'll want to know something about the painting I assume, and the artist."

"I wrote it all down. Here, you give him this and he'll know exactly what I have. You understand you can't tell anyone about this?"

"What happens if we get caught?"

"The only way we get caught is if he says something to the wrong person. Which he won't because I'm going to make sure there is always something else that he'll want from us."

"What do you mean?"

"Collectors are never really satisfied. They always want more. If he's happy with the painting I have he'll want to know what else we have. Especially if he thinks he's getting some sort of inside deal. You know how people are."

"I don't need to tell you how risky this is. We could both wind up in prison."

"What do you say, Pedrito?"

"We're all poor, Roberto, and things are getting worse every day. I'll try and set something up. When do you want to meet?"

"The end of the month. Three weeks from today."

"I'll let Luiz know we plan to meet. If I have any questions after speaking with Mariano, how do I get in touch with you?"

"Stop by Cimex. I get off work at five o'clock. There's a little cafe across the street where we can talk. It's quiet."

"I guess we have a deal then. Unless you hear from me, I'll see you in three weeks," said Pedro.

The two men stood up, shook hands, and embraced once more before saying goodbye. It had been a long day for Roberto who was tired and anxious to return home to deliver the news to Carlos.

The following day Roberto decided he would pay a visit to Anabela, informing her about the success of his meeting with his friend Pedro, who had agreed to contact the Spanish art collector Mariano. He wanted to assure her of his intention to buy the Romanach painting from Carmen.

Roberto's brother Carlos again chose not to make the trip to see Anabela. His unwillingness to make an effort to get past the discomfort generally associated with risk taking was troubling for Roberto. He knew that if and when the time came to leave the island, not only would it be at the very least a monumental emotional struggle for Roberto, but potentially an impossible ask for Carlos.

It was midmorning when Roberto arrived at the home of Anabela, and as he approached the front door, he could hear music coming from inside the house. He knocked on the door, waiting several seconds before glancing up to see Anabela peering down from a window on the second floor, looking somewhat annoyed.

"Roberto! You always show up when I'm getting dressed," complained

Anabela.

"Lucky me," said Roberto, smiling.

"Wait there," she said, pausing for a moment. "I'll be down in a second. I have something for you."

"Oh yeah, what's that?" he asked, excitedly.

"You'll see. Just wait there."

When Anabela opened the door, her demeanor had changed and she was smiling.

"Please, come in," she said, stepping aside and holding the door open for Roberto to walk past.

As Roberto walked through the doorway into the entrance hall, Anabela grabbed his arm and hit him open palm, on the back of the head with her other hand, being certain to make contact with the edge of the ring on her third finger.

"What was that for?" said Roberto, rubbing the back of his head.

"I told you I had something for you," said Anabela.

"Yeah, but," said Roberto, unable to come up with a response.

"Yeah, but, you need to let me know you're coming, or come in the afternoon. Don't you know anything about women?" she said rhetorically. Anabela was smiling now and trying hard to feign annoyance.

"Sorry. I'm a little excited. I met with my friend Pedro yesterday after work and he has agreed to speak with Mariano at Barlovento," said Roberto.

"Oh my god, Roberto. That's fantastic," said Anabela. "I'll make some coffee. Come, sit out back and we can talk."

Roberto followed Anabela to the rear of the house and out onto the terrace where he waited for her to bring the coffee.

"How about a *pastelito con queso*?" asked Anabela from the kitchen.

"Did you make it?"

"I need to teach you some manners, and yes I made them."

"Yes ma'am, I would love one," he said.

Roberto could sense he had reached another level of familiarity with Anabela and was grateful for her trust and friendship. Sitting in what Anabela liked to call, 'her little sanctuary,' he realized that for the first time in four years he felt content. He was surrounded by people with ambition, he thought, whom he could trust and who loved what he loved. He felt strong.

Leaning back in his chair and looking up at the clouds passing overhead swept along by the winter westerlies, he couldn't help but notice a pair of brightly colored birds perched in one of Anabela's mamey trees. He remembered seeing a pair of these birds one day through the open window at the Censam Marin Hospital, where he would sit and talk with the old man Tiburcio. He remembered also how he thought the bird's feathers were the same colors as the Cuban flag.

Anabela was smiling when she emerged from the kitchen carrying a small tray of cheese pastries, hot milk, sugar, and a fresh pot of coffee.

"I'll let you make your own Roberto," she said, sitting down on the opposite side of the table.

"Anabela," said Roberto, pointing up at the two birds. "What do you call these birds?"

Anabela finished stirring some sugar into her coffee, placed the spoon on the saucer beside the cup and looked up at the birds. "That is a pair of tocororos," she said. "They come here in the winter to feed on the fruit. Why?"

"No reason. They're very beautiful."

"Very," she said, looking over at Roberto who was still looking up. "You know that is the national bird of Cuba, right?"

"I didn't know actually," he admitted.

"When you see one, they're supposed to bring good luck," said Anabela.

"If they bring good luck why don't people keep them in their homes?" he asked.

Anabela took a sip of coffee and placed her cup on the table. "Because they die in captivity," she said.

"From what?"

"Sadness."

"Like my friend Tiburcio."

"Yes, like Tiburcio, and many others in Cuba. Roberto, I want to hear about what happened with your friend at Barlovento," she said.

"Well, I have a plan to meet with Mariano in three weeks unless I hear from my friend Pedro that Mariano is not interested," explained Roberto.

"Not only will he be interested, he'll want to know what else you may have to sell," she said. "When do you expect to have the money for Carmen?"

"The day before, on Friday. Can we meet here?" he asked.

"Absolutely. I'll let him know this week. He lives nearby."

"Anabela, I can't thank you enough for all you've done. I need to repay you somehow."

"If you are successful with the painting from Carmen, which I'm sure you will be, as you know, I have a couple of pieces I would like to sell."

"Do you think you would ever leave Cuba, Anabela?"

"Maybe. Why do you ask?"

"My brother and I are thinking about leaving."

"And when do you plan to leave?"

"Not for a few years. It's not possible now."

"Why not?"

"First we need to find a boat that is seaworthy. Which will be expensive. That's why I'm hoping we can develop the business with Mariano."

"You will."

"I wonder, Anabela, do you think it's sustainable?"

"What, selling art?"

"Yes. I mean how much of it still exists in Cuba?"

"Plenty. You have to understand, Roberto, Carmen collected for many years. He knows a lot of people who used to collect and who still have many important and valuable works from before the revolution. You'll see."

"I have a lot to learn," he said. "It's a bit overwhelming."

"It takes time. Besides, you're clever, and you have the right personality for this business. And you're honest," she said. "Have something else to eat?"

"Maybe a little more coffee?"

Anabela stood up from the table, picked up the empty coffee pot and began walking toward the house. Stopping just before she reached the kitchen door, Anabela turned and looked back at Roberto, who was looking up at the tocororos, still perched in the mamey tree above the terrace.

"Roberto, I am grateful for your visit today. It means more than you can know. I truly hope one day you will realize your dream of living in America."

Roberto looked at Anabela but said nothing. He wondered if she had ever been married and why she chose to live alone. He felt sorry for her.

It was nearly dark when Roberto left the home of Anabela. They had talked all afternoon and evening about many things, from the great *maestros* of Cuban art to the cruel illusions and failures of communism, and to a life of freedom outside of Cuba.

XIII

Roberto spent the next three weeks totally dedicated to his work with Colonel de la Guardia at Cimex. He was obsessed with the business and learned quickly, impressing the Colonel, the Colonel's assistant, Andres, and in particular, Andres' daughter, Alina, whom he first met the day he had been hired by the colonel. Roberto had become quite friendly with Alina, and the two had spent several evenings together after work strolling along the Malecon at sunset. Although they had little in common, they genuinely enjoyed each other's company.

Roberto had a particularly long walk to and from work each day which left little time at the end of the day for anything but a quick meal and some sleep. Alina was living with her father, close to work, and had hinted on several occasions perhaps Roberto should consider moving in with her. He thought about the offer but was concerned she would find out about his plan to buy and sell art. He needed to keep it a secret and the fewer people that knew about his plan, he thought, the better.

It was the last work day of the month, pay day, and Roberto was having difficulty concentrating on his work. All he could think about was his meeting with Carmen at Anabela's, later that evening.

Earlier in the day, Alina had approached Roberto about going out after work to celebrate the new job and his first paycheck. He hated having to lie to Alina but buying the painting from Carmen was all that mattered to him, so he told her he had promised the money to his parents for food and would make it up to her the next time they were paid.

As soon as La Tienda Cimex Departamental had closed for the day, he was on his way to the home of Anabela in Habana Vieja.

By the time Roberto had reached Anabela's, it was beginning to rain, forcing him to run the last few blocks to her house. Running up the handful of steps two at a time to the entrance landing, he peered through the front window before knocking, and waived to Anabela who was sitting opposite Carmen facing the window.

"*Hola, Roberto, buenas noches! Que tal?*" said Anabela, as she opened the door.

Anabela was wearing the flowered dress he remembered her having worn the day they first met and she had done her hair. She looked beautiful, thought Roberto, and he wanted to tell her but couldn't find the words.

"What's the matter, Roberto? You coming in or do you prefer

standing in the rain?" she said. Anabela often spoke sarcastically, and he liked that about her. It made him feel comfortable.

"Sorry, I'm a little nervous," said Roberto as he stepped into the house.

"Nervous? About what?"

"Well, tonight is kind of a big deal for me."

"You sit with Carmen. He has something for you. I'm going to bring you something for your nerves."

"Anabela," said Roberto, as he took a seat beside Carmen.

"What is it?"

"You look lovely."

"You're learning, Roberto," said Anabela, pausing slightly. "Thank you. Carmen, show him the painting."

"Roberto. Sit over here," said Carmen, pointing to the chair opposite the one he was sitting in. "The painting looks better from a slight distance."

Carmen turned and reached for the painting which was leaning against the side of the sofa where he was sitting.

"What do you think," asked Carmen.

"What I think is, I can't believe this is finally happening. It's more beautiful than I could have imagined," said Roberto. "What do you know about the woman in the painting?"

"Nothing really, but that's not why the painting is important. What is remarkable about this painting is how Romanach used light to suggest a feeling of melancholy. It's as though the woman is longing for something or someone. It is very subtle. You may not agree, but that is how I see her," said Carmen.

"Clearly I have a lot to learn, Carmen," said Roberto.

"It takes time. The important thing is you have the passion, and you are young," replied Carmen.

"Gentleman, a little something to celebrate with," said Anabela. "I've been saving this for just such an occasion."

"What are we drinking?" asked Carmen.

"*Anejo Quince Anos,*" said Anabela. "I've had this bottle for many years. For special occasions only. You sell a few paintings, Roberto, and maybe we can afford another bottle."

"I'd like to make a toast if I may," said Roberto.

"Please," said Anabela.

"To Anabela, for all that you have done for me, and to the people of Cuba. May we one day be truly free," said Roberto.

No one spoke and Anabela was looking down at her glass. Roberto could see that she was trying not to cry.

"I'm sorry, Anabela," he said.

"No, no, it's okay, Roberto. It's not your fault. To the people of Cuba," she said, wiping a tear from her cheek.

"To art, and to the great masters," said Carmen, smiling.

"*Salud,*" said Roberto.

"What do you think of the painting, Roberto?" asked Anabela.

"I love it, of course. Carmen was just explaining to me about how Romanach would make use of light in his works to create feeling and emotion," he said.

"Yes, he was the master. That's why they call him *el padre de la pintura Cubana,*" she replied.

"So you think Mariano will want to buy this piece?" asked Roberto.

"Absolutely," said Carmen. "Remember, you need to sell it to him as well."

"What do you mean?" asked Roberto.

"You need to give him the full story. That's what salesmen do," said Carmen. "You know, how you fell in love with art, and how you met Anabela and the story of your painting, *El Saxofonista.* He'll probably want to buy that too."

"It's not for sale," said Roberto.

"I realize that. You see, for collectors, the story is almost as important as the work itself. When he returns to Spain he'll surely want to impress all his friends, not only with his most recent acquisition, but the story of how he acquired it. To most Spaniards, Cuba is an exotic place. A tropical paradise of dreams and romance," said Carmen.

"Roberto, when do you meet Mariano?" asked Anabela.

"I meet him tomorrow at my friend Luiz's place," said Roberto. "It's not far from the marina."

"We need to take it out of the frame then. It will be easier to carry and less conspicuous if we roll it up and cover it with paper. It will not hurt the painting, and the frame isn't worth anything, and Mariano will want to have it properly framed when he gets back to Spain," said Carmen.

"Carmen, here is the money. Five hundred pesos, right?" asked Roberto, as he reached into his pocket for the money. "I should be going. I'm anxious to show Carlitos the painting. And thank you for the rum. Carmen, I will remember what you told me about how to sell."

"You'll let us know how it goes tomorrow," said Anabela.

"Of course. You'll be the first to know," Roberto assured her.

Before leaving, with help from Carmen, Roberto removed the painting from the old frame and rolled it up, careful not to crack the paint by rolling it too tight, before wrapping it in several layers of heavy brown paper for protection.

Anxious to return home and show Carlos the painting, Roberto was also nervous about what his parents might say. They knew nothing of his plan and would not be happy if they found out he was involved with making money illegally. He had to keep it a secret.

The rain had stopped by the time Roberto left Anabela's and headed for home. The tree frogs that are common in Cuba, even in the city, were singing loudly as they always do after an evening rain when it is dark. The air was cool from the rain and made for a comfortable walk.

Arriving home Roberto was relieved to find his parents and Carlos sitting out back on the terrace. Not wanting them to see the painting he went straight to his bedroom, hid it under the bed next to the painting of *El Saxofonista*, and went back downstairs to join the family.

"*Buenas noches*," said Roberto to his mother as he entered the kitchen. Rosa was preparing some fresh papaya and shredded coconut with cane syrup for Carlos and Guillermo senior.

"*Buenas noches*, Roberto," replied Rosa. "You are a little bit late this evening. We finished supper several hours ago."

"I stopped off to see Anabela," said Roberto.

"What about Alina? I thought she was your girlfriend," said Rosa.

"I told you, Anabela is not my girlfriend. We enjoy each other's company and we talk about art," said Roberto.

"I will never understand your obsession with old paintings, Roberto. Would you like some *fruta bomba*? I'm making some for Carlos and your father," said Rosa.

"Sure. You remember the books Carlos would bring each time you came to visit me when I was in prison at Censam Marin? Those books—with the old paintings as you say—they saved my life," said Roberto.

"Take this to your father and brother. I'll bring some for you," said Rosa, as she handed Roberto two small bowls of papaya.

Roberto walked out to the terrace, said good evening to Carlos and Guillermo, and gave them each a bowl of papaya.

"Did you see Anabela today?" asked Carlos.

"Yes, I did," said Roberto. Carlos knew about the meeting with Carmen, and the Romanach painting, and wanted to know if Roberto had bought it, but couldn't ask about it in front of his father.

"How is the papaya, *Padre*?" asked Roberto.

"It would be better with a little rum and coconut," said Guillermo.

Roberto waited for the next moment that his father looked down at the bowl of papaya before winking at Carlos, letting him know he had the painting.

"What are you smiling about, Carlitos," asked Rosa as she approached the table.

"I'm happy to see my brother. We haven't seen much of each other the last few years," said Carlos.

"I'm aware of that. He has a problem staying out of trouble," she said.

"I'm all done with that, *Madre*. You don't need to worry any longer," said Roberto.

"I'm not so sure," she said.

"How is Colonel de la Guardia?" asked Guillermo.

"Okay, I think. Although lately he seems a little stressed. He hasn't been around the shop much lately. He spends a lot of time at the Presidential Palace meeting with Fidel, and sometimes Abrantes," said Roberto.

"What about?" asked Rosa.

"I don't know. His personal assistant, Andres, he's acting strange also. The two of them are always talking in Tony's office, and it's not about diamonds," said Roberto.

"Whatever it is, don't get involved," said Guillermo.

"My only plan right now is to stay out of trouble and save a little money," replied Roberto.

"And what are you saving the money for?" asked Rosa.

"I'd like to have my own place," said Roberto.

"You'll be lucky to afford food nowadays," said Rosa. "Everything is scarce."

"We'll see," said Roberto.

Looking across the table at his brother, Roberto could tell the conversation was making Carlos nervous. He was anxious to show him the Romanach painting he bought from Carmen.

"Carlitos, we should visit Maykel this weekend. What do you say?" asked Roberto.

"See if he has any fish for sale," said Rosa.

"I will ask him," said Roberto. "What do you think Carlitos?"

"Sure, I'll go with you. I spoke with Aroldis the other day and he said his father is catching a few wahoo, and he heard a story about a bluefin coming to the dock in Cojimar. I don't know if that's true," said Carlos.

"I think I'm going to get some sleep if you don't mind, *Madre*. It's been a long week. *Padre*, until tomorrow. *Buenas noches*, Carlitos," said Roberto.

"*Buenas noches*," replied Carlos. "We'll make a plan in the morning to see Maykel."

Roberto had trouble sleeping that night. Repeatedly waking up, nervous about his meeting the following day with Mariano and Pedro. He kept thinking about what Carmen had told him that evening about how masterfully Romanach used light in the painting to convey emotion and how important it was to sell Mariano on the story behind the painting. He had never sold anything, he thought, and was beginning to have doubts about his plan.

Rosa and Guillermo often left the house early on Saturdays to wait in line for bread at the nearby government bakery. If you didn't arrive early there was always a possibility the shop would run out of bread before it was your turn.

Before leaving the house, Roberto and Carlos made a plan to meet Maykel at the docks along the Rio Almendares where Maykel kept his boat, near the Malecon on the north side of the city, after Roberto returned from his meeting at La Pescadaria, with the Spaniard, Mariano. With any luck, Maykel would have some fresh fish for sale.

La Pescadaria opened for business around midday, so Roberto, knowing first impressions would be important, left home early, determined not to be late.

When he turned onto the gravel road leading down the hill to the river, he could see at a distance a black Mercedes Benz parked directly in front of the restaurant. What if it was someone from the government, he thought.

To be safe, Roberto decided to enter first through the kitchen. Luiz would most likely be there and he could check with him to see who the owner of the car was.

"*Hola*, Luiz," said Roberto in a low voice as he looked in an open window beside the door to the kitchen.

"Roberto. Pedrito is waiting for you with Mariano. Come around to the front door. It will be better. I'll meet you there," said Luiz.

Relieved, Roberto walked back to the front of the building where he met Luiz and entered the restaurant. Pedro and Mariano were sitting outside on the deck facing the river, each with a beer and had not seen Roberto enter the building.

"Gentlemen," said Luiz as they approached the table. "Mariano, my friend Roberto."

Before Roberto had reached the table Mariano had gotten up from his chair and extended his hand to Roberto. He was younger than expected, thought Roberto, as the two men shook hands.

"Thank you for coming *senor*," said Roberto to Mariano. "*Hola*, Pedrito. *Como estas?*"

"Please, call me Mariano, Roberto. Sit down, sit down," he said. "Pedro tells me you guys used to work together in special forces."

"Yes, we worked at Punto Cero, for El Comandante. More recently I am working for Colonel de la Guardia at Cimex," said Roberto.

"Can I see the painting?" asked Mariano.

"Of course," said Roberto. Carefully, Roberto unrolled the painting from the paper covering and after clearing a space, spread it out on the table for Mariano to see.

"It's fantastic, Roberto. More beautiful than I had imagined," said Mariano as he slowly examined the painting.

"You're familiar with the artist, of course," said Roberto.

"Oh yes. I have a number of his works, but not many this nice. How did you come by it?" asked Mariano.

"It's a rather long story," replied Roberto.

"Well then another round of beers for everyone, Luiz," said Mariano.

"Coming up. What about something to eat?" said Luiz.

"Luiz, I don't have any money and I already owe you," said Roberto.

"No no, *voy a pagar*, Luiz," said the Spaniard.

"You're very kind, Mariano," said Roberto.

"I have some fresh *langosta* from my friend, Joaquin," offered Luiz.

"Fantastic. My favorite. The only time I am able to find them is when I am in Cuba," said Mariano.

"Mariano, it is illegal for me to sell this painting. You are aware of that I'm sure. You must not mention this to anyone. Especially in Marina Hemingway. There are many government officials that go there," said Roberto.

"I understand. You can trust me. I am no fan of Fidel. I come to Cuba because I love the country and I love the people," replied Mariano.

"I have had the painting valued by two friends of mine who have collections and are experts on the subject of the Cuban Masters," said Roberto.

"And what did they tell you?" asked Mariano.

"They said it was conservatively worth three thousand five hundred dollars," said Roberto.

"It's not really about the money, Roberto. You haven't told me the story," said Mariano.

"*Bueno* . . . seven years ago my brother and I had a friend that needed help moving. He was an old man and had no family, so we agreed to help. When we were finished he couldn't pay us. Instead, as payment, he gave us a painting. The only reason we took the painting was because he said it was quite valuable. It took many months of research to confirm what he had told us was true," explained Roberto.

"If he was famous, there must have been some record of his work," said Mariano.

"He was an opponent of the communists and had fled the country after the revolution. The government eliminated all record of him. It was by luck that we found an article in an old newspaper announcing he had been awarded the National Painting award in 1957."

"You're talking about Carlos Sobrino, the Cuban," said Mariano, a bit surprised by what he had heard.

"Yes, you know of him?" said Roberto.

"Of course. He was well known in the expat art community in Spain," said Mariano.

"Well, our research led us to his daughter who lives in Havana," said Roberto. "She introduced me to a good friend who I was able to buy the painting from."

"Your friends, do they have other works for sale?" asked Mariano.

"I believe so," replied Roberto.

"I would be interested to know what else they have for sale," said Mariano.

"But first you agree to buy the Romanach?" asked Roberto.

"Yes, I would love to have it in my collection," said Mariano.

"Something you need to know then. Everything goes through Pedrito. You pay him half and you pay me half. We are partners on everything," said Roberto.

"Understood," said Mariano. "I should tell you, Roberto, I have many friends in Spain who collect and are looking for important works from before the revolution. You and Pedrito could do well. I will contact them if you like," said Mariano.

"I know that I can find other important works that would be of interest to them," said Roberto.

"Gentlemen, your *langosta*," said Luiz, as he reemerged from the kitchen carrying a large tray of fresh grilled lobster, sweet plantains, and some yellow rice with *sofrito*.

"You're a national treasure, Luiz," said Pedro.

"Tell that to El Congrejo," said Luiz with a laugh.

"Thank you," said Roberto. "By the way, I'm a business man now, Luiz, so no more free lunches."

After finishing their meal, Mariano and Roberto made a plan to meet again at the restaurant in two weeks. From memory, Roberto had described to Mariano the three paintings Anabela had offered to Roberto years earlier, the first time they met at La Bodeguita. Roberto remembered that one of the paintings had been done by Romanach and was certain to be of interest to Mariano.

Having been paid in cash Roberto was nervous about carrying around so much money. He was not afraid of encountering common thieves, but should he be stopped by the police on his way home with such a large sum of money, he was certain to be questioned about it and quite possibly arrested.

Feeling grateful to Anabela Sobrino for his good fortune, and thinking she would be excited to know how the meeting with Mariano had turned out, Roberto decided to deliver the news to her, before returning home.

It was nearly sunset when Roberto arrived at the home of Anabela. He stood momentarily at the foot of the stairs before walking up to the front door. Tired from the events of the day, he was relieved to see a light coming from the front window.

He knocked on the door, turned around slowly and faced the street. Looking up he saw, backlit against the pastel peach colored sky, the lavender colored cumulus clouds, typical of late winter, which had built to a great height above the hills to the south of Havana. It was as though someone had painted the sky, he thought.

"Roberto!" said Anabela, surprising Roberto as she opened the door.

"I wanted to come see you. I hope you don't mind," said Roberto.

"You always ask me that. Of course not. Come in, please," she said.

"I have to tell you about my meeting with Mariano."

"What did he think of the painting?"

"He loved it. In fact he wanted to know what else I had," he said. "He also said he has friends in Spain who are looking to add to their collections."

"What did you tell him?"

"I told him about your paintings. Remember the ones you wanted to sell?" said Roberto. "He's particularly interested in works by Romanach."

"He'll buy the Romanach?" asked Anabela.

"Yes, I'm certain of it."

"Did you give him a price?"

"No, because I wanted to discuss it with you. And besides, I don't think money is an issue with him."

"I will sell it for eight hundred pesos. I realize you are assuming all the risk and I know you have to split the money with your friend," she said. "What do you say?"

"I say I'm living my dream, Anabela."

"You are fortunate, and it's no accident. You know they say living is better than dreaming, no matter how grand the dream, but living your dream is always best. I'm happy for you."

"I can pay you tonight for the Romanach if you'd like. Mariano paid me today."

"Well I could certainly use the money. My job, like everyone's job, is not enough to live on."

"I need to leave the painting here for two weeks until I see Mariano again."

"You don't want to take it with you?"

"If I take it home my parents will question me about it. I haven't told them about any of this."

"Not a problem, Roberto. How about a little rum?"

"Sure. We should be celebrating now."

"*Vamos*. Let's sit out back under the stars," she said.

XIV

In two weeks' time Roberto met again as planned with the Mariano, at La Pescadaria, to deliver the Romanach painting he had purchased from Anabela. As promised, Mariano had successfully contacted three other collectors living in Spain and had prepared a list of artists to give Roberto, that they were particularly interested in collecting.

During that time Alina continued to pressure Roberto about moving in together at the home of her father, Andres. Roberto's increasing financial independence and the desire for regular female companionship, something that had been missing in his life, made the decision an easy one.

The home of Andres was conveniently located between Marina Hemingway, where Mariano stayed, the home of Anabela, and Cimex, where Roberto and Alina worked. Alina had shown herself to be pleasantly uncomplicated, easy to be around, and rarely asked any questions. In addition, her father worked long hours for Colonel de la Guardia and was almost never home, so as long as he was able to keep his business with Mariano secret from her, thought Roberto, life would be good.

Over the following months Roberto worked closely with Carmen to expand his network of contacts, not only in Havana, but all the way from San Cristobal in the west to Matanzas in the east. It seemed he couldn't learn fast enough and spent every weekend following leads or meeting with Mariano at La Pescadaria whenever he had something he knew Mariano couldn't live without.

His work appraising and buying jewelry for Colonel de la Guardia at Cimex, was increasing exponentially, as worsening economic conditions resulting from the loss of financial support from the Soviet Union after the collapse of the Eastern Bloc, left many Cubans desperate for cash, and willing to sell family heirloom jewelry simply to put food on the table.

It was a Saturday morning, well before dawn, in early June of 1989, when Roberto and Alina were suddenly awakened by a loud cracking noise that had come from the front of the house and sounded to them like wood splintering. Getting up to investigate the noise, Roberto quickly dressed and began running toward the front room. Once in the hallway that led to the front of the house, he heard someone shout out a command to search the rear of the building. Thinking he needed to warn Alina, he turned to go back to the bedroom. It was too late; they had seen him.

"Stop," shouted one of the men. "Hands over your head and turn around."

Roberto, stopping immediately, turned around and held his hands above his head. Not again, he thought.

"What is your name?" asked one of the men as he stepped in front of the others and faced Roberto.

"Ramos. Roberto Ramos. I work for Colonel de la Guardia, at Cimex," he replied, thinking his affiliation with the colonel would carry some weight.

"Where is Andres?" yelled the man, who appeared to be the commanding officer.

"He's not here. I don't know where he is," answered Roberto. "What do you want?"

"Where does he keep the money?" asked the officer.

"I don't know what you're talking about," replied Roberto.

"You said you work for de la Guardia, at Cimex, right?" said the man.

"Yes, but I have nothing to do with the money there. I appraise jewelry for the colonel. That's it," said Roberto.

Just then, Alina, having dressed hurriedly, came out of the bedroom into the hallway. "What is going on?" she asked.

"They're looking for your father," replied Roberto.

"He's not here. He is with the Colonel at the airport in Varadero," she said.

"Come with me," ordered the man, pointing toward the room at the front end of the house.

Entering the living room, Roberto counted twenty-four heavily armed military police personnel, along with the commanding officer.

"The two of you, sit over here," said the man, pointing to the sofa.

"Roberto," said one of the other men who was standing near the front door. It was a good friend from the military, and he had recognized Roberto.

"You know him?" asked the commanding officer to the man who had addressed Roberto.

"Yes, he is a good friend, Colonel. We served at Punto Cero together," said the man.

Roberto immediately recognized the man as his friend Manuel from their time together in special forces.

"We're looking for Andres, Roberto. This has nothing to do with you," said Manuel.

"What do you want with my father?" asked Alina.

"Your father is in a lot of trouble," said the colonel to Alina.

Roberto could not imagine why the military police had come to the home of Andres, but he was beginning to realize it had nothing to do with him or his black market art business. Whatever the trouble was, it was extremely serious, and Roberto knew, because of his association with Colonel de la Guardia, even though he was simply an employee at Cimex, he needed to be extra careful not to reveal anything about his business dealings.

"Do you know why your father and the Colonel spend so much time in Varadero?" asked the Colonel.

"I assume it has to do with the business with Cimex. They sell the jewelry and the diamonds internationally," replied Alina.

"That's what your father told you?" asked the colonel.

"Yes, what else would they be doing there?" replied Alina.

"It's none of your business," said the officer. "Alright, let's go," said the colonel.

"What about us?" asked Roberto.

"What about you?" said the colonel.

"We work for Colonel de la Guardia," said Roberto.

"I recommend you look for a new job. We're done here," said the Colonel, motioning to his men to leave. After the last man left the house, the Colonel turned around and looked at Alina. "One other thing. I would suggest you not try and contact your father."

Roberto looked over at Alina, putting his hand on her knee. "I'm certain your father has done nothing wrong. He is a dedicated Fidelista and Colonel de la Guardia has the respect of everyone in the military, none more so than Fidel. They are loyal to the revolution," said Roberto in an attempt to comfort Alina and feign respect for Fidel. He looked again at the colonel who was still standing in the doorway.

"Remember what I said," warned the Colonel as he left the house.

Alina was shaking and beginning to cry.

"Roberto, I'm afraid. What if they send my father to jail? He's all I have."

"You have me, don't forget."

"I know. I didn't mean it that way, but we have no jobs. You heard what he said. It's impossible to find work now."

"He doesn't know that."

"Well he sounded pretty certain to me."

"We'll be okay, Alina. Trust me."

"What do you mean, we'll be okay?" said Alina, still crying. "What the hell are we going to do for money. I have no family and your parents can't take care of us. How will we eat?"

Even though Roberto never told Alina he no longer needed the job at Cimex, he had continued working for Colonel de la Guardia, in part because on occasion it provided a way to connect with people who were looking to sell old paintings. In addition he had also developed a reputation locally as somewhat of an expert when it came to valuing precious stones, and in particular diamonds. Working on the side as part of the growing underground economy in Cuba, he was able to capitalize on his expertise, turning it into an informal but lucrative consulting business, as he liked to call it. Charging an appraisal fee for people looking to sell on the black market instead of to the government, which typically paid a fraction of the real value, especially for precious stones, Roberto was, by Cuban standards, becoming rather well off. Money was no longer an issue.

"Alina, I need to tell you something," began Roberto.

"Unless it's good news, I don't want to hear it right now."

"It is good news, but you have to keep this a secret. And I mean from everyone, even your father."

"I'm terrified, Roberto. I may never see him again. You don't have twenty-five armed men break into you home at five in the morning unless you're in serious trouble. They may kill him."

"Alina, I have other ways of making money. Much more money than what the government pays us at Cimex."

"How?"

"You remember I told you about the painting my brother Carlitos and I have? *El Saxofonista,*" asked Roberto.

"What about it?"

"Well, the daughter of the artist connected me with some people, and I was able to develop a business buying and selling old works of art."

"I don't understand. What people? Who in Cuba has money to buy art?"

"I buy from Cubans at a good price and then I sell to several wealthy Spaniards who are collectors. It's a little complicated. I have a good friend at Barlovento who I work with. He delivers the paintings and we split the money."

"What if they catch you? You'd go back to jail."

"I realize that. I'm careful."

"What are you planning to do with this money?"

"What do you mean?"

"People who have money in Cuba always leave. Is that your plan?"

"There's no future in Cuba for me, Alina. I want to live in a place where people are rewarded for hard work. Fidel has created a mentality in Cuba of scarcity. Few people question it. They are resigned. I want to live in a place where people have a mentality of abundance and possibility."

"And what about me?"

"If I make it to the U.S., you can come later."

"What do you mean if you make it?"

"It's dangerous crossing the Straits. Many people don't make it. Besides, I don't even have a boat yet."

"You don't know anything about boats. Where would you even find a boat that is safe enough to make the trip?"

"I know, but one way or the other, I intend to make it happen."

"Roberto, I need to find out what is happening with my father."

"I suspect we'll find out on Monday when we go to work."

"What do we do now?" asked Alina.

"I have to see a friend this afternoon down by the docks at Rio Almendares," said Roberto.

"About a boat?"

"More or less. He's a fisherman and he said he knows someone who might have a boat for sale. You want to go?"

"Well, I'm not staying here alone."

"Alright, let's go. We can take a taxi."

"Now? Isn't it a little early?"

"He'll be there. He wouldn't have gone out today anyway. It's been blowing hard from the south for two days and he won't go fishing again until the wind goes out. He's probably working on his boat. If we're lucky, maybe he can sell us some fish," said Roberto, trying to sound cheerful.

Maykel was below deck in the engine room when Roberto and Alina arrived at the docks just off Calle 24 along the east side of the Rio Almendares, on the northwest side of Havana, where Maykel docked his boat.

"*Hola*, Maykel," yelled Roberto as he hopped down from the finger pier into the cockpit by the port stern.

"Roberto, is that you? asked Maykel.

"No, it's Fidel. You're under arrest for catching more fish than me," replied Roberto, smiling back up at Alina who was still standing on the dock.

"Roberto, please. Under the circumstances," said Alina, clearly not amused.

Maykel, his hands and arms covered in grease, stuck his head out of the engine hatch and looked up at Roberto. "Good morning, Miss," he said looking instead toward Alina. "I am Maykel."

"*Mucho gusto, Senor.* I am Alina," she said.

"Your boyfriend here is quite the comedian," said Maykel.

"Sorry, Maykel, this is my girlfriend, Alina," said Roberto.

"It is my pleasure I'm sure," said Maykel.

"Engine troubles?" asked Roberto.

"No, no—just a little maintenance. The wind is no good, blowing from the south, so I thought I'd take the time to catch up on a few things I've been putting off," said Maykel.

"How's the fishing been?" asked Roberto.

"Good, up until the wind went around. The big fish arrived two weeks ago. I caught five in five days once the bite was on," said Maykel.

"How big was the biggest one?" asked Roberto.

"Well, one went two hundred kilos, but we had a big one on, three days ago, for nearly four hours that would have gone three hundred, easy," said Maykel.

"*Que paso*? asked Roberto.

"Nothing, the hook pulled. You know what happens—the longer you fight those big fish the greater the chance the hook pulls. We hooked him right out in front. The clean water was in close by the Morro. Plenty skip jack and blackfin. Towed us all the way to Guanabo before we lost him. I could have used that meat. You know, helps with the police," said Maykel.

"The big ones always get away. How is your friend in Cojimar?" asked Roberto.

"Gregorio? He's good. You believe he's ninety-two and still goes out," said Maykel.

"When you rest you rust," said Roberto with a laugh.

"What about you?" asked Maykel.

"Not too good. The police came this morning at five, looking for Alina's father."

"What the hell for?

"We're not sure. But it has something to do with de la Guardia. The Colonel has been acting strange lately. We both work at Cimex and I expect Monday we'll be out of work."

"What do you mean?"

"Well, de la Guardia runs that particular Cimex, and Andres, Alina's father, is his assistant."

"What are you going to do?"

"I'll be okay."

"It's getting pretty bad now with the economy."

"Maykel, you remember I asked you if you knew someone who might have a boat for sale?"

"I remember. I spoke to a friend for you who has a good-sized boat for sale. But it isn't cheap."

"What's the price?"

"Twenty-five thousand."

"Why so much?"

"Because it comes with a fishing license."

"Yeah, but I don't need a fishing license."

"I know, but if you have the license, the Coast Guard isn't going to ask many questions if they stop you."

Maykel looked up at Alina who had said nothing and was still standing on the dock by the stern, listening to the conversation.

"It's okay, Maykel. She knows about the boat. What good is the license if I buy the boat? The license is not in my name," said Roberto.

"Because the guy who owns the boat wants to go with you."

"What? Who is this guy?"

"His name is Pedro. He keeps the boat in Cojimar. I told him I might have a buyer. Look at it this way, Roberto. He's an experienced captain. He knows the boat inside and out."

"When can we go see him?"

"We can go now if you want."

"Alina, you want to go to Cojimar this afternoon?" asked Roberto.

"I suppose. It will keep my mind off things."

"We can go in the boat if you'd like," said Maykel.

"*Vamos!*" said Roberto.

"Let me close the hatch and get cleaned up," said Maykel.

"Isn't it a little rough to go by boat?" asked Alina.

"With the wind in the south, we can stay close to shore, in the lee. It will be smooth," said Maykel.

By the time Maykel rounded the point of land where the Rio Cojimar meets the sea and motored past the Castillo de Cojimar, Alina had reached her limit of tolerance with the ocean and couldn't wait to be back on land.

"It's not far now, Alina," said Maykel, realizing now they should have come by car.

"I'm fine. This is only the second time I have been on the ocean and I'm not used to the motion," she said.

The fishing docks in Cojimar were situated to the east of town on a narrow stretch of river, that was protected by an area of mangroves and higher ground to the north from the ocean swells and the occasional storm surge that pushes into the river when there is a hurricane.

"There is a small lagoon ahead on the starboard. He keeps his boat in there," said Maykel.

"What's the name of his boat?" asked Roberto.

"La Rosita, same as your mother and sister, Roberto. It's white, with barber pole outriggers," said Maykel. "He won't be out today in this wind. He lives nearby, so we should be able to find him if he's not at the dock."

"I see her," said Roberto, as they idled into the small lagoon. "She looks small, Maykel."

"She's about seven and a half meters," said Maykel. "I believe I see Pedro also. Yeah, he's here. He's sitting in the cabana. I see my friend

Gregorio also."

Maykel pulled up to the bow of the La Rosita, threw out the stern anchor from his boat, and had Roberto hop onto the La Rosita and tie off to her bow cleat.

"*Vamos*! I'll introduce you to Pedro," said Maykel.

Roberto pulled the slack from the bow line on Maykel's boat, making it easier for Alina to step onto the bow of the La Rosita, and then onto the finger pier leading to the dock.

"*Hola*, Pedrito!" said Maykel loudly, as he approached the group of fishermen in the cabana.

"*Hola*, Maykel! *Que bola?*" said Pedro cheerfully.

"Maykel, I know Pedro!" said Roberto excitedly, as they came closer to the cabana.

"How do you know Pedro?" asked Maykel.

"We were in prison together at DTI," answered Roberto, as they continued walking up the dock. "*Oye*, Pedrito, *acere que bola?*"

Not waiting for them to walk the full length of the dock, Pedro met his visitors half-way down the narrow wooden dock, warmly embracing Maykel and Roberto before being introduced to Alina.

"To what do I owe the pleasure?" asked Pedro.

"This is the guy I told you about who wants to buy your boat. Apparently, you already know each other," said Maykel, smiling.

"Pedrito is my brother, Maykel. I can tell you, we suffered a lot together," said Roberto.

"More than a little I assure you," said Pedro. "Come on, let me show her to you."

Pedro jumped down from the finger pier into the cock pit of the La Rosita and then turned to help Alina come aboard.

"What year is she?" asked Roberto as he peered into the forward cabin.

"She was built in fifty-six," answered Pedro.

"What about the engine?" asked Roberto.

"It's a four-stroke, runs well, but honestly, I think she's a little under powered," said Pedro.

"What would it cost to repower?" asked Roberto.

"Maybe five thousand. The best you could hope for though is a rebuilt engine, with low hours. That's it," said Pedro.

"Maykel tells me you want to leave Cuba as well," said Roberto.

"That's right," replied Pedro.

"Then why am I paying you for the boat?" asked Roberto. "Why can't I just hitch a ride with you?"

"Look at it this way. I have a boat and you don't. I'm a captain and I have a fishing license, which means the Coast Guard doesn't hassle me. I can make any repairs that might be needed and I know the waters. At least the first fifteen or twenty kilometers anyway," said Pedro.

"So basically you're charging me a fee to take me to the U.S., with no guarantees," said Roberto.

"No guarantees. But remember, I'm motivated to get out of the country just as much as you are," said Pedro.

"Understood. How long would it take to find a new motor and install it?" asked Roberto.

"Maybe a few weeks if we're lucky," said Pedro.

"What about the cabin? Does it leak?" asked Roberto.

"That's a strange question. Why?" asked Pedro.

"Just curious. Pedro, I think we have a deal," said Roberto.

"What if we replace the motor. Can you pay me for that as well?" asked Pedro.

"I'll pay you for the boat, then you can look for a motor. When you have that installed, I'll pay you for the motor and the work." said Roberto.

"It's a deal," said Pedro.

Roberto shook hands with Pedro and then looked at Alina who was looking down at the deck.

"I think we'll take a taxi back home, Maykel, if you don't mind," said

Roberto.

"I was going to suggest you do that," replied Maykel.

"Pedrito, I'll see you next Sunday. You'll be here?" asked Roberto.

"I'll be here all day. You can meet me by the cabana," said Pedro.

On the ride back home, neither Roberto nor Alina had much to say to each other. Roberto's plan to leave frightened Alina and she knew, even if he was successful in his attempt to make it to the U.S., there was little chance she would ever leave Cuba.

As the cab came to a stop in front of Andres' home, they could see Andres' red Chevrolet Deluxe parked in the narrow driveway beside the house.

"It's Father, he's home!" said Alina loudly.

The cab driver turned around, looked at Roberto and held out his hand. "Four pesos, *senor*," he said.

Roberto paid the driver, then quickly hopped out the passenger side of the cab and held the door open for Alina, who wasted no time running up the walk and into the house.

"*Gracias, senor*," said Roberto, as he shut the car door, tapping twice on the roof before the cab drove off.

In a hurry to find her father, Alina, upon entering, had left the front door open. It was hanging from a single hinge, having been damaged by the police break-in earlier that morning.

"Alina," yelled Roberto, as he entered the house.

"I'm here, in the kitchen," said Alina.

Roberto secured the door to the front of the house as best he could and made his way to the kitchen. Andres, looking disheveled, was seated at the kitchen table, staring motionless at a glass of rum he was holding in his right hand. A half empty bottle sat on the table in front of him.

"What happened?" asked Roberto.

"They took Tony away," said Andres.

"What for?" asked Roberto.

"They arrested him because he followed orders," replied Andres. He looked up at Roberto who was now seated next to Alina across the table from her father.

"Andres, you need to tell us what is going on," said Roberto.

"*Padre*, what did they do to you?" asked Alina.

"Nothing Alina. I'm fine. I've not been involved in any of this, but I know what's going on. Tony told me a couple weeks ago he expected to be arrested," said Andres.

"That's why he has been acting so strange lately," said Roberto. "What is he being charged with?"

"Treason, basically. From what I've heard, more than a dozen people were arrested. General Ochoa, Tony, Captain Martinez, Major Padron, many high-level people," said Andres.

"Treason? That's impossible," said Roberto.

"That's just what they call it. They were smuggling," said Andres.

"Smuggling what?" asked Roberto.

"Diamonds, ivory, sugar, even rare wood, anything of high value. But mostly, it was cocaine, and the quantities were not small," said Andres.

"What the fuck, Andres," said Roberto. "From where?"

"From Colombia, where else? From Colombia it went to Panama, then here by plane and then to the U.S. by boat. Tons of it. They also received money from the Colombians for the use of Cuba as a staging ground for the shipments to the U.S.," said Andres.

"There's no way in hell Fidel was not running that operation," said Roberto.

"Of course he was. Nothing happens in this country without the permission of Fidel. Tony told me every time he was in Fidel's office the last few months for a meeting, Fidel would have Sanchez turn the recorder off. Everything that was said in that office since 1960, Fidel would record. I mean everything, except this. I'm telling you, Tony is a dead man," said Andres, as he poured himself another shot of rum.

"But General Ochoa and Tony are war heroes. You honestly believe they'd give them the death penalty?" asked Roberto.

"No one is safe from Fidel, except his family. Don't forget, Fidel had Cienfuegos murdered, and after that he threw Huber Matos in jail for twenty years. Che and Raul wanted to send Matos before the firing squad. Then, years later, Fidel abandoned Che, who ended up being killed by the Bolivians," said Andres.

"Why did they come here if they weren't going to arrest you?" asked Alina.

"They were looking for money and probably thought Tony was hiding it here," replied Andres.

"What about our jobs?" asked Roberto.

"I don't know, but if I were you I wouldn't show up on Monday. The police will be there," said Andres.

"What about you, Andres. Are you going in to work?" asked Roberto.

"I have to. It's all I have. And besides, I've done nothing wrong," he replied.

The situation with Colonel de la Guardia was much worse than Roberto had imagined, and he didn't want to show his concern in front of Alina. She was younger than Roberto and hadn't lived or suffered as much as he had. He saw her happy-go-lucky manner more as a denial of the reality of everyday life in Cuba, where most people didn't expect much and were content simply to live day by day, sharing their misery in ways only the oppressed know how to do. He felt terrible about the situation and was worried about his friend Colonel de la Guardia, but there was nothing he could do. Now more than ever his vision for the future was clear.

The next morning Roberto was awake and in the kitchen making coffee when Alina came down from the bedroom to join him.

"You have any plans for today now that we are out of work?" she asked.

"I need to see a friend of mine," replied Roberto.

"What about?" she asked.

"About a painting," answered Roberto.

"You know, eventually the government is going to find out what you're doing Roberto," warned Alina.

"Have a *colada*, Alina. I think you worry too much. Besides, I'll be leaving Cuba soon with Pedrito."

"Well, it makes me nervous. What if the government finds out and they arrest you? I could be arrested as well."

Roberto could see that Alina was more than a little agitated and could feel the conversation becoming increasingly tense.

"That's ridiculous, they wouldn't arrest you. What am I supposed to do? I don't have any options, Alina. It's only for a few more months," said Roberto. He was beginning to lose his patience.

"It's not ridiculous," said Alina, raising her voice. "I don't want to be a part of it. I don't care how much money you make."

"What are you saying?"

"I'm saying I thought about it and I don't want to be a part of it," said Alina. She looked directly at Roberto, unblinking.

"Well I'm not throwing my future away because you're nervous. Nothing has happened," he said.

"That's my decision," she said. Alina refused now to look at Roberto. She sat with her arms folded and stared down at the cup of coffee on the table in front of her.

"You're sure? Because I'm not turning back."

"I'm sure," she said.

"What the hell, Alina? You want me to leave now?"

Alina didn't answer him and continued staring at the table.

"Okay then, I'll leave," he said.

With Alina refusing to say anything, Roberto knew it was useless to continue the conversation. Their relationship was over. In the last twenty-four hours he had lost his job; his boss, Colonel Antonio de la Guardia had been arrested; he committed to buying a boat; his girlfriend had broken up with him; and now he needed to find somewhere to live. Life in Cuba was anything but predictable, he thought.

After gathering a few items of clothing, he awkwardly attempted to say a last goodbye to Alina, who was still sitting at the kitchen table. The day was not going as expected and with few options and not knowing what else to do, Roberto decided to stick with his plan to visit Carmen.

XV

Despite the events of the last two days, he was excited about seeing Carmen, whom he had not seen or spoken with in more than two weeks. The last time they had been together, Carmen had promised to contact an old friend who lived in the countryside, two hours' drive from Havana, who Carmen recalled having a small collection of paintings from the time before the revolution. It sounded to him like a good buying opportunity and Roberto was anxious to see if Carmen's efforts had paid off.

Carmen lived alone in a large, single-family home that had been converted into apartments, in Habana Vieja, not far from where Anabela lived. Like most of the aging baroque and neoclassical buildings in Old Havana, the building Carmen lived in was in a constant state of decay. It was not unusual to see large pieces of concrete in the street, having fallen from the building's crumbling facades, often after a heavy rain, sometimes blocking the sidewalks, and occasionally injuring the unlucky passerby.

When he arrived, he found Carmen, who lived on the first floor, sitting alone on the front stoop, having a coffee. Carmen had opened the window beside the steps and was listening to Tommy Dorsey's recording of "I'll Never Smile Again," sung by Frank Sinatra. Carmen spoke little English, and didn't understand the lyrics, but loved listening to music, and in particular, American popular music from the 40's and 50's.

"Carmen, *mi hermano, como estas?*" said Roberto, holding his arms open slightly and smiling.

"Roberto! I've been thinking I should get in touch with you. How are you, man?" asked Carmen.

"Not too bad, although things have been a little crazy the last couple days."

"What's with the backpack?"

"I broke up with my girlfriend, or actually she broke up with me."

"What the hell happened? I thought you guys were pretty tight."

"She thinks I take too many risks."

"Risks?"

"You know, the paintings."

"Maybe, but the government has more important things to worry about right now than our little business venture."

"Yeah, like how the hell to feed everyone."

"It's getting bad, *es verdad*."

"It's about to get a lot worse, Carmen."

"What do you mean?"

"Rumor is General Ochoa and Colonel de la Guardia were running a smuggling operation that El Jefe says he knew nothing about. Apparently it included drugs."

"El Jefe is a liar. If there was a smuggling operation you can be sure he was running it."

"The military police showed up at my girlfriend's house yesterday morning before dawn looking for her father, Andres. They broke the door down. Andres is the Colonel's assistant. At first I was sure I was being arrested again. Fortunately one of the policemen, a friend of mine from the military, recognized me and said they were looking for Andres. I'm not sure but I believe they thought he had money hidden in the house."

"What now, Roberto?"

"I'll sleep at my parents' house until I find something. I help with the bills, so they won't mind having me around until I get a place."

"You're welcome to sleep here. I wouldn't mind the company."

"Thanks, I'll think about it. Carmen, did you manage to speak with your friend in the countryside? The one with the painting."

"I did. That's why I wanted to get in touch with you. He says he has something you might be interested in. He didn't tell me the name of the artist, but he claims the painting is very valuable."

"Everyone claims what they have is valuable. When can we go see him?"

"I'll call him now if you want. It's Sunday. He'll be home," said Carmen, as he stood up and turned to go inside. "Come in, Roberto. You want some coffee?"

"I'm okay, thanks. Remember to ask him the name of the artist. Oh, how are we going to get there? You said he's a couple hours from the city," said Roberto.

"I have a friend who agreed to drive us there. You pay for the gas, and he'll take us," said Carmen.

"You mind if I look at your record collection while I wait for you to call your friend?" asked Roberto.

"Not at all. I collected mostly American jazz. I love *La Voz*, as you can see," said Carmen.

"Wasn't he involved with the Mafia before the revolution?" asked Roberto.

"He may have been, but if you went to a nightclub in Havana in the 40's, you can be sure the Mafia was nearby. I mean, hell, they ran the city. Just because you're in the same club with criminals doesn't make you a criminal. I don't think about that though, I just love his music."

"Did you ever hear him sing live?"

"Just once. In the ballroom at the Hotel Nacional. A friend of mine who worked there got me in. I'll never forget it."

"Do you know if he's still alive?"

"Yes, I believe he's something like seventy-three, and still performing from what I understand. It will be a sad day in Cuba when he dies," said Carmen. "I'm going to call my friend. I'll be right back."

Several minutes later Carmen returned to the living room, having spoken with his friend, who lived outside the old city of Pinar del Rio, two hours southwest of Havana.

"I spoke with Arturo and he's expecting us," said Carmen.

"What about your friend with the car?" asked Roberto.

"I spoke with him also and arranged for him to drive us there."

"How much for the painting? I don't have much money with me."

"He said five hundred, but I think you can negotiate. If I were you I would bring a little more. You never know what else he may have. He collected for many years like me."

"Then I will need to stop by my parents' house in Santos Suarez. I keep the money there."

Roberto knew his parents would be upset by the news about Colonel de la Guardia and the end of his relationship with Alina. Perhaps it was better this way, he thought. He could devote more time to look for paintings to buy and sell, and besides there was the boat he was going to buy in Cojimar. He would have to sell additional paintings in order to pay for the boat which he promised his friend Pedro he would pay for the following weekend.

Arriving at his parents' home, Roberto wasted little time collecting the money, which he kept in two old Cohiba boxes made of Spanish Cedar, hidden in his bedroom on the second floor in the bottom of an old single door *caoba armario* he inherited from his grandparents.

After saying hello to his parents and promising to return later that evening to explain his surprise early Sunday morning arrival, he rejoined Carmen who had decided to wait in the car with his friend Maceo, whom they had hired to drive the two hours to Arturo's home in the country, near Pinar del Rio.

Carmen had arranged for them to meet Arturo near the center of the city in front of the Museo Ciencias Naturales, on La Calle Celestino Pacheco.

When they arrived at the museum, the only car parked anywhere nearby was an old white MG Roadster convertible with the top up.

"Maceo, pull up behind that car," said Carmen pointing to the MG.

"That's your friend?" asked Roberto.

"I'm pretty sure that's him. He told me he inherited a sports car recently from his father. That must be it," said Carmen as he stepped out of the car.

"*Hola*, Arturo!" said Carmen. The man sitting in the MG stuck his hand out of the window and shook hands with Carmen. Judging by the gestures the two men were making it was clear to Roberto, Arturo wanted them to follow him.

"We'll follow him to his house," said Carmen, as he opened the passenger side front door. "He lives just outside of town."

"Nice car," said Roberto. "I don't think I've ever seen one of these."

"Yeah, they're pretty rare," replied Carmen.

Arturo lived in a small and very old wooden house on a hillside overlooking the Vinales Valley, twenty kilometers north of Pinar del Rio. Although Roberto had never visited the valley, he was familiar with the region from the stories his father told of the famous tobacco grown in the Vuelta Abajo area near the town of San Luis.

Maceo pulled into the driveway next to Arturo's MG, turned off the motor and turned around to address Roberto.

"I hope the trip will be worth your time and money, Roberto," said Maceo.

"We'll, I guess we're about to find out," said Roberto, stepping out of the car.

"*Hola, amigo*," said Roberto to Arturo. "Lovely spot."

"*Gracias*, Roberto, *y mucho gusto*," he replied. "Thanks for coming."

"The pleasure is mine," said Roberto.

"Arturo, my brother, how have you been?" asked Carmen.

"Nice car, Arturo," said Roberto. "What year is she?"

"She's a fifty-six," replied Arturo. "Come on, let me show you the painting."

"Arturo, if I may ask. Who is the artist?" asked Roberto.

"Sobrino," replied Arturo.

"Carlos Sobrino, from Cuba?" asked Roberto, who was somewhat surprised by the answer.

"Yes, it is signed Sobrino, at the bottom," said Arturo.

Arturo led Roberto and Carmen up the half dozen steps in the front of the house leading up to the porch, before turning around once more to admire the view.

"Arturo, what is the name of the mountains in the distance?" asked Roberto. "They're unusual looking."

"The mountains are the Sierra de los Organos, and the limestone rock formations, they are called Mogotes. This is one of the only places on the island where they're found," said Arturo.

"They remind me of the landscape in the north of Puerto Rico, near the old city of Manati," said Carmen. "I had many friends there. I remember we would go to La Mar Chiquita on weekends for parties. I would give anything to go back one day."

"I remember now, you used to travel there, Carmen, when you worked for Bacardi," said Arturo.

"You're fortunate to live in such place," said Roberto.

"The Vinales Valley is one of the most beautiful places in Cuba. I love to do photography. That's one of the reasons I live here. That and the people here are wonderful. This is old Cuba. Why don't you have a seat on the porch, and I'll bring the painting for you to look at. The light is better," suggested Arturo. "And how about some coffee?"

"I would love some. With sugar only, no milk," said Roberto.

"Same for me," said Carmen.

"I'll bring the painting, and you can have a look while I make coffee," said Arturo.

Re-emerging from inside the house with the painting, Arturo handed it to Roberto, who had taken a seat on the railing bench which bordered the edge of the porch. With his back toward the valley for better light, he placed the bottom edge of the frame on his knees and held the painting out at arm's-length for a better look.

"Arturo, this was not done by Carlos Sobrino," said Roberto.

"What do you mean? It's signed right here," exclaimed Arturo.

"I see that, but this painting was done by Carlos Sobrino Buhigas, the Spanish painter, not the Cuban Carlos Sobrino," said Roberto. Their styles are completely different. Buhigas was a great painter but he was not Cuban. The signatures of the two men were different as well. Carlos Sobrino Rivero signed his name Sobrino only, no C in front of the last name. I mean the painting is very nice but I'm really only interested in Cuban artists."

"How do you know all this, Roberto?" asked Carmen.

"I learned mostly from Anabela, but my brother Carlitos also does a lot of research," replied Roberto.

"Have another look while I bring the coffee," said Arturo.

"Sure, we're in no hurry," said Roberto.

Roberto waited until Arturo was back inside in order to speak privately with Carmen.

"I'm sorry, Carmen, but I'm simply not interested in buying this painting. It's truly lovely but not what I'm looking for. I'm sure as a collector you understand," said Roberto.

"No, I understand completely. It happens sometimes," said Carmen. "I have to tell you, I'm impressed with your knowledge."

Arturo came back onto the porch carrying a small tray of coffee along with several *buenuelos de viento*, one for each of them.

"I'm sorry to disappoint you, Arturo," said Roberto.

"No, I understand. You're looking for Cuban artists."

"Do you have any other paintings you might be interested in selling?"

"No, nothing I want to part with right now. Almost everything I have I inherited from my father who passed away recently."

"Why then did you want to sell this one?"

"I really need to do some repairs. The house is old and in need of repairs. My father never wanted to spend any money on the house."

"Selling this painting wouldn't pay for much."

"I realize that, but at least it would be a start."

Roberto had been thinking about Arturo's MG Roadster since the moment they parked behind it in the driveway, and now, realizing Arturo was hard up for cash, Roberto was seriously considering making an offer on the car. He had never bought a car before and the only thing he knew about MGs was they had a reputation for frequently breaking down. It was out of his mouth before he knew it.

"What about the car, Arturo?" said Roberto, pointing in the direction of the MG. "Would you consider selling it? It would certainly pay for all your house repairs."

"I don't think so. It was my father's."

"Twenty-five thousand. I have it with me," said Roberto. Leaning back against the post on the corner of the porch, he pulled his feet up on the bench, stretched his legs in front of him and crossed his arms, waiting for Arturo to respond.

Carmen looked at Roberto in disbelief, surprised to hear that he was willing to spend that kind of money on a car he had just seen and knew nothing about.

"These cars can be a lot of trouble, Roberto," said Carmen. "My brother had one years ago and he went broke trying to keep it on the road."

"What do you say, Arturo?" repeated Roberto, undeterred by Carmen's comment.

"I have to keep it. I rode in that car with my father when I was a boy. I'm sorry."

"Thirty thousand," said Roberto, confidently. He could see the new number had gotten Arturo's attention.

"If you make it thirty-five, we have a deal," said Arturo, leaning forward in his chair and holding out his hand out.

"Deal," said Roberto, standing up to shake Arturo's outstretched hand. "I have the twenty-five thousand with me and I can return later in the week with the other ten."

"No problem. I trust any friend of Carmen's," said Arturo. "You have time for some rum? Maybe a cigar."

"How about we go for a little drive first, then celebrate?" asked Roberto.

"Absolutely. I'll put the top down. Carmen, you good here?" asked Arturo.

"Sure, if you bring me a little rum, I'll wait here with Maceo," he said.

"You think you should put the top down, Arturo? It's looking a little squally over the mountains," said Roberto.

"It always rains in the mountains. The skuds as we call them, don't roll into the valley until evening. We'll be drinking rum by then Roberto," said Arturo, smiling. "*Vamos.*"

XVI

Sometime after midnight, Roberto, behind the wheel of his nineteen fifty-six MG Roadster, parked in front of the home of his parents in Santos Suarez, and turned off the engine. The last few kilometers the car had been running hot and he was relieved to have made the two-and-a-half-hour trip back to Havana without breaking down.

The house was dark except for a light coming from the kitchen, and Roberto, stepping lightly along the edge of the hallway, in an effort to convince the old wooden floor boards not to give away his arrival, made his way back to the kitchen, hoping he'd find some leftovers in the icebox from the family meal his mother always prepared on Sunday.

"Lazaro!" whispered Roberto, surprised to see his younger brother, who he had not seen in several months, sitting at the kitchen table. "What are you doing here?"

"I was waiting for you," he replied. "Carlitos said you were coming home tonight."

"Waiting for me? What for?" responded Roberto, sitting down at the table across from Lazaro.

"Carlitos told me about your plan to leave the country," said Lazaro.

"It's still just a plan. Besides, I don't even have the boat yet."

"Carlitos said Maykel had a friend with a boat."

"Yeah, I met with the guy a couple days ago. Turns out he's a friend of mine. We spent time together in DTI," said Roberto.

"Did you buy the boat?"

"I committed to buying it, yes. I'm going to pay for it next week."

"Where is she docked?"

"In Cojimar. She's solid but needs a bigger motor, according to Pedro."

"He's the owner?"

"Yes. He fishes for a living, and he has a license, which is important because the Coast Guard tends to leave him alone when they see him out on the water. He wants to leave as well, with his wife and two kids."

"Is the boat big enough?"

"She's seven and a half meters long and has a small wheelhouse. Pedro says she's seaworthy and can make it across," said Roberto.

"I want to go with you."

"What the hell are you going to do Lazaro, once you're in Florida?"

"Same as you. I'll figure it out when the time comes. You know it has to be better than staying here."

"You haven't said anything to *Madre* have you?" asked Roberto, somewhat agitated.

"No, of course not."

"Good. You can't mention this to anyone. Understood?"

"*Entiendo*," said Lazaro, looking down at the table.

"What about Carlitos? I don't think he wants to go," said Lazaro.

"I know. He's too afraid. His autism is so debilitating. He suffers a lot. Maybe once we're there we can get some legal help and figure out how to get the rest of the family to the States. You should get some sleep, Lazaro. Don't you have to work tomorrow?"

"I suppose. I was going to sleep here but *Madre* would ask too many questions if she knew I spent the night. What about you? Don't you have to work in the morning?"

"I'm pretty sure I don't have a job any longer."

"What happened?"

"Colonel de la Guardia, General Ochoa and something like a dozen other officers were arrested. According to Alina's father Andres, they were running a smuggling ring that included among other things, a lot of cocaine. The Colonel ran the branch of Cimex where I worked. They broke into Andres' house at five in the morning on Saturday. Must have been twenty-five guys and they were heavily armed. I thought I was going to be arrested again, but one of the guys was a friend of mine from when I was in special forces and told me not to worry, they were looking for Andres. The Colonel in charge of the break-in told us we would be wise to look for new jobs."

"Alina must have been freaking out. What happened to her father?"

"He was questioned and released. He was at home when we returned from Cojimar that evening. That's how I know about the smuggling. He said they were looking for cash when they broke in."

"What are you guys going to do now?"

"Me, I have my business selling paintings and I'll do some gemstone appraisals. I don't know about Alina. We broke up. She said my lifestyle made her nervous. I also need to get the money to buy the boat from Pedro. Oh, and I just bought a car today. An MG Roadster," said Roberto, casually.

"You broke up with Alina and you bought a sports car? Are you nuts?" exclaimed Lazaro, loudly.

"Not so loud. I know, the timing isn't the greatest, but the car is in great shape and I'm sure if I have to I can sell it for more than what I paid for it."

"You know, Roberto, that's the kind of thing that attracts the attention of the government."

"I'm not worried. Besides I can register it in *Padre's* name. He won't care."

"What if he says no? You take too many chances."

"Look, I'm tired. I'm going to bed. We'll talk about this later. And remember, don't say anything to anyone about all this."

"Trust me, I'm not going to talk to anyone. I have a stake in this now too, don't forget."

"If you want you can come with me next weekend to Cojimar and have a look at the boat. I promised my friend Pedrito I'd pay him. Unfortunately, I spent most of my money on the car so I'm hoping he'll agree to take a deposit."

"He'll take it. There's no way he'll find someone else to buy the boat. I'm working at the restaurant on Sunday. I can go with you to Cojimar later, after you buy the boat."

XVII

It was mid-day when Roberto finally woke, got out of bed, and went downstairs for something to eat and to speak with his parents. By now his father had probably seen the MG parked in front of the house and would surely want an explanation. His parents would want to know why he wasn't at work, and when they found out he no longer had a job, what he planned to do with his time. It was going to be a difficult conversation and he was not looking forward to it.

"*Hola, Madre, como tu ta?*" said Roberto cheerfully, as he entered the kitchen.

"The question is, how are you?" replied Rosa. "Your father is outside. He's been waiting to speak with you."

"Do you have any coffee from this morning?" he asked.

"No, but I can make some. I'll bring it out to you. You need to speak with your father," said Rosa.

Roberto walked out onto the patio from the kitchen and sat down at the table with his father who was reading the newspaper and didn't look up at Roberto.

"*Buenos dias, Padre,*" said Roberto.

Guillermo stopped reading, folded the paper, and placed it on the table in front of him. "People in Cuba don't have enough to eat and you think it's important to have a fancy sports car," said Guillermo.

"It's an investment. I don't intend to keep it forever. Besides, I needed a car," replied Roberto.

"You realize when you drive a car like that you attract the attention of the police," said Guillermo. "They will confiscate that sort of thing."

"I know. I was thinking I could register it in your name," said Roberto.

"So then I go to jail instead of you," said Guillermo.

"The police are not going to question you," replied Roberto. "The worst that could happen is I lose the car. There are plenty of nice old cars in Havana. They can't put everyone in jail."

"So, why are you here and not with Alina?" asked Guillermo.

"She broke up with me."

"Broke up, why?"

"She said my lifestyle was, I don't know, too risky politically."

"What about your job at Cimex? Why aren't you at work?"

"Tony was arrested on Saturday," said Roberto. He looked at his father and waited for a response.

Guillermo picked up the newspaper, unfolded it, and held it out in front of him with both hands in such a way that Roberto could read the headline.

"What's the real story, Roberto? And I assume, since you are sitting here that it doesn't involve you," said Guillermo.

"No, I'm not involved. Believe me, I'm not involved," said Roberto emphatically. "From what Andres told me, Tony, along with Ochoa and some others, were running a smuggling ring."

"So it's true, what is reported here?" asked Guillermo.

"What does the paper report?" asked Roberto.

"It says they were smuggling diamonds, elephant ivory, and let me see, rare woods. Is that true?" he asked.

"Small detail, but they left out the most important part," said Roberto.

"And what is that?" asked Guillermo.

"Here, Roberto. Have a *colada*," said Rosa, who had come out onto the patio from the kitchen, carrying a tray with a plate of warm guava *pastelitos* and a *moka* of hot coffee.

Roberto leaned forward, poured himself some coffee, sat back in his chair, and took a sip. "Thank you, Mother. *Es perfecto*," he said, looking up at Rosa. "Cocaine, from Columbia," he said, as he turned and looked in the direction of his father.

"El Jefe must have known," said Guillermo.

"What did you say?" asked Rosa. "Did you say cocaine?"

"Yes, and Andres said he's certain Fidel was running the operation," replied Roberto.

"Let me get this straight. De la Guardia is arrested for drug smuggling, you lose your job, Alina breaks up with you, and the first thing you do is buy a fancy sports car. Apparently, you enjoy torturing your mother," said Guillermo.

"I had nothing to do with losing my job and I told you, that car is a good investment. You'll see," said Roberto.

"What do you plan to do with the money when you sell it?" asked Rosa who was now sitting at the table.

"Probably buy more paintings. I'm making good money now with that," said Roberto.

"Maybe you can still work at Cimex," said Guillermo.

"Look, if it's okay with you, I need to get going," said Roberto.

"Will you be staying with us tonight?" asked Rosa.

"If you don't mind. It's just until I can find something," replied Roberto.

"Suit yourself, but you need to pay for food. We can't afford to feed you now," said Rosa.

"That's not a problem. In fact, here is some money for the market. I know you like to go on Mondays," said Roberto. He handed his mother five twenty-peso notes and kissed her on the forehead. "I'll stop and see Maykel this evening. Maybe he'll have some fresh fish."

"You be careful," said Rosa, looking down at the money, then holding up one of the bills for Roberto to see. "You're gonna end up like this guy," she said pointing to the image of Cienfuegos on the front of the twenty-peso note.

Roberto had enough money hidden at his parents' house after making the deposit on the MG to buy three or four more paintings from Carmen, depending on the size and quality. If Carmen could locate several works of high quality, Roberto was certain Mariano, the Spaniard, would buy them. That way he could make enough money to pay Arturo the rest of what he owed on the car, along with making a sizable deposit on the boat.

Carmen, having expressed regret for the deal with Arturo not working out, had promised Roberto he would contact an elderly friend living in Mariel whom Carmen remembered as having owned several important works by the famous Costumbrismo artist, Antonio Sanchez Araujo.

After stopping for gas, he also checked the coolant level in the radiator, which he found to be low, then headed north, toward Habana Vieja, to see Carmen.

Roberto was feeling good about life and realized, as the car came to a stop in front of the apartment building where Carmen lived, that he hadn't thought about Alina all day, and wondered if she was regretting her decision to break up with him. In the end it was better he thought. Alina was the type of person that always wanted to know how cold the water was before jumping in. Roberto was not, and he knew it was only a matter of time before they would have parted ways. His focus now was on the future, and his freedom.

Roberto knocked on the door and waited for Carmen to answer, turning around slightly, he looked over his shoulder, admiring his new car.

"*Hola*, Roberto! Long time no see," laughed Carmen, as he placed his left hand on Roberto's shoulder, then motioning for him to come in with his right hand. "I'm sitting out back in the cool, on the patio, with a young friend of mine. Come, I'll introduce you."

Following Carmen through the house and outside onto the patio, Roberto had not known Carmen to have many friends. He was a rather private person and generally kept to himself.

"Maura, *me gustaria presentar a mi buen amigo*, Roberto," said Carmen. "This is the guy I told you is my business partner. Roberto, Maura helps out around the house a couple days a week."

Roberto was stunned. She was one of the most beautiful women he had ever seen, and in Havana, where there were many beautiful women, it was easy to forget just how beautiful they were, and Maura, was exceptionally beautiful.

"*Encantada, senorita*," said Roberto, rather formally. He was normally not so formal, and was trying to be as casual as possible, but he could tell she had sensed his surprise.

"The pleasure is mine I'm sure," she said. "Won't you join us? Please, sit down."

"Maura has family in Miami," said Carmen.

"Why do you still live in Cuba?" asked Roberto.

"Like everything here, as you know, it's complicated, but I'm planning on leaving as soon as I can find a safe way," answered Maura. "Carmen tells me you're also thinking about leaving."

"That's the plan," he said, answering Maura and then turning to address Carmen. "Carmen, the reason I am here is, I need to visit your friend in Mariel. You remember, the one you told me about with the works by Araujo."

"Yes, Castillo. I spoke to him and he is interested in selling four paintings. The three I mentioned by Araujo, and one by Armando Garcia Menocal," said Carmen.

"Then the subject matter is of a more traditional nature. Mariano has rather conservative tastes, as you know," said Roberto.

"He'll be very interested, I assure you Roberto," said Carmen. "Two of the works by Araujo are *paisajes* and the other two are *retratos*."

"Mariano is always interested in landscapes, so that is good, but I don't believe I have sold him any portraits. Did you make arrangements for us to see him?" asked Roberto.

"Yes, he said he would come to Havana if it was easier. He has family here and doesn't have a chance to see them very often. I thought maybe we could meet here and then go to La Bodeguita," said Carmen.

"Roberto, how do you know so much about art?" asked Maura.

"I had a lot of free time to study the last four or five years..." answered Roberto, pausing slightly before continuing . . . "in prison."

"I assume for political reasons," said Maura, coolly.

"No, not exactly. I was never a very political person, I just had a few problems on occasion with my superiors. I became somewhat of a security risk, and was discharged after my last year in DTI, in Havana," said Roberto. "Then shortly after I got out of prison, Carmen and I started working together."

"Roberto, I am going to call Castillo. He may be able to come to Havana today. Maura, are you busy later? Maybe you would like to go with us to La Bodeguita," said Carmen.

"I can't really afford to go out, Carmen, but thanks," she said.

"What if I ask you to go? *Puedo pagar*," said Roberto, with a coy smile.

"You should go with him, Maura. He's rich," laughed Carmen.

"We can go in my new sports car," said Roberto proudly. He wished he hadn't said anything about the car.

"I should be going, but thank you, Roberto. Maybe some other time," she said. "Carmen, I'll be back later in the week."

Roberto politely said goodbye to Maura and waited on the patio while Carmen showed her out. He regretted having asked Maura to go with them later that evening. Perhaps he had been a little too forward, and in so doing ruined any chance he may have had of seeing her in the future. He would have been more upset with himself, he thought, had he not tried.

Carmen returned several minutes later from inside the house, carrying two small glasses and an unopened bottle of Havana Club *Siete Anos*.

"I spoke with Castillo. He said he could be here in two hours. He sounded excited. He has an impressive collection, Roberto. I'm telling you, you could do well with him. He's getting older and is interested in selling a good portion of his collection," said Carmen, who then, taking a small knife from his pocket, cut the seal that ran around the top of the rum bottle, uncovering the cork, and after carefully twisting it free, offered some to Roberto who nodded his approval.

"You know, if it wasn't for you..." Carmen stopped mid-sentence and poured some rum into one of the glasses for Roberto... "paying me a commission, I couldn't afford the good stuff, like this," he said, finishing his sentence while pouring some for himself. "I'm going to miss you, Roberto."

"Maybe there's a way you can come to the U.S. someday," said Roberto.

"Maybe. I'm getting old, though, and I have very little money. I would have no way to support myself in the U.S.," he replied.

"You can work for me," said Roberto, smiling.

"Listen, when Castillo arrives, don't get too excited when he shows you the pieces. I know he's anxious to sell, but he can be difficult with the price," said Carmen.

"I understand. Don't worry. I developed a few negotiating skills when I was in prison," said Roberto.

More than four hours had passed before Castillo arrived at the home of Carmen. Roberto and Carmen were well into the bottom half of the bottle of Havana Club, and because events are more important than time in Cuba, especially weekend events, hadn't noticed that Castillo was so late to arrive.

All four paintings were small, and Carmen had easily fit them into a single wooden box that Roberto volunteered to carry into the house for Castillo from his 1953 two-door Buick Special.

Once inside, Roberto, remembering his friend's advice not to appear too anxious, waited for an introduction from Carmen.

"Castillo, this is my friend Roberto, the one I have been telling you about," said Carmen. "Roberto, my good friend, Castillo."

"My pleasure sir. Thank you for coming," said Roberto.

"No need to be formal. The pleasure is mine I'm sure," said Castillo. "I must tell you, I was quite surprised when Carmen told me he had a young friend who was interested in buying several pieces from my collection. It is only a handful of older people, like us, who care about such things anymore. There is so much history that is being lost today in Cuba. It is truly one of the great tragedies of the revolution. I have to ask Roberto, where does your interest come from?"

"My brother and I, quite by chance, acquired a painting by Carlos Sobrino. I'm sure you are familiar with him. Basically, our interest grew from that one painting. While I was in the army I had some disagreements—shall we say with my superiors—and ended up in prison. I spent one year at Censam Marin, and during that time my brother would bring art books for me to study. Those books saved my life Castillo. I don't know what else I can tell you, except that, for me, art is freedom. I look at the world more objectively, now that I realize every artist's vision is unique and I would say my appreciation for life's possibilities is much greater," explained Roberto.

"Let me show you what I have. There are three Araujos, and one Menocal. The Araujos are the more valuable, but the Menocal is my favorite," said Castillo.

One at a time, Castillo handed Roberto the paintings for him to examine. They were everything he had hoped they would be. The subject matter was exactly what Mariano was looking for, and each of the pieces was in near perfect condition. If Roberto could reach an agreement with Castillo on price, he thought, he would have more than enough from the subsequent sale to Mariano to pay off the car and the boat.

"Do you have a price in mind, Castillo, for all four?" asked Roberto.

"If you were to take all four, I was thinking two thousand pesos. Carmen said you are always fair with him, and I want to be fair with you. I know you have, shall we say, business expenses to consider," said Castillo.

"I do. I have a partner I am obligated to pay half the profit. He's my connection with the buyer," said Roberto. "I'm comfortable with the two thousand."

"I am grateful, Roberto," said Castillo. "Today I have no money and I had no food at home. I had to borrow money for the gas to drive here. If you had not agreed to buy the paintings, I was planning on selling my car. I have an extensive collection of paintings and would be happy to sell more, if you are interested."

"I'm sure that my friend Mariano and some of his fellow collectors in Spain will be very interested. They have traditional tastes in art, so I believe they will be quite happy to buy more," said Roberto.

"Castillo, we plan to go to La Bodeguita del Medio this evening. You're welcome to join us," offered Carmen.

"I haven't been in years, and I would love to, but my wife is ill and I should return to Mariel," said Castillo. "Next time for sure."

"Here's is the money, Castillo," said Roberto. "May I keep the box?"

The three men shook hands and walked outside onto the street together, pausing long enough for Roberto to admire Castillo's car, and promising to meet again before Castillo headed out of the city, back to Mariel.

Back inside, Roberto and Carmen carefully looked at the paintings again, one by one, before rewrapping each with the burlap cloth and placing them back in the wooden box.

"I think he's going to be a great contact for you," said Carmen. "He knows all of the old families on the north coast from the time before the revolution who had the love of art and the means to collect."

"I feel sorry for Castillo. He's an old man, his wife is sick and now he has to sell the thing that brings him so much joy and happiness simply to put food on the table. It's not right, Carmen," said Roberto.

"I understand, but that is the life we have been given by the communists. I prefer not to talk about that now. We planned to go to La Bodeguita, right? So let's go," said Carmen.

"*Vamos*," said Roberto.

In a little while the sun would be setting, and Carmen suggested they walk east, toward Havana Harbor, to watch the sunset across the water, opposite the Castillo del Morro. The sky to the east, above and behind the old fort, was a dark charcoal color ... all that remained of a heavy, late-day thunderstorm that had moved in from the ocean, and was now raining itself out, over Cojimar.

Arriving on the Avenida del Puerto, by the water's edge at the mouth of the harbor, just before the moment the sun set, they could see in the distance the stone walls of the Morro, brilliantly lit against the fading remnant curtain of dark clouds of the dying storm.

When the last rays of evening sun had burned out, and their light, reflecting off the glass at the top of El Morro lighthouse had dimmed and been replaced by the lights from Habana del Este, shining on the now still harbor water, the two friends walked the half dozen short blocks south to La Bodeguita for a drink.

The popular bar was always crowded, and this evening was no exception. It was early in the week, and from the look of the crowd it appeared to be mostly locals who had come for the music. Too late to find a table, or even a seat at the bar, Roberto edged his way within earshot of the bartender and ordered a mojito for Carmen and a *ron anejo* for himself, while Carmen got lucky and found an empty piece of wall near the musicians where they could enjoy their drinks.

"Roberto, keep an eye out for someone leaving," said Carmen. "I'm going to look in the back room to see if I can find a table."

"Who is the guitarist, Carmen?" asked Roberto.

"That is Manuel Galban. He is one of the best guitarists in Cuba, or the world for that matter. I'll be right back," he said.

"You're like a music encyclopedia," said Roberto.

Carmen smiled before turning and making his way to the next room to look for a table. He wasn't gone long when Roberto noticed him weaving his way back through the crowd to the front of the bar. Rather than fight the crowd, Carmen stopped half-way, and motioned for Roberto to follow him to the back room.

"We're in luck," said Carmen, as Roberto joined him.

"What do you mean?" he asked.

"You'll see," said Carmen, smiling from the side of his mouth. "Please, I'll follow you."

"Entering the back room of the bar, which was only slightly less crowded, Roberto couldn't see anywhere to sit.

"I thought you said there was a free table," said Roberto, turning around to face Carmen.

"You see the young woman at the table in the far corner, with her back to us? Maybe she'll let us sit there," said Carmen.

"You're lucky you're with me tonight, old man," joked Roberto.

"I'm pretty sure it's the other way around, but let's see," replied Carmen.

Roberto walked up to the table where the young woman was sitting and stepped around to the opposite side where she could see him.

"I thought maybe you decided not to come," said the young woman. It was Maura.

"We stopped along the way to watch the sunset," was all Roberto could think to say.

Maura had put on a modest, and for her, an unnecessary amount of makeup. She was wearing a floral print tank dress, which, along with her abundant natural beauty, had a mild paralyzing effect on Roberto, leaving him at a loss for words.

"And how was *la puesta del sol?*" she asked.

"Uncommonly beautiful," answered Roberto, somehow managing to maintain eye contact with Maura.

"Would you like to sit down? I saved two seats," she said.

"You're very kind to do so," said Carmen, trying not to smile. "Isn't she wonderful, Roberto?"

"*Claro,*" said Roberto, as he pulled back the chair next to Maura and sat down. "So what made you change your mind."

"I was thinking about the conversation we had earlier today regarding leaving Cuba," she said.

"What about it?" asked Roberto.

"I can't stay here much longer. Roberto, my life here is shit, and I'm afraid of the government," she said.

Maura covered her face with her hands and began to cry. Roberto had been a little suspicious of Maura when they first met but could see now she was sincere.

"Look Maura, I don't even have a boat yet, and the one I am looking at is not that big," said Roberto. "Have you ever even been on the ocean?"

"No," she said. Maura wiped her eyes and looked up at Roberto.

"What do you think, Carmen," asked Roberto.

"I've known Maura since she was a little girl, and I know her family. There is no problem with trust. Her father has done well in Miami and could be helpful if you make it. You have no contacts there, Roberto, and you don't speak English. You don't have American dollars and Cuban pesos are worthless outside of Cuba," replied Carmen.

"I plan to take some paintings with me. As many as possible—to sell," said Roberto.

"My father sends me money. I can help," offered Maura, careful not to be too aggressive but sensing Roberto was beginning to soften.

"When I have the boat we can talk about it," said Roberto.

Maura smiled. "You won't regret it, Roberto. I promise you," she said.

By the time the bartenders had come to the back of the bar and begun to move the last of the patrons toward the front and onto the street in order to lock up for the night, it was well after the official midnight hour closing.

They were all surprised at how quickly the time had passed, and Maura's mood, to the delight of Roberto, had continued to improve throughout the evening, aided in part by a number of Agustin's finest mojitos.

Before parting for the evening, Roberto promised Maura he would take her to Cojimar the following weekend in order to see firsthand the boat he agreed to buy from his friend Pedro. By showing her the boat, he thought, the reality of an attempt at crossing the Straits of Florida in such a small vessel, possibly in the middle of winter, at a time when the northers would be at their strongest, would force her to think twice about going with him.

XVIII

By the end of the week Roberto had sold Mariano the four paintings he had purchased from Castillo, giving Roberto the money he needed to pay off Arturo for the car. Most of the remaining money he would use to pay Pedro for the boat, and what was left he set aside to buy more paintings.

His personal collection was growing steadily, now numbering ten paintings, including *El Saxofonista*. His plan was to have at least fifteen by the time he left Cuba.

The only thing Roberto knew for certain about Florida, from the numerous stories he heard growing up, was that many of the Cuban nationals who emigrated to the U.S. had become prominent and wealthy business people in south Florida. Confident in the quality of his collection, Roberto was certain he could parlay all but *El Saxofonista*, which he planned on keeping, together with the nostalgia the expats surely felt for the Cuban homeland, into a modest art business. That was his plan.

It was Sunday and Roberto was looking forward to his meeting with Pedro in Cojimar. With help from a friend he had been able to solve the problem he'd been having with the MG overheating, and by noon was on his way to pick up Maura, who lived near Carmen in Habana Vieja, for the short ride to the docks along the Rio Cojimar.

He was excited to see Maura again, and in the days leading up to their getting together, had allowed himself to wonder if she had intentions other than simply using Roberto as a means to leave Cuba. He had no illusions about his chances with a woman as beautiful as Maura, and was determined, no matter where their relationship ended up, to maintain his self-respect.

When he came to a stop in front of the house where Maura lived with her grandmother, she was waiting outside on the sidewalk. Roberto could tell she was excited but appeared relaxed and genuinely eager to see him again. It was what he had hoped for, and her mood gave him confidence.

"You sure you're up for this?" he asked, turning sideways in his seat and placing his arm on the back of the empty seat, in an effort to look relaxed.

Maura began walking toward the car but did not respond to Roberto's question. She was slender, although not too slender as to be uninteresting or unattractive, and very tall, nearly one meter eighty centimeters. The low profile MG sports car appeared lower, parked next to the street curb, making Maura look even taller alongside. Roberto, not remembering her to be so tall, began to feel intimidated.

"Here, let me get the door for you," he said.

Roberto barely had time to open the driver's door before she had gracefully slipped into the seat beside him, and without interrupting her motion, leaned over and kissed him on the cheek.

"I'll take that as a yes," he said, more than a little surprised, his face now flushed.

"One thing you need to know about me, Roberto, I am a very straightforward person. So you should believe me when I say this day means more to me than you can imagine," she said.

"I'm getting that impression. I will try not to forget."

"How about, for the rest of the day, we are only serious when we need to be."

"I can manage that."

"Why do you have such a small car?" she asked.

"I don't know, I just always wanted a sports car. I plan to sell it before I leave," he said.

"A car like this tends to attract the attention of the authorities. You must know about *la Operacion Maseta*."

"No, what is that?"

"It's a government operation that identifies people, with the help of our beloved neighborhood snitches, that they believe have too much money, and must have attained it by illegal means. They've been putting people in jail recently."

"The only way someone can attain anything of value in Cuba is by illegal means. I'm not worried. They can't put everyone in jail. Besides I registered the car in my father's name."

"Why did you do that if you're not worried?"

"Just in case. My father is almost seventy and the government tends to leave the older people alone. I thought we were saving the serious conversations for later."

"Sorry. I'm a bit paranoid these days. With my family having escaped to Miami, I feel like the government is always watching me."

"Why didn't you go with them?"

"My boyfriend at the time didn't want me to leave, I had a decent job, and was feeling good about my life."

"But no longer?"

"No, like I told you, my life is shit. The hollow promises of the revolution are a cruel illusion, perpetrated by the great *estafador*. My father has told me if I make it to Miami, I'll have no trouble finding work as a model."

"I don't doubt that," said Roberto, pausing for a moment before continuing. "Please don't misunderstand, Maura, but I think you're one of the most beautiful women I have ever met."

"Thank you. You're a gentleman. But I knew that already," she said.

"Here we are Maura," said Roberto. The old boatyard in Cojimar, along the river next to La Playa Cojimar, faced northwest, with an unobstructed view downriver all the way to the ocean.

"I love this place, Maura. I don't know what it is, but when I come here, I always feel content, and hopeful. Probably because I am a fisherman at heart."

It was midday and the force of the water from the young flood tide, pushing in from the sea against the river's flow, was beginning to ripple the water in the middle of the river where the current was strongest. Roberto noticed a large school of passing jacks, common along the coast in late June, beating to the east, just inside the point near the Torreon.

"It's only a short walk from here to the docks," he said, cheerfully.

"This is the first time I have been in Cojimar," she said. "I like it here. It's quaint."

"I'm sure you know Cojimar was made famous by Senor Hemingway, and his long-time friend and first mate, Gregorio Fuentes," said Roberto.

"Come on Roberto, really? I am Cuban," she said, slapping him on the back of his arm with the back of her hand.

"Senor Fuentes lives here," he said.

"He's still living?" she asked.

"I'll introduce you. He should be by the dock unless he's out fishing," he said.

The narrow sand path leading from the boatyard down the hill to the cabana at the end of the pier by the dock where Roberto met with Pedro the week before, was bordered by a tangle of sea grapes, and shaded by a canopy of tall almond trees. The ground beneath was damp and scattered with many large holes made by the big land crabs that were more active in June after a rain, and when caught out in the open feeding, would run noisily across the dead leaves in a sideways motion, toward their burrows.

At the end of the path where it met the river, the bush opened up into a loose stand of coconut palms, protected from the unrelenting trades by a dense thicket of red mangroves that grew on both sides of the river. The coconut palms grew tall and straight and Roberto had a clear view to the cabana.

"Good, Pedrito is here," he said to Maura, who was following close behind.

"Those crabs creep me out," she said holding onto Roberto's arm.

"They're more afraid of you than you should be of them," he said. "Haven't you ever eaten *cangrejo de tierra*."

"No, and I don't care to. They're ugly," she replied.

"*Hola*, Pedrito," shouted Roberto, spotting his friend.

"*Mi hermano*! *Como tu ta*?" said Pedro. "Every time I see you man, you have a new girlfriend."

Maura released her grip on Roberto's arm, stepped back, folded her arms and looked instead at Pedro. "I'm not his girlfriend," she said.

"Alina broke up with me the day after we were here, Pedrito. This is my friend Maura. We met recently," said Roberto.

"So who is this Alina? And why did she break up with you?" asked Maura. She was not convinced and wasn't about to let Roberto off the hook without an explanation.

"Because she didn't think much of my plan to leave the country," he said. "Look, you asked to come here today. I didn't ask you."

"She knows?" asked Pedro, pointing to Maura.

"Not only does she know, she wants to come with us. That's why she's here. I told her she needed to see the boat before making a decision," said Roberto.

"Pedro, I'm Maura. It's a pleasure. Before you get too worried, I have family in Miami. I can be of help once we get there," she said.

"My apologies, Maura. My pleasure, I'm sure. I don't mean to be insulting, but you don't look like the boating type," said Pedro.

"I'm not, and I don't plan on becoming a fisherman any time soon either. I just want to get the hell out of Cuba," she said.

"There's already five of us in the boat now Roberto, and it's a small boat," said Pedro.

"Six," said Roberto.

"Who is the sixth?" asked Pedro.

"My brother Lazaro. Maura would make seven. I don't think that's too many. We plan to leave when we know the weather is good. At nine or ten knots, we could make it to the U.S. Keys in nine or ten hours," said Roberto.

"Sure, if nothing goes wrong. You know, Roberto, you've been out in the winter. The Stream is unpredictable, even in good weather," said Pedro.

"I'm willing to take my chances," said Maura.

"Have you asked around about a motor?" Roberto asked Pedro.

"As a matter of fact I believe I may have found one. It has nearly double the horsepower and the guy says he only needs thirty-five hundred for it," said Pedro.

"Tell him we'll take it. I have the money for the boat with me. You can use what you need for the motor out of that and when you have it installed, I'll give you the money to cover the motor and your labor," said Roberto.

"You're a good man," said Pedro.

"I'm not so sure about that. I'd like to know more about the girlfriend," said Maura, now smiling.

"Maura, let me show you the boat," said Pedro.

Maura and Roberto followed Pedro to the end of the dock where the La Rosita was tied off at the end of a short finger pier with several other smaller fishing boats.

"You can change your mind at any time, Maura," said Roberto.

The tide was dead low and the boat was resting partly on the bottom which made her tilt to one side. Maura stepped down onto the finger pier and walked out to a point alongside the boat where she had a better view into the wheelhouse.

"How can you go anywhere with the boat stuck on the bottom?" she asked, turning in the direction of Pedro.

"The river is tidal. When the tide is high, depending on the phase of the moon, it will come up to here," he said. Pedro pointed to the top of one of the heavy pine poles that supported the finger pier, where the barnacles and algae were growing. "When tide's high the barnacles are covered, and when we have the King Tides, the water will come even higher."

"And you think this boat will make it to Florida in one day?" she asked.

"No problem. I've spent thousands of hours aboard her. Not many boats her size are as sea kindly," said Pedro.

"What do you mean, 'sea kindly'?" she asked.

"It means she's comfortable even when it's a little choppy," replied Pedro.

"You don't have to decide today, Maura," said Roberto. "We don't plan on leaving until after the new year."

"It's going to take some time to swap out the motor and we need to sea trial her after that. I'd like to fish her as many days as possible with the new motor this fall. That way if there's any kind of problem we'll have plenty of time to fix it," said Pedro. "I'll let you know, Roberto, when I have the new motor installed. We can run her together."

"I'll be waiting. Pedrito, Senor Fuentes around today? I wanted Maura to meet him," said Roberto.

"No, he's gone out. With all the Passing Jacks that we're seeing lately he told me he was going with Maykel. Try and catch a big one," replied Pedro.

"Maybe next time, Maura. Pedrito, *mi hermano, muchas gracias,*" said Roberto.

"You care for a cigar before you leave?" asked Pedro.

"Always, but it's up to Maura," said Roberto.

"I have no plans and I'm rather enjoying Cojimar," she said to Roberto. "I would like to sit somewhere out of the sun."

"We can sit in the cabana, in the cool. *Vamos,*" said Pedro.

For the rest of the afternoon and into the evening Roberto and Maura sat with Pedro in the shade of the thatch cabana. It was always the coolest place to sit along the river in summer.

The wind had gone out the day before and was light but still strong enough to keep the sand flies from biting. Pedro and Roberto talked briefly about the time they spent together in prison, but like every small village by the sea everywhere in the world, the conversation always came around to fishing, the weather, who was catching, and why they were catching fewer fish than in past years.

By midafternoon the local fishermen who had gone out early and been successful, began returning to the harbor. One by one they tied up to the floating dock anchored at the end of the pier, just outside the low tide line, to clean their catch. The daily fish cleaning in Cojimar was always an event, and because today was Sunday there were more people than usual. All of them were watching; most quietly hoping for a little fish, although few were able to pay.

After cleaning, and then cutting the head off each fish, the fisherman would dump the bony, mostly meatless carcass overboard, where it would sink to the bottom for the grey snappers, that lived in great numbers under the dock when the weather was warm, to pick clean, before the sharks, that came in from the ocean after dark, finished off the rest. The fish heads were given away first to the elderly and then the poorest for making soup, with the rest divided among the local fish potters for bait.

Roberto noticed a young man and woman on the edge of the crowd with two small children, who watched the fishermen as they cleaned their catch. They had been sitting by the dock since the fishermen began returning from the ocean earlier in the afternoon. The children's clothes were little more than rags and they were thin for their age. He asked Pedro about the couple and Pedro said he knew them, and that the man had recently been released from prison and was unable to find work, and they had come hoping for a few scraps of fish.

"Pedrito, do you have a couple of large plastic bags? Maybe onboard the boat?" asked Roberto.

"What for?" asked Pedro.

"I want to buy some fish for that family," said Roberto, pointing to the couple with the two children."

"It's not necessary. Someone will give them some heads," said Pedro.

"They need more than fish heads. You know the boat that just came in?" asked Roberto.

"Sure, that's Mario. He'll have something. With this light wind he probably went mutton fishing. I'll introduce you," said Pedro.

"Maura, you mind waiting here?" asked Roberto.

"Certainly not. I'm a little thirsty though. Some coconut water would be nice," she said.

"Tajo," said Pedro to one of the young boys who had been sitting with them in the cabana listening to their conversation. "Take the cutlass and gather some coconuts for us, please. Be careful not to cut the ones with the brown tops."

"I know which ones to cut," said Tajo, annoyed that Pedro didn't trust he knew to cut the young ones with the clean tops. "*Cuantos?*"

"Cut eight. You be careful when you climb, Tajo, and give some to that family," said Pedro, pointing to the couple with the two children. "Cut the bottoms so they can drink them now."

Roberto followed Pedro to the end of the pier and did not speak to the family when he passed. By the time they reached the dock where the men were cleaning fish, Mario was beginning to unload his catch.

"*Hola,* Mario. I see you went mutton fishing again," said Pedro.

"Yes. It's getting near the end of the spawn but we got all we wanted," said Mario.

"Where did you go?" asked Pedro.

"To the bar, off La Playa Santa Maria," he answered.

"Mario, this is my good friend Roberto. We were in prison together. You remember I told you about the guy who put his commanding officer in the hospital? Well this is the guy," he said.

"It is a great pleasure, Roberto," said Mario.

"The same, I'm sure," replied Roberto. "Mario, would it be possible to buy some fish? I can pay you right away."

"Not a problem. It's five pesos a kilo. One fish weighs about four kilos. How many you want?" asked Mario.

"Give me four. No, make it eight. I need to take some to my mother," said Roberto.

"You want me to get the scale and weigh them or you take my word for the weight," he asked.

"I'll take your word. Pedrito, can you get me the bags? Four, if they're kit size," said Roberto. "Here's the money, Mario. You can pick out the fish for me."

Roberto and Pedro watched as Mario finished unloading his cooler and then picked out eight of the largest muttonfish for Roberto. Because the fish were large and heavy spawning-size adults, two were enough to fill one of the plastic bags from Pedro. Roberto then tied a large knot in the open end of each bag, making them easier to carry.

As Roberto turned to walk back to the cabana, Mario asked if he wanted one of the two barracuda he had caught that day.

"You think they're poison?" asked Roberto.

"I don't know. Honestly, I never eat them. I only keep them because they make good bait," he said.

"I'd rather not take the chance, but thanks anyway, Mario," said Roberto.

As Roberto walked back up the pier toward the land, he noticed the man who had just been released from prison was watching him intently. Roberto, thinking he might humiliate the man in front of his family by offering him the fish, began to have doubts about giving him the fish, but quickly changed his mind when his eyes went again to the children.

"Sir, this is for you and your family," said Roberto, when he stopped to address the young man.

The man looked at his wife before standing up to take the fish from Roberto. The woman stood up also, smiled and placed her hand on her husband's shoulder, which seemed to comfort him.

"I was released from prison only a few days ago sir. When I was in prison it was very hard on my family. I don't normally accept charity, but we're in a difficult situation until I can find work," said the man.

"I understand. I've been in your shoes. I was in prison twice in the last four years," said Roberto.

"God bless you, my friend," said the man.

"You as well, sir," replied Roberto, reaching out to shake the man's hand before walking back to the cabana.

"How is the coconut water, Maura?" asked Roberto.

"Refreshing, thanks. That was very kind, what you did," she said.

"They are suffering. Anyway, I'll sleep better tonight. We need to leave soon. The fish won't last long in this heat," said Roberto.

"I'm ready," she said.

"Pedrito, always a pleasure. You let me know when you have the new motor installed. I'd like to be here when you sea trial her," said Roberto.

"I'll let you know, don't worry. Maura, it was nice to meet you. Keep him out of trouble," said Pedro.

"I don't have that kind of influence, Pedrito. Not yet anyway," she said.

By the time Roberto and Maura arrived at Maura's grandmother's in

Old Havana, the sun had set and the air in Habana Vieja was beginning to cool from the light north breeze still coming off the ocean. Her grandmother was sitting outside the house and looked suspiciously at Roberto's car as it came to a stop in front of the house.

"*Buenas noches, Mima,*" said Maura from the car. "Roberto took me to Cojimar today."

"What for?" she asked sternly. Maura's grandmother was protective of her granddaughter. She hadn't wanted to leave Cuba with the rest of the family and now Maura was all she had.

"Here, take her some fish," whispered Roberto. "Maybe it will improve her mood."

"You don't need to make jokes about my grandmother," she said.

Maura leaned over and kissed Roberto on the cheek before stepping out of the car and closing the door. Stooping down to the height of the car door she placed her arms on the top of the door with her chin resting on the back of her hands.

"I'm going with you," said Maura in a voice that was barely audible, not wanting her grandmother to hear what she was saying.

"You seem certain."

"I'm more certain about this than anything in my life. Remember, I told you I'm straightforward, so there is no need to second-guess what I'm telling you."

"Then I can be confident your answer will be honest if I ask you if you have plans for next weekend."

"I have no plans."

"Have you ever been to the city of Cienfuegos, in the south?"

"I've never been anywhere."

"I've always wanted to go there. It's two hundred fifty kilometers from Havana," said Roberto. "I've heard it's very beautiful."

"Then I need to pack a toothbrush," said Maura, smiling.

"Probably a good idea. I'll pick you up Saturday morning," he said.

"What time?" asked Maura.

"10:00," he said.

"Where will we stay?" she asked, having to speak above the noise of the engine when Roberto started the car.

"We'll find something. See you Saturday," said Roberto.

Roberto had questions about Maura's intentions even though he believed her to be sincere and genuine. Still, she was unusually independent and had little trouble making decisions. He liked that about her and it gave him confidence.

Never one to have any illusions about himself, especially having to do with women, Roberto knew the basis of their relationship, at least for now, was their mutual determination to leave Cuba. It was something he could live with, he thought, and if successful, could lead to other possibilities. There was no need to think of it any other way.

XIX

Ever since the arrest of General Ochoa on the twelfth of June in 1989, and the subsequent arrests of a number of other high-ranking military officers, including Colonel Antonio de la Guardia, the country had been riveted to the daily, state-run television broadcasts of the sham trial, held before a Military Honor Court in Havana.

It came as no surprise to Roberto, when on the eighth of July, the official mouthpiece of the communist state-run newspaper, La Granma, reported that the military tribunal had found officers Ochoa, de la Guardia, Martinez, and Padron, guilty of drug smuggling and corruption and sentenced them to death by firing squad.

Only a handful of people in Cuba knew the truth about the Castro brothers' cocaine smuggling operation and the risk it posed to the future of the Cuban revolution should the government of the United States find out it was solely the work of Fidel. Roberto was one of those people.

Even the casual observer witnessing the alleged defense testimony had no trouble understanding why the details of the operation were never revealed by the accused. When reference was made to even the slightest involvement on the part of the so-called "highest authority," the testimony of the accused was swiftly discredited.

It was speculated by many in Cuba, that had the truth been told by any of the defendants during the trial, all of whom were highly respected throughout the ranks of the Cuban military, as well as the civilian population, and possessed enough political leverage to challenge the Castros, that the lives of the family members of the accused would have been in peril.

Not since the murder of Camillo Cienfuegos had the actions of the *estafadors*, masquerading as benevolent Marxist father figures, posed such a danger to themselves. This scandal however, even more than the Cienfuegos affair, had the potential to seriously threaten their thirty-year stranglehold on power.

Early on the morning of July fourteenth, Roberto, while still living with Rosa and Guillermo, awoke and went downstairs to join his parents for coffee and something to eat on the terrace.

Rosa was making a second pot of coffee and Guillermo was sitting outside with Carlos when Roberto walked into the kitchen.

"*Buenos dias, Madre,*" he said cheerfully.

Roberto's mood could not have been more ebullient. In recent weeks he had sold a number of paintings to Mariano before the Spaniard had returned to Spain for the summer, providing him with more than enough to live on until Mariano returned the following winter.

His black-market business appraising precious stones, while increasingly risky due to the government campaign, *Operacion Maseta*, which was intended to root out ordinary citizens suspected of so-called criminal capitalist activities, had become quite lucrative, providing him with a backup cash flow during the months when Mariano was not in Cuba.

"You may not feel quite so cheerful after you read the paper," said Rosa.

"Why?" asked Roberto.

"Your father has the paper. I'll bring you some coffee," she said.

Roberto walked outside and sat down next to Carlos, across the table from his father. Guillermo leaned forward and slid the morning edition of La Granma to a position on the table in front of Roberto where he would be able to read the headline.

Slowly, without picking up the paper, Roberto leaned over and read the headline reporting the death sentence by firing squad for General Ochoa, Colonel de la Guardia, and the two other officers, Martinez and Padron, had been carried out the previous day, before dawn, at the Tropas Especiales military base in Baracoa, West Havana.

"Now the truth will be buried in the ground forever," said Roberto.

"What do you plan to do now?" asked Guillermo.

"What do you mean?" replied Roberto.

"I mean I think you should consider giving up your black-market activities. The government is on high alert looking to jail anyone they consider involved in counter-revolutionary activities. We're worried you'll be imprisoned again, and for a much longer time. Remember, you have a serious record," said Guillermo.

"I'm aware I have a record. Look, I'm careful and I don't plan on doing this forever," said Roberto.

"What do you plan on doing?" asked Guillermo.

"I haven't figured that out yet. There are not a lot of options right now with the economy," said Roberto. "Maybe I'll become a fisherman."

"At least it's honest work," said Guillermo.

"I think my work is honest," said Roberto. He was annoyed with the way his father had characterized his business dealings and wanted to change the subject. "We are being squeezed now more than ever and this is not going to help." Roberto picked up the newspaper and pointed to the headline.

"That's what I mean. The Castros are nervous. We lost the support of the Soviets and Fidel is determined not to adopt any of Gorbachev's policies of Perestroika. Look, all we are saying is now is not the time to take chances," said Guillermo.

"I understand. Did you receive the car registration?" Roberto asked, again trying to change the subject.

"Yes. You need to keep it with the car in case you're questioned by the police. The police should have stopped you by now. They're not doing their job," said Guillermo.

"Quite the comedian," quipped Roberto.

Rosa finished making the coffee for Roberto and had joined them on the terrace. "It's sickening what the Castros did to your friend Tony," she said.

"It is, but it was expected. I feel bad for his wife and children. He was a good person. It's not easy to be a good person in Cuba," lamented Roberto.

"He was smuggling drugs for *El Jefe*. That's not being a good person," said Rosa.

"I know but he had no choice. He refuses, he goes to jail. That's the way Fidel operates," said Roberto.

"What about this *nueva novia*. Is she nice?" she asked. Roberto knew this was Rosa's way of asking if Maura could be trusted.

"She's no nonsense, I can tell you that. She lives with her grandmother," replied Roberto.

"What does she do?" asked Rosa.

"She works part time for my friend Carmen, and for other people in the neighborhood. Whatever she can find. Her parents live in Miami," said Roberto.

"The two of you planning to leave for Miami?" asked Rosa.

"No, we're not planning to go to Miami," answered Roberto. Roberto was a terrible liar and not telling his mother the truth made him uncomfortable. He could see out of the corner of his eye that his brother Carlos was looking at him. Worried Carlos might slip and say something that would reveal his plan to leave with Pedro, he distracted him with a question.

"Carlitos, have you been to see Maykel lately? I heard from a friend in Cojimar he has been fishing most days with Senor Fuentes" said Roberto.

"Yes, I have gone to the docks several times recently, in the afternoon when the boats are coming in. He and Gregorio have not always been lucky, but the days when they are, it has often been a big one. The *dorado* run has been over for at least a month now, but the big marlin have been steady. Maykel always asks me when you are coming fishing again," said Carlos.

"Maybe we can go a day later in the month," said Roberto. He knew it was unlikely they would go fishing with Maykel, perhaps ever again, but he wanted to give Carlos something to look forward to. The brothers had spent little time together in recent years and despite Carlos's difficulties in communicating his feelings to his brother, Roberto could tell their time apart was taking a toll on their relationship.

The family sat on the terrace late into the morning, talking and drinking coffee and though the talk was mostly about the news of the day, the intensity lessened as the conversation evolved more toward the comfortably mundane. Roberto had no plans for the day and was happy and comfortable spending it with his parents and Carlos.

By mid-afternoon the coffee had given way to rum and the family had been joined by Roberto's brother Lazaro and his sister Rosa. From the patio they could hear the sound of thunder coming from the summer squalls, building slowly since early afternoon, as they passed steadily to the north over the old city. While no rain fell in Santos Suarez, the cooling effect from the wind that came with the squalls as they brushed by, along with the fresh sweet smell of the nearby rain, provided just enough inspiration for the tree frogs, safely hidden in the banana plants that bordered the terrace, to begin singing.

XX

Sometime during the summer after the political turmoil over the Ochoa affair had subsided, Roberto and Maura decided to move in together, and found a small apartment near his parents' house. The move was a disappointment to her grandmother, and a difficult thing for Maura to do, but she knew if she was going to leave with Roberto, she had to put some emotional distance between her and her grandmother.

It was early the following spring when Pedro finally telephoned Roberto to tell him he had completed the installation of the more powerful motor in the La Rosita and was waiting for Roberto to come to Cojimar for the sea trial. The work had taken Pedro much longer than expected, which was always the case in Cuba, because replacement parts, especially mechanical ones, were impossible to find, and required everyone to have the ability to fabricate parts they couldn't buy.

Roberto agreed to meet Pedro on a day when the weather would be favorable and the wind light. On a flat ocean they would be able to run the La Rosita at full speed, knowing that if something was going to fail in the motor, there was a better chance it would happen when she was at full throttle.

Roberto and Maura went together to Cojimar the day of the sea trial. She had never been on the ocean and he wanted her to get a feel for what it would be like. Even though the wind was light and the sea would be calm, he needed to know how she would react to being in deep water, too far out to swim ashore if something went wrong.

When they arrived in Cojimar, Pedro had readied the boat and was waiting under the cabana. It was overcast and the air was still, the breeze had fallen out to a dead calm after a brief early morning shower. With no movement in the damp humid air, it made life easy for the sand flies.

"The nippers are thick this morning. If you'd been much longer, I believe they'd have carried me into the bush and finished me off," laughed Pedro, while brushing the outside of his legs with his hands in a futile effort to rid them of the tiny insects.

"*Vamos entonces,*" said Roberto.

"I've already taken everything to the boat in the buggy. You can put your drinks in the cooler," said Pedro.

Pedro, hopping aboard first, turned around and took the two cloth bags with the food and drinks Roberto had brought. The tide had come up, bringing the boat's washboard even with the dock, making it easier for Maura, who had never been in a boat, to step on board.

"You plan on fishing today, Pedrito?" asked Roberto, noticing the four fishing rods Pedro had already rigged and placed, one each, in the boat's four rod holders. Pedro had outfitted the boat with two gunnel mount outriggers, that when turned outward, made it possible to troll four baits at once.

"The wahoo have been thick, and since we're going out I thought we'd troll the ledge and see if we can pick up a couple. Besides, if we look like we're fishing the Coast Guard should leave us alone. You need to troll a little faster if you want a wahoo to bite. This way we can see how she does at a higher speed for a couple hours," said Pedro.

"I don't understand, why does the Coast Guard care what we're doing?" asked Maura.

"If they see you going fast, they get suspicious," said Pedro. "I'm not worried if they stop us. I have all my paperwork—fishing license, boat license, everything—onboard."

Pedro and Roberto untied the dock lines, one from the bow and one from the stern, before Pedro eased her out into the middle of the river. The tide had just turned and was beginning to fall, increasing the speed of the current, making it possible to run at a fast idle most of the way to the ocean.

"She runs smooth, Pedrito, and quiet," observed Roberto.

"For a boat that's more than thirty years old she's solid as you want," said Pedro.

Slowly, they motored downriver, eventually turning north with the river, past El Castillo. When they had cleared the reef that narrowed the channel at the mouth of the river where it met the ocean, Pedro motioned for Maura to hold on before increasing the speed and putting the La Rosita on a plane.

The sky was overcast, and with no wind the surface of the ocean was oil calm, except where the current rips formed from the deep-water eddies that spun off the Gulf Stream pushed against the ledge that ran along the northern edge of the island. The fishermen called the eddies, "boils," and on calm days when the conditions were best for drift fishing the bar, the sound made by the water "boiling" to the top could be heard at a great distance.

Pedro slowly increased the speed, encouraging the bow of the La Rosita to settle into the ocean. As she passed easily over the low smooth swells, the stream of water thrown from the spray rail, hitting the surface of the ocean, sounded like a pulsing windblown shower of rain.

"I want to run her a little out in front here before we start fishing. She sounds good but we need to be sure before we get too far from Cojimar," said Pedro to Roberto, above the noise of the engine. "We're only going to fish two rods Roberto."

"Why only two?" he asked.

"Like I said, we need to troll fast, at least ten knots and the outrigger clips won't hold at that speed," said Pedro. "We'll fish a naked ballyhoo with a weight in front on each rod. Let me know if you see any breaking fish."

"What's a breaking fish?" asked Maura.

"It's when you see a splash from a fish breaking the surface of the water," said Roberto.

"You mean like those splashes over there?" asked Maura, pointing to a school of skipjack tuna that had just surfaced and were beating two hundred yards off the port stern beyond where the indigo blue water of the Gulf Stream came in to meet the dark green water flowing out from the river.

Roberto and Pedro had been looking in the opposite direction and had not seen the school of small tuna surface. Roberto was impressed with how quickly Maura seemed to catch on to what he had told her. Pedro, however, was embarrassed, because Maura, who had never been fishing, or been on the ocean, had seen them first.

"Aren't you going to try for them?" she asked, when Pedro did not slow down.

"Too small. I'll wait until we find some bigger ones," he said, not looking in Maura's direction.

Maura smiled at Roberto. She wasn't bothered by Pedro's response, knowing his ego, like that of most men, and fishermen in particular, didn't allow him to acknowledge that she had seen the school of small tuna first.

Several hundred yards before Pedro reached the area where he planned to start fishing, he slowed the boat and dropped the two baits overboard along with the lead cigar trolling weights that kept them at a depth of fifteen feet, one off each side of the stern. Then, he gradually brought the boat back up to a speed of ten knots.

Pedro knew fishing in and out of the current, where the rips were forming on the surface, concentrated the bait fish above the ledge and would give him the best chance of catching a wahoo.

The flying fish had been plentiful in recent months and had been joined by good numbers of small squid that when startled by the noise from the engine would launch themselves free of the water, in groups of ten and twenty, by means of a water jet at the base of their mantel. As they ran out of water stored inside the mantel for propulsion, and before reaching the apex of their flight, they would flare the fins at the top of their mantel along with their tentacles, helping them to gain additional height above surface, making it possible to cover a distance of up to thirty meters in the air before collapsing their fins and tentacles to minimize the impact upon reentering the water.

It wasn't long before the starboard rod bounced once, then bent over and quickly began to dump line, followed by the port rod.

"Roberto, you take the fish on the starboard rod, but not before I tell you to. I'll fight the other one once we slow down," yelled Pedro. "Put on a belt. These are both good-size fish."

Pedro wanted to make sure the fish were solidly hooked and kept the line tight by going ahead before easing off on the throttle.

Maura, surprised by the sudden force of the strikes, along with Pedro's somewhat manic reaction, had moved to the forward end of the cockpit just inside the cabin in an effort to stay out of the way, deciding to watch from a seat on the cooler.

"Ease off on the drag a little before you take it out of the rod holder and then push it back up to where it was, once you have it in the belt," instructed Pedro. "Don't try and horse him. These fish have plenty power."

Roberto followed Pedro's instructions carefully and once he had the rod set firmly in the gimbal belt, he slowly began to lift the rod with his left hand while alternately winding with his right as he lowered the rod back down toward the water's surface.

"Don't lift too high. That old Lee bamboo is brittle and the fish is a big one. The higher you lift the more pressure you put on the tip and it could break. Keep the tip low and use the butt to lift," said Pedro.

"Feels like he wants to run, Pedrito," said Roberto loudly.

"Then let him go then. We have all day," replied Pedro.

"All right, I feel like I have him stopped now," said Roberto. "I can feel him shaking his head."

"They'll do that to try and cut the line. They have teeth like razors. They can't cut that heavy wire though. Just keep the pressure on him," he said.

Steadily Roberto was able to gain line, sometimes having to stop for a few seconds when the fish would burst unexpectedly. Fortunately the two fish had gone in opposite directions when they began to run hard, eliminating the possibility of the lines crossing, which sometimes resulted in one line cutting through the other, losing one of the fish.

"I'm going to need the gaff in a second," said Pedro. "Maura, can you hand me the gaff that's underneath the washboard next to where you are sitting?"

"What's a gaff?" she asked, slightly panicked.

"Look under the washboard, next to Roberto's knees. The thing with the long wooden handle and the curved metal tip. That's a gaff. Quickly," said Pedro.

Pedro tightened the drag on his reel and set the rod in the forward rod holder, next to the one holding the port outrigger. The fish was on its side, held under the surface by the heavy trolling weight, just behind the stern, and the fight was out of him now.

Taking the gaff from Maura with his right hand, Pedro hooked the wire leader behind the weight with the metal hook on the end of the gaff and pulled it in where he could reach it with his left hand.

He could clearly see the neon blue vertical stripes, common to all pelagic game fish, spaced along the fish's side, through the prop wash. The fish's mouth was fully open and the hook was firmly lodged in the hinge of the jaw.

"Maura, I'm going to need your help," said Pedro. "When I tell you, slowly pull down on the line toward the reel, and crank at the same time, until I tell you to stop."

"Pedro, you want me to help?" asked Roberto.

"No, no, you stay on your fish and keep him coming," yelled Pedro. "Maura can handle this."

With each turn of the reel handle Maura made, Pedro was able to slide his hand down the line in the direction of the fish. Finally he was able to grab the weight and gain control of the fish.

"Damn it," yelled Pedro. "You bastard."

"What happened?" shouted Roberto, turning around to see.

"Big tiger," answered Pedro. "He's at least fourteen feet."

In a single motion Pedro slid the meter and a half long fish up to the surface along the side of the boat and stuck the gaff deep into the thick shoulder meat behind the gill plate. Just before he was able to pull the fish from the water, the shark struck, taking most of the tail and a section of meat from the underside behind the caudal fin.

Before the shark could hit again Pedro dropped the weight, then gripped the gaff with both hands as near as he dared to the hook end of the gaff in order to gain more leverage, safely lifting the fish clear of the water onto the deck where it lay quivering, its' mouth frozen open.

"Good job Maura, like a pro," said Pedro. "Alright, let's get this other fish in. Stay away from the fish's mouth Maura. Remember what I said about the teeth."

"Pedrito, my fish is on top," said Roberto.

"That shark is probably on him too," replied Pedro. "I'm going to swing the boat around and head toward the fish. You crank as fast as you can and don't let any slack come in the line."

"I see him now, Pedrito," he yelled. "He'll go a good fifty kilos!"

In no time Pedro had closed on the fish and made up most of the line still out on Roberto's rod, and now had him less than ten meters from the boat. Roberto, although tired from the fight, continued to reel aggressively, knowing the big tiger could easily end things at any moment.

"Keep him coming, Roberto. Okay, step toward the bow and raise the rod a little," said Pedro calmly, as he grabbed the line. "As soon as I gaff him you back off on the drag."

Before Pedro finished giving Roberto the instructions they saw the great shark emerge from under the boat. It swam slowly a short distance directly away from the stern, then again picking up the scent of the struggling fish, made a quick turn back toward the wahoo, which Roberto now had alongside the boat.

"Stick him," yelled Roberto.

At the precise moment Pedro sunk the gaff into the wahoo, the tiger struck, slamming Roberto's fish into the side of the boat with enough force that it broke the wire leader.

"I don't have him anymore, Pedrito," yelled Roberto.

"Get the other gaff. It's under the washboard on the port side," said Pedro.

Pedro struggled to keep the limp body of the wahoo, which had been cut nearly in two at a point on the body below the dorsal fin, out of the water and away from the shark. The shark had let go after biting off and swallowing whole a two-foot-long section of belly meat and was coming again.

"Try and gaff the tail, Roberto. Quick!" shouted Pedro.

Again the massive, one ton tiger struck. This time from under the boat, tearing off the back half of the fish before Roberto could sink the gaff.

Pedro, his shoulders slumped, lifted what remained of the big wahoo over the washboard and let go of the gaff with his left hand as the fish thumped onto the deck, bloody and lifeless, next to the first fish, then sat down on the port washboard to catch his breath.

"Damn, Pedrito, I'm sorry," said Roberto.

"It's not your fault," said Pedro. "We were lucky to get as much as we did. The bastard was big enough he could have eaten that wahoo whole if he'd come at it from either end. What do you say, Maura? You like fishing?" Pedro was smiling and could see Maura was still trying to process what had happened.

"I'm just happy to be in the boat and not in the water. I had no idea there're creatures that big living down there," she said.

"All the more reason to be sure she can make it across the Straits," said Pedro, patting the side of the boat.

"I think the sea trial was a success, Pedrito!" said Roberto.

"*Por supuesto que si*, Roberto," replied Pedro. "I think we need to head back to the dock. The cooler isn't big enough to hold them and I'd like to keep the meat as fresh as possible. We'll run the twenty kilometers back to the river mouth. I'd like to see what she'll do at top end. With these conditions we can run full throttle and still be comfortable."

After cleaning the fish blood off the deck with buckets of sea water and stowing the two fishing rods, Pedro swung the bow of the La Rosita around and began heading west toward Cojimar.

There was a light breeze no more than five kilometers an hour from the southwest and Pedro could feel the Gulf Stream current, which flowed from the west, pushing against the bow of the boat as he increased the speed. Even though the current was not in their favor, if they could make fifteen knots or better, it meant they would reach the mouth of the Cojimar River in forty minutes.

It was when they reached the eastern point of land at the mouth of the river, across from the Torreon, and began to slow the boat before entering the channel that they saw the boat from the Tropas Guardafronteras steaming toward them. Pedro saw them first and although he wasn't worried, he couldn't imagine why they would be approaching. He always kept his fishing license on board in case he was stopped by the Coast Guard and it would be obvious to them once they came along side and checked the boat that they had in fact been fishing.

"Pedro, you see them?" asked Roberto, pointing to the boat.

"I see them. I can't imagine what they want but I have all my paperwork. I'll do the talking. I know some of these guys and they know I fish," said Pedro.

Pedro, easing up on the throttle, brought the boat to a stop, mid-channel just inside the Torreon, and waited. Not wanting to make the situation any worse, Pedro was careful to stay in the deeper water of the channel where the larger coast guard vessel would not hit bottom. As the boat approached they could see several military personnel standing on the bow looking at the La Rosita through binoculars.

When they neared the La Rosita, the captain of the Coast Guard boat put the port engine in neutral and gave the starboard engine a little fuel, bringing her stern around to a position alongside and parallel with the smaller vessel.

"Captain," yelled the commanding officer from Coast Guard vessel.

"You seem to be in a hurry. Why?"

"I'm trying to get back to the dock as quickly as possible. As you can see, we have been fishing and I don't want the meat to spoil," said Pedro, pointing to the two wahoo laying on the deck.

"I'm going to have one of the men throw you a rope. Tie off your vessel and come aboard. Be sure to bring your papers with you," said the officer.

"What do you think he wants?" whispered Roberto.

"I don't know, but I can't believe these sons of bitches don't have anything more important to do than harass fishermen," said Pedro, now clearly annoyed. "Roberto, would you pour some sea water on the fish while I find out what they want. Hopefully this won't take too long."

After retrieving the plastic bag from under the console beside the steering wheel that held his boat license, government identification, and fishing license, Pedro boarded the Coast Guard boat and disappeared into the wheelhouse with the commanding officer.

Maura was sitting on the cooler, deliberately not making eye contact with the men still standing on the bow. "I don't like the way those pigs are looking at me Roberto," said Maura. "Can't you do something?"

"Gentlemen," said Roberto, addressing the men. "My girlfriend would appreciate it if you would stop staring at her." Roberto crossed his arms and waited for a response.

"Tell your girlfriend if she would like to know what it's like to be with a military man, I'd be happy to accommodate her," yelled one of the men, laughing above the noise of the idling engines from the bigger boat.

Maura looked nervously at Roberto but said nothing. It was then that he remembered the military SS badge in his wallet. He had discovered it recently in his parents' house, having accidentally left the badge there while on leave several years earlier and had not turned it in after being released from prison thinking perhaps someday it may be useful. It had proved invaluable once before, making it possible for Carlos and him to gain access to the restricted archives in the Jose Marti Library, when they were looking for information about Carlos Sobrino.

"I don't believe my boss would appreciate your comments," said Roberto casually.

"Yeah, and who is your boss?" asked the crewman, still laughing.

Roberto didn't answer. In a deliberate motion, he reached for his wallet and pulled out the Secret Service badge, holding it in the sunlight where the man could see it clearly.

"Secret Service. Punto Cero. Maybe you are acquainted with the gentleman that lives there," said Roberto as he slid the badge back into his wallet.

The crewmen stopped laughing and stared at Roberto in disbelief. Roberto briefly waited for one of the men to say something before turning toward Maura who was having trouble processing what was happening.

"Roberto, what are you doing?" she asked excitedly but in a voice low enough that the men onboard could not hear.

"Don't say anything," he whispered back. "I'll explain when we get to the dock."

Just then the commanding officer emerged from the wheelhouse with Pedro.

Before Pedro stepped back onto the La Rosita, the officer returned the plastic bag of identification papers to Pedro and motioned for him to return to the La Rosita.

Back onboard, Pedro quickly untied the rope connecting the two boats, threw it up to one of the servicemen and pushed the La Rosita away from the Coast Guard vessel, before starting the engine and putting her in gear.

"What the hell was that all about, Pedrito?" asked Roberto.

"You're not going to believe this, Roberto," said Pedro. "The commanding officer is telling me the boat is too fast."

"What do you mean too fast?" Roberto asked.

"I told him I was having trouble with the old motor, which is true, and replaced it with one that has more power," said Pedro.

"So what's his problem?" asked Roberto, still not understanding.

"He said the boat is too fast and we have to put the old motor back in, and he will be stopping by the dock in two weeks to make sure we comply," replied Pedro.

"Are you fucking kidding me?" said Roberto loudly.

"I wish I was," said Pedro.

"The old motor isn't going to get us to Florida, Pedro. You know that," said Roberto, slightly panicked.

"I'm aware of that, Roberto," replied Pedro.

As they made the turn into the lagoon, Pedro could see the tide had gone out and there was only enough water to make it to the outer end of the main pier in the center of the creek.

"We'll tie up here and I can move her back to my finger pier when the tide comes in. I want to get the fish on ice," said Pedro, as he threw out the stern anchor. "I'll get the fish, Roberto, if you can grab the cooler. There is a large chest with ice, in the shed beside the cabana. We can put the fish in there and I'll clean them later."

Pedro, along with several of the other fishermen in Cojimar had built a small ramshackle building next to the cabana under the shade of a large almond tree, where they kept their fishing tackle and where they would store their catch on ice before selling it.

After Pedro had finished emptying the boat and had put away all the tackle he came out of the shed carrying a plastic bag with three bottles of beer he had put in one of the ice chests in the building before they had left the dock that morning.

"I need to sit down," said Pedro as he walked underneath the cabana and sat down in one of the plastic chairs that surrounded a long wooden table. "Here, have one. They're ice cold."

"Maura, you having one?" asked Roberto.

"What I'd like is an explanation for what happened with those guys on the Coast Guard boat. And yes, I'll take a beer," she said, sitting down at one end of the table.

"Something happened when I was in the wheelhouse?" asked Pedro.

"You could have gotten us arrested, Roberto. What the hell were you thinking?" asked Maura.

Roberto took the wallet out of his left rear pocket and showed Pedro his Secret Service badge.

"And?" asked Pedro.

"You know the three guys standing on the bow? Well they were pricks, and were rude to Maura. So I told them I worked for Fidel, at Punto Cero, and I showed them my old badge. I figured that would shut them up," said Roberto.

"What did they say?" asked Pedro.

"Nothing. It shut them up," he replied.

Roberto leaned forward in his chair and pressed the lip of the top to the beer bottle at a slight angle against the edge of the tabletop, then hit the top of the bottle with his right hand. After popping the top off, he leaned back hard in his chair and drank half the bottle before stopping.

"I wish you wouldn't take chances with my liberty, Roberto," said Maura.

"You asked me to do something. So I did," he replied.

"That is not exactly what I had in mind," she said.

"What are you going to do, Pedrito, about the motor?" asked Roberto.

"I'm going to put the old one back in. I have no choice," he said.

"But the old motor will never take us across the Straits," replied Roberto.

"Look, we know the new motor runs good. I'll put the old one back in, and just before we plan to leave, I put the new one back in and we go. It's not like the Coast Guard will be coming to Cojimar every few days to inspect the boat. I realize it's a lot of work but I either do what they say or they confiscate the La Rosita," said Pedro.

"You still interested in going with us, Maura?" asked Roberto.

"I trust what Pedro says, so yes, I'm still going," she said.

"Pedrito, you know I don't know much about boat motors, but I would be happy to help in any way," said Roberto.

"I have two guys who helped me install the new motor and I will have to pay them again. You can help pay expenses," said Pedro.

"I can do that," said Roberto.

"Pedro, may we have some fish to take home?" asked Maura.

"I'll clean some for you now. How much do you want?" he asked.

"Half of what is left of the big one will be plenty, Pedrito," said Roberto. "If you steak the fillet, I can butterfly them before cooking."

Pedro went to the shed and took the half fish they managed to save from the tiger shark out of the ice chest and laid it in the buggy headfirst along with a machete for cleaning and a large bucket to put the meat in.

"There's plenty meat left here," said Pedro.

"May I watch?" asked Maura.

"Of course," said Pedro.

"I'm staying here in the cool," said Roberto.

When Pedro finished filleting the wahoo he cut the skinless fillets into the size pieces Roberto had requested which filled the twenty-liter bucket to the top.

"We would have had more than two buckets full if the shark hadn't taken the rest," said Pedro to Maura as they walked back up the pier to the cabana.

"Do you see many tiger sharks when you are fishing?" she asked.

"Not many. Tigers are not common. Mostly we see *el tiburon toro*. The bull shark is the dangerous one." he said. "You must see sharks sometimes when you are swimming."

"I never swim outside the reef so if I see one it's always a small one," she replied.

"Roberto. What do you think?" asked Pedro, as he ducked underneath the cabana and held the bucket in front of Roberto for him to see.

"*Bonito*! What I think is we are the luckiest damn fishermen in Cuba.

I haven't tasted wahoo in many years. We'll eat well tonight, Maura. Like kings," he said.

"You mean queens," she replied.

"We should be going, Maura. Pedro, you let me know what happens with the Coast Guard.

"I will. We need to start planning," he said. "It's going to be tricky, even if we leave at night. These bastards are always patrolling."

"Another reason to have as few people involved as possible," said Roberto. "I don't like being responsible for other people's lives."

"Pedrito, *hasta la proxima vez*," said Roberto. "You be careful."

It was growing dark when they left to drive back to Santos Suarez. Stopping on the outskirts of Havana—when a squall of rain forced them to put the top up on the MG— Roberto noticed a car that had been following them since they left Cojimar, had also stopped several blocks away.

"Maura, don't turn around," said Roberto as he got back in the car.

"What?!" she exclaimed, looking in the side view mirror.

"See that black Chevy? They've been following us since we left Cojimar," he said.

"It's probably someone from the CDR. I'm telling you Roberto, this car is like catnip to those guys," she said. "Please don't do anything stupid with me in the car."

"I think I'll make a few extra turns and see what they do," he said.

When they reached the Nuestra Senor de la Caridad, Roberto turned right and headed toward the Tunel de la Habana and around the harbor in the direction of Old Havana. If the men in the car didn't know where he and Maura were living, and continued following them, there was a chance he could lose them in one of the back streets of the old city and at least make it back home where he could hide the car in the alley behind their apartment.

"They turned off. Damn it!" he said.

"Roberto, let's just go home," said Maura frantically. She had seen many times in her old neighborhood how the government informants from the Comites de Defensa de la Revolucion operated and knew they had no chance of escaping.

"Let me see what happens when we get to the Castillo. If they are still following us when we get there, I'll turn around at the Gomez Monument and head back to Santos Suarez," he said. "Shit, they're coming up beside us."

"You need to pull over, Roberto," said Maura loudly.

"All right, all right. I'll pull over,' he replied.

They had just passed the Brazilian Embassy on the Tunel de la Habana, when Roberto slowed the car and turned off the road into a small roadside parking lot beside the harbor and waited for the car that was following them to pull up behind them.

"Whatever you do, don't show them that SS badge," said Maura.

"I'm giving it to you in case they arrest me. Here, hide it somewhere. Quickly," he said. "I'm getting out."

Roberto opened the door and stepped out of the car, closed the door, and waited for the officers to approach.

"CDR, you're under arrest. Turn around and put your hands on top of the car," said the officer.

"What the hell for?" asked Roberto.

"Do as you're told!" barked the officer.

The two assisting officers had drawn their guns and walked to a position at either end of the car. Roberto turned around and looked through the open window at Maura, before putting his hands on the roof.

"Put your hands behind your back," said the officer sharply.

"Can you tell me why I am being arrested?" asked Roberto.

"Where do you keep the money?" asked the officer.

"What are you talking about, I don't have any money," replied Roberto.

"Then how did you pay for this car? I see your girlfriend has nice clothes. They're not cheap," said the officer looking through the window at Maura. "You need to tell us where you hide the money."

"I told you I don't have any money. The car is my father's. He lets me drive it," said Roberto.

"Get out of the car, and stand over there," he said to Maura, pointing to the seawall beside the parking lot. "Search the car."

The arresting officer led Roberto over to where Maura was sitting and ordered him to sit down, then waited for the two other officers to search the car.

When the two officers were finished, one of them held the plastic bag containing the wahoo up for the officer in charge to see. "There's nothing sir. Only some fish," said one of the officers.

"Put the fish in the other car," said the officer in charge.

"You normally make it a habit of stealing from ordinary citizens?" asked Roberto.

"Shut up, Ramos!" said the officer.

"How do you know my name?" he asked.

"We know everything about you," he said. "Put him in the car."

"Where are you taking him?" asked Maura loudly.

"El Combinado del Este," he replied.

"What about me?" she asked.

"You're free to go. Someone will come tomorrow for the car. You make sure it's available, unless you'd like to join your boyfriend in prison," the officer said.

"I told you, it's my father's car," said Roberto from inside the car.

"He'll have to take that up with the government," said the officer as he opened the passenger side door.

"What a fucking government," said Roberto under his breath.

"What did you say?" yelled the officer looking at Roberto from outside the car looking through the rear window. "*Vamos.*"

"Roberto, I will tell your mother and father what happened," said Maura, walking beside the car as it started toward the exit of the parking lot back onto the Tunel de la Habana.

"Tell my mother I love her," were the last words he yelled to Maura through the car window before they sped off in the direction of the prison.

XXI

The notorious Combinado del Este prison was the largest detention facility in the country, housing over five thousand prisoners. Many of whom while starving during the so called, "special period," and after being caught stealing food, were sentenced to multiple years behind bars. Roberto had friends who were or had been incarcerated there and he heard many stories about the treatment they had received while imprisoned. The damp, rodent infested, mildew covered cells were small and often overcrowded, with as many as eight men to a cell.

Roberto knew firsthand how cruel the government could be and remembered how he had suffered when he was in DTI. He knew also it would take more than that to break him and that he had much to live for and was prepared to suffer once again if it meant he would one day have a life of freedom.

When they arrived at the prison Roberto was taken to building number one at the western end of the sprawling complex where political prisoners and criminals considered to be a security risk were taken to await a hearing, which in many cases meant they had to wait for a year or more before their case was heard.

At all hours of the day and night it was a loud place. The constant noise from the prisoners yelling could be heard echoing throughout the concrete and steel structure.

That night, Roberto was placed in a small cell with three other men. One of them had been in prison several years, having also been arrested for allegedly engaging in black-market activities and having a lifestyle that "exceeded state limits." He was the only one of the three who had previously been in prison. Roberto could tell by the look on the faces of the first timers—who had been there less than one year—they were on the verge of being broken.

One of the prisoners appeared to be no more than sixteen or seventeen years old. He was small and frail looking and had not spoken since Roberto had been placed in the cell. Roberto wanted to know why.

"What is your name?" asked Roberto of the boy.

The boy looked at him but did not speak. He sat in one corner of the cell with his legs drawn up to his chest and his arms wrapped tightly across his shins. He had on a tattered tank top and a pair of shorts that were several sizes too large. The homemade flip-flops he was wearing were paper thin and no longer large enough to protect his heals.

"I understand your fear," said Roberto. "This is the third time now the government has put me in jail."

The boy lifted his head from his knees and looked directly into Roberto's eyes.

"The first time was for nearly killing my commanding officer. Honestly I'm surprised I made it out alive," said Roberto.

"You're not going to hurt me, are you?" asked the boy.

"Of course not," said Roberto smiling.

"What happened with your commanding officer?" asked the boy.

"He threatened me, and I warned him not to do it again," said Roberto.

"And then what happened?" the boy asked.

"He became enraged and slapped me with the palm of his hand across my face. He was a big guy, much bigger than me and he almost knocked me over. I should tell you I was a national champion in Karate and Taekwondo and wasn't about to be intimidated by the guy. Anyway I lost control, my training instincts took over and I put him in the hospital. They arrested me and I was taken to DTI and then to Censam Marin. Altogether I've been in jail for something like three years. It could have been a lot worse. Oh, and they tried to kill me the second time I was in jail. Didn't end well for those guys either," said Roberto.

"And today. Why were you arrested?" asked the boy.

"For having a nice car," laughed Roberto. "What about you? Why were you arrested?"

"I was arrested for assaulting a police officer. I mean look at me, I could never be a threat to anyone," said the boy. "I had been stealing mangos from a local farmer. I have no family, and I was hungry. I pleaded with the farmer not to turn me in. I think he may have been working for the CDR."

"Where is your family?" asked Roberto.

"My father was killed in Angola and my mother married another man who was violent. So I decided to take my chances on the street," he said.

"What is your name?" Roberto asked.

"My name is Yoel. And you, what is your name?" the boy asked.

"Roberto. Roberto Ramos. As long as we're in the same cell I won't let anyone harm you," he said.

The boy reached out with his right hand in the direction of Roberto. "Thank you. There is little kindness in here," he said.

By morning the cell was cold. Roberto and Yoel slept back to back, leaning against one of the end walls and one another in an attempt to keep warm.

An hour after sunrise two guards appeared at the door to the cell carrying four small bottles of water they claimed was for drinking along with four steel cups, each half full of sugar.

Roberto was hungry and hadn't eaten anything since the morning of the day before. He took the water bottles one at a time from the guards and handed one to each of the other three prisoners, then took the four cups of sugar.

"What about something to eat?" he asked the guards.

"I just gave it to you," said one of the guards who seemed annoyed with the question.

"You have to be joking. Sugar? They gave me more than this at DTI," said Roberto loudly.

"Then maybe you should have stayed there," said the guard who then turned and went on to the next cell.

"Roberto, I wouldn't do that if I were you. They've beaten me for saying less," said the man who had been imprisoned the longest and whose name was Francisco.

"I'm not afraid of them," said Roberto.

"I realize that, but you can't fight the entire Cuban army," replied Francisco.

"They only feed you sugar in the morning? You can't survive on this. The water looks pretty bad also," said Roberto.

"It's typical. Sometimes you get sick when you drink it. But if you complain too much, you get nothing," said Yoel.

"What about in the evening? What do they feed you?" asked Roberto.

"Mostly rice and beans," said Francisco. "You have to be careful though because you never know what they put in it. Sometimes we find roaches."

"I understand. I saw it all at DTI. I'll deal with it. Do they let you exercise or have family visits?" asked Roberto.

"It depends on your behavior. If you don't piss off the guards, maybe every two months you can see your family, and then only three family members at a time," answered Francisco.

"Do they allow conjugal visits?" asked Roberto.

"Yes, but I wouldn't recommend it," replied Francisco.

"Why not?"

"Because sometimes they'll strip search your girlfriend before they allow her in. Especially if she's attractive," Francisco explained. "Is she attractive?"

"Very."

"Then tell her not to come if you can stand it."

"Have any of you had a hearing?" asked Roberto.

"No, none of us," said Yoel. "When you ask, they just keep telling you 'soon.'"

"Have you seen a lawyer?" asked Roberto.

"A lawyer? That's a joke," said Francisco.

Roberto sat back on the sagging canvas cot that was black with mildew and leaned against the cold concrete wall. He could not still his mind and he was beginning to fear the worst. His plan had been a good one and it had all been working.

They had planned to leave from Cojimar by the end of the year, soon after Pedro would have replaced the new motor with the old one as demanded by the Coast Guard.

Everything was now in doubt. Roberto had his doubts also about Pedro, who had a family to consider. How long was Pedro willing to wait before attempting to escape, not knowing if or how long it would be before Roberto would be released from prison.

And then there was Maura and his brother Lazaro who were depending heavily on him. If it was up to Pedro, he thought, perhaps Pedro would decide not to let them go. After all the boat was small and the more people wanting to leave the more complicated and potentially dangerous the trip would be. They were all desperate.

Roberto knew the government's evidence provided by the neighborhood CDR snitch was little more than hearsay and was certain he could convince a judge of his innocence if only he could have a hearing.

Roberto's cell was on the second floor and had a direct view across a narrow hallway through the heavy vertical concrete slated ventilation wall overlooking one of the prison exercise yards. He noticed that most of the prisoners when released into the yard simply sat in the shade of one of the concrete walls that surrounded the yard.

He thought back to his time in DTI and how important it had been to his survival to maintain at least a minimum level of physical fitness and wondered why so few of the prisoners took advantage of their time in the exercise yard.

"Francisco. The men in the yard. Why do they spend their time just sitting? They have no interest in exercising?" asked Roberto. He thought, of the three men in his cell, Francisco had been here the longest and would know better the daily prison routines.

"Most of them have only ever known baseball and soccer. They know nothing about physical training. Most of them are just happy to be outside. So they sit," he replied.

"How often are you allowed onto the yard?" asked Roberto.

"Every day unless the weather is bad," said Francisco. "The guards should be coming soon to take us there."

"Roberto, maybe you can train us in martial arts," said Yoel.

"For sure. I don't plan on sitting when it's my turn in the yard. But we could have a problem with the guards," said Roberto.

"Can we begin today?" asked Yoel.

"Absolutely," replied Roberto. "Francisco, are you interested?"

"I'm not much of an athlete, and I'm in poor shape after being here for three years and doing nothing," he said.

"We'll start slow. It's a process. It takes a long time to master. One thing we have plenty of is time," said Roberto with a smile.

When the time came later that day to go out onto the exercise yard, Roberto had already given Yoel, Francisco, and the other man in the cell whose name was Benito, a brief lesson in the ten basic movements in Taekwondo.

Of the three men, Benito showed the most promise. He was not too tall and had a naturally powerful body with a low center of gravity, perfectly built for martial arts. He reminded Roberto of his former commander, Colonel Charon. He was a muscled pocket version of Charon. The biggest difference though, was Benito had a quiet and pleasant personality. He seemed disciplined and steady.

As the new guy in the cell block, Roberto immediately drew the attention of several of the other inmates as he made his way onto the exercise yard with the three men from his cell.

"I want to go to the other end of the yard, where there is some shade, by the wall," said Roberto to his cell mates. "We can train there."

Out of the corner of his eye Roberto could see two other inmates approaching as he made his way across the yard. Choosing not to make eye contact he continued walking toward the far end of the enclosure.

"Excuse me," said the bigger of the men as they approached. "Where are you going?"

Roberto stopped, turned in the direction of the two men and faced them head on. "We are going to train," responded Roberto.

Benito stepped in front of Roberto and pointed at the two men. "I wouldn't recommend it if I were you, Renier," said Benito.

"Yeah, and why is that?" said the man crossing his arms in an effort to make himself look larger.

"It's okay, Benito. Come on," said Roberto.

Benito hesitated briefly, looked at Roberto then continued walking toward the wall at the far end of the yard. Letting Benito go ahead, Roberto paused, looked at the man, and then turned to join the others.

When Roberto heard the sound made by the sudden movement of the man's feet on the loose gravel covering the dirt yard, he knew it could only mean one thing. Having noticed the way in which the man had crossed his arms, Roberto knew he was likely right-handed and would come at him leading with his left, leaving that side vulnerable to a counterattack.

Roberto made one quick step to his left, then pivoted on his left foot, raised his right knee, and landed a solid roundhouse kick to the backside of Renier's torso. The power from the blow sent him face first onto the ground, knocking the wind out of him.

Roberto's cell mates hearing the sound made by the blow to Renier's ribs and then the sound of his body hitting the ground, wheeled around and rushed toward Renier, expecting to help Roberto should Renier come at him again.

"No," yelled Roberto. "Leave him alone."

"I should have warned you," said Benito.

"You probably should have warned him," said Roberto pointing to Renier who had rolled over onto his back and was gasping uncontrollably, having had the wind knocked out of him.

"I did," said Benito.

Roberto walked over to Renier who was beginning to breathe easier and slower and with increasing regularity. He knew he could have seriously injured Renier and even killed him. It was his intention not to.

"Where did you learn to do that?" Renier asked, coughing slightly and still lying on his back.

"I trained with the top two Taekwondo teachers in the world from Korea for three years," replied Roberto. "I was national champion in Taekwondo and Karate multiple years."

"Well, you were a good student," said Renier. "You're strong for someone who is not very big."

Roberto leaned over and offered his hand, helping Renier to his feet. "It's not about superior size. You're bigger than me and much stronger but you don't know how to control your strength," said Roberto.

"You could have seriously hurt me. Why didn't you?" asked Renier.

"Because the situation didn't require it. Without self-control I lose control of the situation. Besides, I don't know you and have nothing against you. To be good at Taekwondo, you need to have a conscience and understand the limits of your ability," said Roberto.

The altercation had attracted the attention of several guards who were now walking toward the group of men who had gathered around Roberto and Renier.

"What's the problem here," yelled one of the guards as they approached.

"No problem," said Renier as he stepped between the guards and the other men.

"Renier, you know the consequences of fighting. Perhaps you should explain that to your new friend," said the guard.

Roberto stepped beside Renier. "This is a Taekwondo training class," said Roberto to the guard.

"And who authorized you?" asked the guard.

"No one. But I know the prison rules and there is no rule that says Taekwondo training is prohibited," replied Roberto. "Look around. Most of these guys, they just sit here and do nothing. This gives them something positive and constructive to look forward to each day."

"I doubt the warden would appreciate you teaching martial arts skills to prisoners. I suggest you find something else to do," said the guard.

"On the contrary I believe he would see the value in it. In the Taekwondo oath one commits to building a more peaceful world, where students learn respect for authority," said Roberto. He could see his words were having an effect on the two guards and continued. "They learn self-control and humility. How could that be a bad thing? Maybe you could speak to the warden."

"What is your name?" asked one the guards.

"Roberto Ramos," replied Roberto.

"What makes you think you're qualified to conduct Taekwondo training?" asked the guard.

"I was national champion several years running. Taekwondo and Karate. I trained Comandante's son, Antonio. I trained also with the Comandante's personal assistant, Juan Sanchez while I worked at Punto Cero," said Roberto.

"Come with us, Ramos. The Colonel Soto will make the decision," said the guard.

"He should be handcuffed," said the other guard.

They left the exercise yard, one guard in front of Roberto and one behind. The warden's office was in a separate building, several hundred yards from building number one, near the main entrance to the prison complex.

"Ramos, I suggest you speak only when you are asked a question by the warden. He is intolerant of prisoners who think for themselves.

Understand?" asked one of the guards upon entering the building.

"Understood," said Roberto.

Roberto waited in the hallway outside the warden's office, watched by several guards deployed within the building, while one of the guards from the yard went in the office to speak with the warden. It all felt very familiar to him, and he wasn't nervous.

"Ramos," barked the first guard. "The warden will see you."

"Ramos," said the warden upon seeing Roberto. "Take his handcuffs off, guard. Have a seat, Ramos. I understand you're claiming to have been a national martial arts champion and were deployed at Punto Cero. Is this true?" asked the warden.

"Yes sir, it is all true. I trained with the assistant to El Lider Maximo, Juan Sanchez. I also trained Comandante's son, Antonio."

"What happened to your military career?" asked the warden.

"I was arrested for possessing American dollars," said Roberto. "It was a foolish mistake."

The warden leaned back in his chair, puffing slowly on his freshly lit cigar. "You believe in the revolution?" asked the warden after blowing the smoke from the cigar to the side.

Roberto hesitated then moved to a position on the edge of his chair. "Sir, I am not a political person. I am a Cuban trying to survive, like all of us. I'm not interested in causing trouble for you or the men who work for you," he said.

Roberto continued talking in an attempt to distract the warden's attention away from the fact that he had not directly answered the warden's question. "The political people—I believe you call them 'intransigents'—I can assure you, I am not one of them." Roberto sat back in his chair, trying to appear relaxed, and waited for the warden's response.

"You're an interesting young man, Ramos. What else can you tell me about yourself?" he asked.

"Not too much, sir. I would say I love my family, I love to fish, and I have a nice girlfriend," said Roberto. He knew any mention of his love of art or his modest collection of paintings would be dangerous and would certainly lead to a long prison sentence.

"Ramos, you're in building number one. Many of your fellow prisoners there are dangerous. You think it's a good idea to teach them martial arts. Why?" asked the warden.

"I can teach them discipline and respect for authority," said Roberto.

"Go on," said Soto.

"I believe if the men have something to look forward to each day they will be less likely to cause problems for you. In the principles of Taekwondo, the first things you learn are humility and self-control. They would be less likely to fight among themselves," said Roberto.

"What happens if one of the prisoners uses what you have taught them and decides to experiment, shall we say, on one of my guards?" Soto asked.

"They will never train with me again and they suffer the consequences," replied Roberto.

"Ramos, I'll tell you what I'm going to do. I'll give you a month. If after a month there have been no problems, you can continue," said the Colonel.

"I can assure you Colonel Soto I will not tolerate any *mierda*. You have my word. One question."

"What is that?"

"When do I get a hearing?"

"What are you charged with, Ramos?"

"Lifestyle exceeding state limits."

"Are you guilty?"

"No sir. The CDR thinks I have money because I drive my father's old MG sports car. I have no car and he lets me use it," said Roberto.

"You'll have to wait your turn with the judge. We'll speak again in a month," said Soto. The Colonel stood up and held out his hand. "We have a deal then."

Roberto stood up and shook the Colonel's hand. "Yes, we have a deal," he said.

"The guards will take you back to your cell," said the warden, gesturing to the guard to handcuff Roberto.

The warden sat down and relit his cigar, drawing slowly on the cigar until the end was glowing red. "Don't disappoint me, Ramos," he said looking at the cigar and not Roberto.

"That will never be my intention, sir," said Roberto.

By the time the guards had returned Roberto to building number one his cell mates had been taken back to the cell. While waiting for the evening meal, they had been speculating as to what may have happened to Roberto when he met with the warden and were surprised to see him being led back to the cell.

"Roberto!" exclaimed the boy when he saw him standing in front of the cell. "We were worried. What happened?"

Roberto waited until the guards had let him back into the cell, locked the door and had left the cell block before answering.

"I had a little chat with Colonel Soto, and he agreed to let me conduct the training for one month. If it goes well, he'll let us continue," he said.

"What's he like?" asked Francisco.

"Oh, you know, cagey, just like you would expect. Dresses like Fidel, smokes expensive cigars and looks like he hasn't missed many meals lately," replied Roberto.

"You think he'll keep his word? asked Benito.

"I think so, but we'll see. We'll start tomorrow," said Roberto.

"You impressed Renier, I can tell you that," said Benito. "He wants to train with us."

"He's a natural athlete, but he needs discipline," said Roberto. "What's his story anyway?"

"I've heard rumors, but honestly, I don't know. He has a temper," Benito said.

"I had the same problem. It's a useless emotion to have if you want to live in Cuba," said Roberto. "You're permitted to have a temper only if your name is Fidel."

"After the guards took you to see the warden, many of the other men in the yard were asking about you," said Benito.

"What did they want to know? asked Roberto.

"They want to train with you," replied Benito. "You're a celebrity now," he laughed.

"I'll train anyone who is serious and committed to being disciplined. If they cause trouble, they're out," responded Roberto.

"I believe after seeing how you handled Renier, they have no intention of causing any trouble," said Yoel.

"The guards are coming," said Yoel. "Time for some of that good Combinado home cooking. You must be hungry, Roberto?"

"They feed us in the canteen in the evening?" asked Roberto.

"Remember what I said this morning," said Francisco.

"What was that?" Roberto asked.

"Check the *congri* for cockroaches before you eat it," he said with a wry smile.

XXII

In the weeks that followed Roberto successfully established a regular training routine for anyone in building number one who was interested in participating, with the exception of the political prisoners held in solitary confinement, who were never permitted time outdoors or to exercise.

For his efforts, Roberto slowly began to gain the respect of the warden and many of the guards. The daily training routine however—which would sometimes last for hours in the hot sun, and when the wind was blowing, made worse by the choking dust stirred up from the exercise yard—was beginning to take a toll physically.

Knowing it could be months before being granted a hearing and possible release, he knew the debilitating physical effects from the lack of food would be a danger to his health, and so one day boldly made a demand for increased food rations. To his surprise and good fortune, the request was personally granted by the warden.

Roberto's cell mates never thought to hold this against him, and he was grateful for their understanding and shared the extra food with them as much as he could. The quality of the food was better also and when they were in a particularly good mood, the guards would sometimes bring Roberto chicken or fish.

It was almost two months before Roberto received a visit from anyone. It was his brothers, Lazaro and Pedro, who had come. They had been trying for many weeks to arrange a visit ever since Roberto had been arrested. His mother and brother Carlos were reluctant to come to Combinado del Este, having heard too many horror stories about the treatment received by family members of inmates.

The visiting room was long and narrow with wooden tables bordered on both sides by concrete benches. It was there, after going through multiple security checkpoints, that the two brothers, sitting opposite Roberto, were able to talk with their brother. Visitation was always no more and no less than two and a half hours.

Several guards patrolled the room eavesdropping on conversations and ogling the wives and girlfriends who came to visit and had braved the security checks, which often included humiliating same sex strip searches. Roberto was relieved that Maura had not come with his brothers.

"How is Mother?" asked Roberto first.

"She is worried, as always," replied Lazaro. "She doesn't understand why you are always the one going to prison."

"I take more risks I suppose," said Roberto. "How is Maura?"

"She is worried also, but she is young and can handle the stress better," answered Lazaro.

"And Pedro, how are you?" asked Roberto.

"Struggling and sick of life, like everyone now," he said. "Roberto, Lazaro has told me about the boat and your plan."

"That's a little uncertain. At least for now," said Roberto.

"I want to go with you," said Pedro.

"That would make eight now assuming I ever get out of here. I don't know if the boat is safe with that many people. Have you been to Cojimar to see the boat? Have you spoken with Pedrito?" asked Roberto. He knew all too well the look of desperation in his brother's eyes.

"We went to Cojimar last week to see Pedrito. He said he switched the motor and that the Coast Guard had come to check," said Pedro. "He said everything was fine with the Coast Guard and he would take his chances and put the more powerful motor back in just before leaving."

"The guard is coming. I know him, but wait until he passes," said Roberto.

"Pedrito is worried, Roberto," said Lazaro after the guard had passed.

"About what? He's not the one who is in prison," said Roberto. He was becoming suspicious.

"He's worried you may be in prison for several years. He said he has known of people imprisoned here who have waited for years to get a hearing, much less a trial," said Lazaro.

"I have a good relationship with the warden and the guards. I don't think it will be much longer," said Roberto.

"But what if they sentence you to several years?" asked Pedro.

"That isn't going to happen. They have no evidence," said Roberto.

"Pedrito says he wants to leave soon, that he doesn't want to wait," said Lazaro, then waited nervously for Roberto's response.

"What do you mean he doesn't want to wait? He can't do that to me," said Roberto trying not to raise his voice and attract the attention of the guards. "Besides, he has no connections in Florida."

"He says he doesn't care what happens when he gets to Florida. That he just wants the hell out of Cuba," said Lazaro.

"You have to convince him to wait, Lazaro. I have more invested in this than anyone. It's not fair. What does Maura say?" he asked.

"She doesn't want to leave without you," replied Lazaro.

"Ask her to talk to Pedrito. Jesus, I can't believe this is happening," said Roberto.

"I'll go to Cojimar with Maura and talk to him," promised Lazaro.

"You're allowed to visit again in three weeks. Ask Pedrito to come with you. I want to talk with him directly," said Roberto.

"You want Maura to come?" asked Lazaro.

"No. I don't want her inside this shit hole," said Roberto.

"Time's up, Ramos," said one of the guards loudly as he walked past the table where they were sitting.

"You have to tell Pedrito not to leave without me Lazaro," whispered Roberto. "This is my only chance."

With that Lazaro and Pedro stood up from the table, said goodbye to Roberto and were escorted out of the visitation room to the prison exit. Roberto was returned to his cell. He had little to say to the others who wanted to know how the visit went with Roberto's brothers and if there was any news from the outside.

Roberto explained that the visit with his brothers had not gone well, and he was not in a mood to talk and apologized to the others for it, explaining that he needed some time to think.

It was evening and a heavy, slow-moving thunderstorm had settled in over the Combinado del Este prison complex, breaking the heat and bringing some relief to the prisoners who were now in their cells for the night. The cells on the lowest level, where even a strong breeze was never felt, were always hot, even at night, except in winter when the wind came from the sea and it was cold, and then they were always cold. The men in these cells suffered the most. Roberto remembered when he was in solitary confinement how the cold had made it impossible to sleep for many days and nights.

By the middle of the night Roberto had not slept and had memorized every crack in the leaky, crumbling, concrete ceiling. The frustration he felt from being trapped in a situation that was out of his control was building, and he was becoming angry. His relationship with the guards and the warden was a good one, he thought, and would eventually work in his favor, but how long would it be before he was released and would Pedro and the others wait for him?

XXIII

As the months passed, Pedrito, along with Lazaro and Roberto's brother Pedro, had been regular visitors at Combinado del Este. During these visits, Roberto had, over time managed to convince Pedrito not to leave Cuba without him, by promising to help him financially once they arrived in Florida. Roberto knew Maura's family in Miami was well off and would have connections and perhaps Pedrito, whom Roberto knew to be a great fisherman, could work in the seafood business supplying fresh fish to the best restaurants in the city.

His plan when the time came to leave Cuba, was to take as many paintings as possible with him, stored safely in the ceiling of the small wheelhouse of the La Rosita. Once he arrived in Florida, and was released from U.S. Immigration, thought Roberto, he could then sell them to wealthy expats living in Miami or connect with a gallery that would have many customers. The paintings, if they were the right ones and good ones, would easily sell themselves once people heard the story of their journey.

A whole year had passed, and Roberto was still waiting for word from the warden when he would be granted a hearing with the judge assigned to Combinado del Este.

Yoel, the boy, had been released several weeks earlier and there had been others whom Roberto had known from his Taekwondo training that had also been released after having a hearing with the prison judge.

There was speculation among the prisoners that the worsening economic conditions in Cuba were making it difficult for the government to afford the increasing cost of imprisoning so many of its citizens.

The quality of the food in recent months had begun to deteriorate further and although Roberto had enjoyed special meal privileges, he was losing weight and constantly battling skin infections brought on by the damp and filthy living conditions. Unless you were near death, and not always then, would you be allowed to see a doctor.

When the guards came that evening it was a surprise as they never came in the evening after the prisoners had been locked in their cells for the night. There were two of them and they had a relaxed look about them which they rarely had because the job of working in the prison, especially for the guards in building number one where the most dangerous criminals were housed, was a miserable and dangerous one.

"Ramos, get your things together," said one of the guards as the other unlocked the door to the cell. His tone of voice was upbeat and it surprised Roberto.

"Where are you taking me?" he asked.

"The judge is going to hear your case," said one of the guards. "Bring your things."

"Francisco, Benito, whatever happens, know that I will never forget you. God bless you," said Roberto, who quickly gathered his few possessions, putting them in a burlap sack given to him by one of the guards.

The guards then escorted Roberto to a small building near the entrance to the prison complex housing the courtroom where the cases were heard for all prisoners awaiting pretrial hearings except those being held for crimes against the government. These men, unless they reaffirmed their commitment to the revolution and allegiance to Fidel, were condemned to a life of unimaginable misery, suffering, and eventually death, inside Combinado del Este prison.

The courtroom, which could hardly be described as a courtroom, was small, and dimly lit, with a single long table at one end where the judge was sitting when Roberto arrived with the guards, and there were no lawyers present.

The judge was sitting on one side of the table wearing green army fatigues and the trademark Cuban military hat made famous by Fidel, and did not look up when Roberto was led into the room.

He was short, middle aged and overweight. His prosperous appearance was no doubt the result of a favorable rating from his superiors, which meant that he was tough. He did not immediately speak to Roberto and was reading from a black notebook laying on the table in front of him.

The guards led Roberto to a place directly in front of the table opposite where the judge was seated and instructed him to remain silent and wait for the judge to address him and to answer all of questions the judge asked.

When the judge had finished reading from the notebook he sat back in his chair and looked up at Roberto.

"You are, Roberto Ramos?" asked the judge.

"Yes sir, I am," he replied.

"According to this report, Mr. Ramos you were arrested for having a lifestyle that exceeded state limits supported by black-market activities," said the Judge. "Is that true?"

"No sir, it is not," asserted Roberto.

"Why were you arrested then if that is not the case?" asked the judge.

"I believe because at the time I was driving a car the CDR thought I could not afford based on my state salary," said Roberto. "But I was not the owner of the car."

"Who was the owner?" asked the judge.

"My father is the owner. They would have realized that if they had checked the registration, but they didn't. They kept asking me where I kept all the money. I told them, I don't have any money. They kept saying I was lying and that's when I was taken into custody and brought here," said Roberto.

"So am I to understand that you are telling me you were arrested simply for driving your father's car and that there is no evidence you are involved in *actividades del mercado negro*?" asked the judge.

"Yes sir, that is what happened, Your Honor," he replied, looking directly at the judge, not wanting to break eye contact.

The judge looked down again at the notebook without saying anything. Roberto could feel his heart rate increasing. He waited for the judge to say something. Trying to stay calm he kept his eyes on the judge. With every breath he noticed more the pounding, pulsing feeling from the blood running through the veins in his temples and he tried to relax. Finally the judge closed the notebook, looked up at Roberto, and stood up from the table.

"Ramos, based on the lack of evidence presented to me as well as your record of good behavior while in prison, I see no reason for you to be detained any longer. You're free to go," said the judge.

"Thank you, Your Honor," replied Roberto in disbelief.

"Where does your family live?" asked the judge.

"In Santos Suarez, Your Honor," he replied.

"Well you better get going. It's a long walk to Santos Suarez," the judge said. He handed Roberto an envelope and motioned toward the door, "Keep this paper on you at all times in case you are stopped by the police or anyone from the CDR. Your ID card they took from you when you were processed after your arrest, is in the envelope. The guards will take you to security at the main gate."

"Yes sir," said Roberto. The guards who had brought Roberto to see the judge, and had been waiting in the back of the room for the judge to make a decision, came forward and walked Roberto outside the building. They then took him to the main security check point where he was officially cleared for release and set free.

Roberto walked through security out onto the entrance road that led to the main highway and did not make eye contact with any of the guards who were stationed at the gate.

Still in disbelief at the sudden and unexpected turn of events, he wasn't taking any chances and did not turn around as he walked. Finally after walking several hundred meters he stopped where the road made a slight bend to the right and looked back in the direction of the prison.

It was early December and the first of the winter cold fronts had arrived and settled in over the northern half of the island. The sky was cloudless, and the air was dry and pleasant and wonderfully cool. A young waxing moon rose clear above the prison.

He knew he had a long walk to his parents house but didn't care and was happy to be anywhere outside of the prison. Roberto stood motionless on the side of the road looking in the direction of the prison and thought about Francisco and Benito and tried to imagine how they must be feeling not knowing what had happened to him and he wondered what would become of them.

As he turned around to continue walking, he noticed a pair of tocororos flying just above the treetops along the edge of the road to his right and remembered the time he had first seen them from the window when he was in the hospital at Censam Marin and then again at Anabela's in the garden and that she told him the name of the bird and how if you saw one they would bring good luck.

He began to feel excited as he walked and realized he hadn't felt excited about anything since being arrested and he thought about his paintings and of Maura and of the boat in Cojimar and about his plan to leave Cuba.

When he arrived in el barrio de Santos Suarez, it was dark and he was very hungry but not tired because he was looking forward to seeing his parents and for news about Maura, whom he had not seen in more than one year.

Turning the corner onto the street where his parents lived, he could see at a distance in the low light, the silhouette of his MG parked in front his parents' house.

Stopping for a moment to look at the car before going inside, he knew then he had to sell the car as quickly as possible. It would be easy to sell he thought, remembering that many people had asked if it was for sale. Even if he did not make a profit it would easily provide enough money to buy four or five more high-quality paintings to add to the ten he already had.

He walked up the steps and stopped on the top step and stared at the front door. It was the third time in five years he had been released from prison. His parents, especially his mother, had always welcomed him home but he knew the second time had been more difficult for them than the first and this time would be no different and probably worse, he thought. He decided not to knock and opened the door and walked in.

There was a single light on in the front room, but the room was empty, and Roberto could hear voices and the faint sound of music coming from the back of the house. One of the voices he thought was Maura's. He quietly shut the door and set the burlap sack with the handful of things from the prison by the door.

When he walked into the kitchen there was no one in the room. There was a radio playing music and everyone was on the terrace. Roberto stepped into the doorway leading to the terrace and stopped.

"*Buenas noches,*" was all he said.

Guillermo and Rosa were sitting on one side of the table opposite Lazaro and Carlos, with Maura seated at the near end facing away from Roberto.

When Maura heard Roberto's voice, she put her face in her hands and began to cry and did not turn around.

Roberto walked over to the table and put his hand on her shoulder.

"*Madre,* if I tell you how sorry I am will it make you feel any better," was all Roberto could think to say. He kept his hand on Maura's shoulder.

"I suppose it never hurts to say it," said Rosa.

Maura stood up and turned around to hug Roberto. She was still crying but not uncontrollably. Then she kissed him and stepped back slightly, folded her arms, and looked at him up and down.

"You look awful, and you smell terrible," she said smiling and wiping the tears from her eyes.

"It's temporary," he said and hugged her again. "May I take a shower, *Madre*?"

"Of course," Rosa answered. "What do you want to eat?"

"Whatever you have, and a little rum if you have some, *Padre*. Carlitos, how is Maykel? You need to tell me all about how the fishing has been when I come back from a shower," said Roberto, trying to sound cheerful.

"When did you find out you would be released," asked Lazaro.

"Today. They never said anything about a hearing. They just took me to see the judge, I explained what happened with the car and that I didn't have any money and he said I was free to go," said Roberto.

"That car has been nothing but trouble," said Guillermo. "You should get rid of it."

"I plan to sell it as soon as possible," said Roberto.

"Go and get a shower. You're disgusting," said Rosa sternly.

When Roberto returned to the terrace everyone's mood was better and Maura was no longer crying and was smiling. Rosa had a steaming hot plate of *platillo moros y cristiano* waiting for him and a tumbler of dark rum.

"*Gracias, Madre.* I forgot what actual food looked like," said Roberto.

"This is the last time, Roberto," said Guillermo.

"What do you mean?" he asked.

"We can't take the stress anymore," said Guillermo.

Roberto took a sip of rum and set the glass back on the table. "I can promise you *Padre*, for certain, I will never go to prison in Cuba again," he said.

Maura and Lazaro both looked at Roberto but said nothing. They had kept the plan to leave Cuba a secret and were caught off guard by Roberto's comment to his father.

"You need to have a normal job," said Rosa.

"It will not be easy for me. With my prison record, who would want to hire me?" asked Roberto.

"Many people who have been in prison find jobs. If that was a reason not to hire someone, then half the people in Cuba couldn't find work," said Rosa.

"The economy is so bad now it will be difficult," said Roberto. "The rice and beans are perfect, mother."

"Where do you plan to live?" asked Rosa.

"I haven't thought about it," replied Roberto.

"It's worse now than before and we don't have the money to feed you," Rosa said.

"I'll catch fish," he said.

"That's not making a living," said Guillermo.

"I realize that but it's something to eat. Jesus, I was just released from prison," said Roberto. He was becoming annoyed and changed the subject. "Maura, what would you like to do tomorrow? Maybe we could go to the beach."

"Roberto, your parents are afraid. You need to consider the feelings of others sometimes. They simply don't want any more trouble. You're so stubborn," she said.

"So what do you want to do tomorrow," he asked, ignoring Maura's comments.

"The weather is nice. Maybe go to the beach in Alamar. There's never anyone there and it's not too hot. We can go swimming," she replied.

"Good, we can see Pedrito on the way. He was loyal and good to me when I was in prison. He didn't have to be and I need to thank him," said Roberto.

"Why are you such good friends with this guy anyway?" asked Rosa. "How do you know him?"

"We were in prison together. He's just a friend, that's all. We enjoy fishing together," said Roberto.

"Well, if you see your friend, ask him for some fish," said Rosa.

"I will. Carlitos, you haven't said anything. How is Maykel?" asked

Roberto.

"I'm sorry I never came to see you in prison," was all Carlos said.

"It's okay. It's not a place you want to go. I'm sure Lazaro and Pedro told you all about it," replied Roberto.

"I haven't seen Maykel for a couple of months. He doesn't fish in the Gulf Stream this time of year. The water is cool and the *dorado* don't arrive until late next month. You should visit him. He's always asking about you," said Carlos.

"We can go together. Maybe next week," said Roberto.

"I should be going, Roberto," said Maura. "*Mima* worries when I am out late."

"You went back to live with your grandmother?" he asked.

"Yes. I couldn't afford to live on my own after you were arrested. Don't worry, I have all of your things at grandmother's," she said.

"I'll go with you," said Roberto. "*Madre*, thank you for *la comida*. I won't be late. I need a good night's sleep. It was always impossible to sleep in prison."

"We'll see you in the morning then. I'm too tired to wait up," said Rosa.

When Roberto returned from the home of Maura's grandmother, his brother Lazaro was waiting for him, alone on the terrace.

"*Hermano,*" said Lazaro to Roberto when he walked out onto the terrace. "Here, sit down, have some rum. We need to talk."

"What are we having?" asked Roberto.

"Santiago de Cuba, *Anejo Superior*. I can't afford much more than that," said Lazaro.

"I'm not going to complain," said Roberto.

"I have been talking to Pedrito quite a bit recently. He's very anxious to leave as you know and things have become a little more complicated," said Lazaro.

"Is there something wrong with the boat?" Roberto asked.

"No, no, nothing like that. The boat is ready to go. The problem is there are other people that want to go with us," he said.

"Who, and how many? It's too small a boat and there are already six of us and Pedrito's two children, which makes eight," said Roberto.

"Six others. You know the doctor, Ernesto? Well he and his wife Alena and his brother Omar and his wife Yamilet. And then there are two friends of Pedrito's, named Armando and Frank. I don't know them. They live in Cojimar. I think they fish," said Lazaro, looking down at the glass on the table, knowing Roberto would not be happy with what he had told him.

"Seriously, that's fourteen people! The boat can't hold that many," said Roberto. "I have to talk to Pedrito."

"He says the boat is big enough. Besides, if we tell them they can't go they may go to the police. They have leverage now and they're just as desperate as we are. Pedrito says it might be good to have a doctor with us in case something happens," said Lazaro.

"Oh yeah, sure. Maybe someone will need surgery in the middle of the ocean," replied Roberto.

"Look Roberto, it's not up to me and it's not my boat. I just want the fuck out of here before everything really turns to shit! Just like you. What am I supposed to do?" asked Lazaro.

"I know, I know. I'm sorry. It's just that when you have so many people everything becomes more complicated. You can't simply load fourteen people in a boat and head north. If the Coast Guard sees more than a few people in a boat, they'll arrest everyone," said Roberto. "Even if we leave at night, it's too risky. If I'm arrested one more time I'm done. They'd put me away for a long time. That would be it for *Madre*. It would kill her. I need to speak with Pedrito."

"He told me he has a plan to get everyone on board safely so even if the Coast Guard sees him leaving they won't be suspicious," said Lazaro.

"And what is his plan?" asked Roberto.

"You know the beach at Alamar?" he asked.

"Sure, I've been there many times. Maura and I are going there tomorrow," replied Roberto.

"Well his plan is to take his wife and two kids in the boat as though they were going fishing. His wife would hide in the engine compartment and if he was stopped by the Coast Guard he would tell them he was only taking his kids fishing," explained Lazaro.

"And what about the rest of us? How the hell do we get onboard?" asked Roberto.

"Well, that's a little more complicated," said Lazaro.

"How complicated?" he asked impatiently.

"Well, Pedrito told me he knows of a few other boats that had the same problem. Too many people wanting to go, increasing the risk of being stopped. As he explained it, the way everyone managed to get onboard was, they waited until dark and using truck tire inner tubes, they swam offshore from Alamar Beach a mile or so out in the ocean and the boat would meet them and pick them up. Then they would head north as hard as they could go," said Lazaro.

"Wow, Maura is not going to be happy. She's terrified of sharks even when she's in the boat. And at night. Jesus," said Roberto. "What if we get out there and Pedrito can't find us or something happens to the boat, or the Coast Guard picks him up? It would all be over."

"Pedrito said all the other boats he knew that tried it, were successful," said Lazaro.

"Seriously? What, did they call when they got there? He couldn't have known if they made it," said Roberto.

"Come on Roberto, I'm just the messenger," said Lazaro. "Give me a break. You should take some more rum. It will calm you down."

By the time the brothers finished the bottle of rum it was late and the roosters in the neighborhood were beginning to call to one another. Their calls carried far in the heavy damp December air.

"I never understood why people keep roosters," said Roberto. "They're useless."

"That's what grandmother used to say about grandfather, remember?"

laughed Lazaro. "She would call him the rooster and he would strut around when he would put on his clean *guayabera*."

"I remember," said Roberto. "Lazaro, the rum is finished and I need to rest before I go to Cojimar and to La Playa Alamar. It's been a crazy day."

"Sure, we can talk tonight after you see Pedrito. I have to be at work at the restaurant by eleven," said Lazaro.

When Roberto awoke it was almost noon and he was late to pick up Maura. Cojimar was too far to go on foot, which left the MG as his only transportation option, provided it was in running order. After dressing quickly, he went downstairs to look for his father and to ask for the keys to the car.

Roberto found Guillermo outside sitting at the table on the terrace having coffee with Carlos, who was reading the morning paper aloud for his father to hear.

"*Buenas dias*," said Roberto.

"I thought you were going to Cojimar with Maura," said Guillermo.

"I am. I over-slept. Lazaro and I were talking nearly until dawn. *Padre*, is the MG running?" asked Roberto hurriedly.

"She's running. You need to check the coolant if you want to go to Cojimar. The keys are on the table by the front door. If the CDR arrests you again, tell them they can keep the car. I don't want it. It's cursed," said Guillermo loudly.

"I'll be back in time for *la comida*. I'll see if Pedrito has some fresh fish," said Roberto as he walked to the kitchen for some water to put in the radiator of the MG.

"Take some extra water. Just in case," said Guillermo.

Maura was waiting in front of the house when Roberto arrived at her grandmother's. Roberto could see her grandmother who was standing just inside the door in the shadow of the entrance. She never looked happy and today she looked less happy than all the other times Roberto had seen her.

"*Hola,*" said Roberto from the car. "*Estas listo?*"

"My favorite car! Wonderful," said Maura walking up to the car.

"I see your grandmother looks happy as ever," he said.

"Save the commentary. I brought some fruit and some bread and some *jugo de maracuya.* I thought we could have a picnic on the beach," said Maura smiling.

"I'm sorry for what happened."

"What do you mean?"

"I mean for the last year. I know it's been hard for you. When we get to the U.S. life is going to be so different, Maura."

"We're not there yet. A lot can go wrong. Remember, many people have died trying to make it across."

"I want to stop on the way and talk to Pedrito before we go to the beach," said Roberto. "He doesn't know I was released. When he first visited me in prison he kept saying how he didn't want to wait much longer to leave, and that he might have to leave without me."

"What did you tell him? I mean the boat is yours. You paid him. He has to wait."

"I said it would be much better for him if he waited because I could help him get established once we were in Florida."

"How do you plan to do that? You don't know anyone in Miami. You don't have family there."

"I told him your father has connections."

"You promised Pedrito my father would help him?"

"Look, if Pedrito had left without me you'd have been stuck here too," said Roberto. "What was I supposed to tell him? At the time it was all I could think of. I'm telling you, he would have left without us, Maura!"

"Alright, alright. Please let's not argue anymore today, Roberto."

"I'm sorry," he said. "Pedrito is going to be surprised, and happy."

"When do you think he will want to leave?"

"I'm sure as soon as possible. Probably right after Christmas," he replied as they came to a stop in the parking area near the path that led down to the harbor in Cojimar.

They came to the end of the path where it opened up from the bush and could see the door to Pedro's shed next to the cabana was open and there was a light on inside.

"Pedrito!" exclaimed Roberto, sticking his head inside the door.

"What the hell! Roberto! When did they let you out?" he asked loudly. Pedro stepped outside the shed and the two men hugged. "Sorry, my hands are a little greasy. I was working on the motor."

"Yesterday. It happened all of a sudden. I had a hearing, pled my case and that was it. The judge told me I was free to go. Something wrong with the motor?" asked Roberto.

"No, no she's fine. Just changing the oil," he said. "This is good news Roberto. We can start planning now."

"I was already talking with Lazaro last night," said Roberto.

"Then you know about the others. I couldn't help it Roberto. Ernesto found out and he told his brother. You know how these things happen," said Pedro.

"I understand. Who are the other two guys Lazaro told me about, Armando and Frank? You never mentioned them before," said Roberto.

"Armando is a friend. He's a fisherman and lives here in Cojimar. I don't know Frank, but he is a fisherman and friend of Armando," said Pedro.

"You trust them?"

"I trust them, yeah. They're good seamen."

"Lazaro told me your plan to get everyone in the boat."

"It's the only way, Roberto."

"I understand."

"What plan?" asked Maura.

"I'll explain when we get to the beach," said Roberto to Maura. "Pedrito we need to talk details, but not today. When are you thinking of leaving?" he asked.

"Well, after New Year's, but it will depend on the weather. It can be unpredictable this time of year. You know how it is in winter. You get a strong norther and it could be a week, or maybe only a few days before the sea flattens out," replied Pedro.

"That's fine. I need time to sell the car and I plan on buying more paintings. Then I have to figure out how to tell *Madre*, three of her sons are leaving Cuba. That will be the difficult part," said Roberto.

"Come back right after Christmas and we'll work everything out," said Pedro. "If you go to the beach in Alamar, there is a little cabana out on the point surrounded by some madera trees. No one ever goes there. You'll have a sea breeze there today. Wait, take this cutlass. You can cut some coconuts."

"*Vamos*. See you in two weeks, Pedrito. I'll bring this back when I come," he said, holding up the machete Pedro had given him.

"You know the way Roberto?" asked Pedro. "Take the bridge across the river. Turn left on the main road and then take your first left. That will take you around to the point."

"*Gracias*, Pedrito," said Roberto. "Oh, Pedrito. Do you have any fish? I promised my mother I would ask."

"You stop on the way back and I'll have something for you."

After turning off the hard road on the other side of the river from Cojimar, they drove out the sand road to Alamar Beach, all the way to the point to the cabana where Pedro had directed them to go. As far as they could see along the outer beach to the east there was no one. The breeze was from the north coming in off the ocean and was strong and dry, which made it feel cool in the shade of the madera trees.

"Let's sit in the shade," said Maura. The midday tropical sun was directly overhead. Even though it was December the sun's intensity could still be felt on the skin, but in the shade, it was cool enough to need the cover of a heavy towel to be comfortable.

"Don't be upset if I fall asleep. Sitting here looking out at the ocean I'm suddenly very tired," said Roberto.

"It's the stress leaving your body," she said. "I don't mind if you fall asleep. I love being here with you and that's enough."

"The water here is so clean. You see where turquoise-colored shallows end and the water becomes dark blue? That's the edge of the bar. Remember, we fished along there with Pedrito for wahoo," said Roberto.

"Yes, and I remember how I saw the school of skipjack before either of you and how Pedrito didn't like it much."

"I remember. How could I forget? So, Mrs. Santiago, what do you see now?" he asked, testing Maura.

"I see beautiful blue water all the way to the horizon and beyond I see a land where there are no dream police," she replied. "What do you see?"

"I'm not sure I see all that, but I do see a big cuda in the shallows and three war birds heading out to look for fish," Roberto said smiling.

"I'm trying to be romantic and you want to talk fishing. We're like oil and water sometimes, Roberto," she said. "Take a nap. I'm going to walk up the beach."

"It's probably more interesting this way," he said. "Wake me up when you get back."

When Maura returned Roberto was no longer asleep and was sitting up on the blanket, staring intently toward the horizon to the northwest.

"What are you looking at?" she asked.

"A Coast Guard boat, on the horizon. You see it? They went several miles to the east then turned around and are heading back west toward Havana. They must be on regular patrol. I wonder when the last patrol is each day," he said.

"I see it now. Why do you want to know?" she asked.

"Maura, I have to explain something to you. When we leave Cuba, there will be fourteen of us. If the Coast Guard were to see a boat with that many people in it, what do you think would happen?" he asked.

"We'd go to jail I suppose," she replied. "So we leave at night."

"There's more to it than that. If I go to jail one more time, that's it for me. I'll never get out," said Roberto still staring intently at the Coast Guard boat.

"You mentioned something about a plan to Pedrito. What is it?" she asked. "I can tell already I'm not going to like it."

"This is how it has to go. Pedrito goes out late evening as though he is taking his kids fishing."

"What about his wife?"

"She hides in the engine compartment. There's a lot of room below deck, all the way to the bow. The engine doesn't take up much space. The rest of us, once the sun is down, leave from here."

"What do you mean, leave from here?" she asked, raising her voice.

"We'll have inner tubes and we swim out and meet Pedrito offshore. Maybe a kilometer or more. That is why I want to know when the last patrol is each day," he said. "So we know when it is safe to get in the water."

"What?! Are you kidding me?! Safe to get in the water! I mean, swimming in the ocean doesn't bother me, but at night! That far off out. What about sharks? I saw that tiger when it cut the wahoo in half," she said loudly.

"It's the only way, Maura," said Roberto. "Look, you can sit in the inner tube if you have to and paddle backwards. We'll all be together. If it makes you feel safer, I'll hang a dead chicken off my tube. That way if they come, they'll hit me first," he said smiling.

"I'm not amused," was all she said. Maura leaned back against the madera tree they were sitting under and crossed her arms, staring out at the water.

"You don't have to go you know. I don't like it much either but this is our only option," he said.

"I hate that man with the heat of a thousand suns," said Maura, still looking toward the ocean.

"Who, Pedrito?!" asked Roberto in disbelief.

"No! Jesus Roberto, I'm talking about Fidel. That bastard put me in this situation. He needs to be fed to the sharks, not me," she said.

"I can tell you Maura, I fear Fidel much more than I fear the sharks," he said.

"I'm going. I don't care what happens. Life here is worse than death and we don't need to talk about it anymore," she said. Maura laid down on the blanket next to Roberto and closed her eyes.

"You're an amazing woman," he said and laid down next to her.

XXIV

Every day for the next 28 days Roberto returned to the beach at Alamar to drift fish and to watch for the Coast Guard patrols boats. The fishing was a cover. He wanted to know for sure, when the last patrol would pass for every day of the week.

He would fish each day with a hand line—sitting in an inner tube, out in the deep water near the edge of the reef when the ocean was not rough—until he thought the last patrol had passed. Occasionally when the patrol passed close to shore, and he was outside the line of the surf, he would wave innocently to the crewmen and they would wave back. Only once he saw them pass after seven o'clock in the evening.

Roberto and Pedro continued to meet regularly to discuss their plan to escape. Pedro had finally introduced Roberto to the other people who would be going with them, and although he wasn't happy knowing there would be fourteen people in such a small boat, Pedro repeatedly assured him it was safe and would take no more than ten hours to reach the Florida Keys. Gradually, he thought about the situation less and less.

Pedro was leaving nothing to chance and meticulously inspected every part of the motor and drive train. He had taken the newly renamed, in honor of Roberto's mother and sister, Rosita II, out a few times in recent weeks—only enough to keep her fresh—and when he did, was careful never to run her at full throttle remembering the trouble it brought after attracting the attention of the Coast Guard the previous year.

They were days away from leaving by the time Roberto finally found a buyer after weeks of looking, who was willing to pay his asking price of $40,000 pesos for the car. He made arrangements to meet one last time with Carmen at La Bodeguita, to buy four additional paintings, which would bring the total for his collection to fourteen, with an estimated value in excess of half a million U.S. dollars.

Carmen had asked Roberto to meet him at La Bodeguita del Medio instead of his home in Habana Vieja. Roberto had been watched closely by the local CDR since being released from prison, and Carmen knew it would be safer to meet in La Bodeguita. Roberto had not been to the old bar in more than a year.

Maura and Roberto deliberately arrived early, before the music had started at a time when there would be fewer people in the bar. Roberto wanted to find an open table in the back room where they could talk quietly with Carmen without anyone eavesdropping on their conversation.

"Good evening," said the waiter. "What would you like to drink?"

"Agustin, right?" asked Roberto.

"Yes, that's right. I remember, you're friends with Anabela," said the waiter. "She'll probably be here later. Usually she comes in when Rafael is performing."

"Yes, I'm friends with Anabela. I am Roberto, and this is my friend, Maura," said Roberto.

"*Mucho gusto*, Maura," said Agustin.

"*Mucho gusto*, Agustin, I'm sure. Actually, I'm his girlfriend. You see he has a tiny fear of commitment. At least for some things," she said smiling.

"I'll have a Havana Club, *Siete Anos*. And for the comedian?" asked Roberto, looking at Maura.

"A mojito will be fine, Agustin, thank you," she said.

"You're so independent, Roberto. Your mother was right," said

Maura, turning away. She was trying not to smile and pretending to read the notes from the tourists who come from around the world, written on the wall behind the table where they were sitting.

"Yeah, and what did she say about me?" he asked.

"I learned plenty while you were on vacation at Combinado. Don't you worry," she replied.

"*Oye*, Carmen is here! You're in luck. You won't have to testify," smiled Roberto.

"Roberto!" said Carmen as he walked up to the table. "We were so worried about you."

"I know, I know, I'm sorry, I should have contacted you sooner. How have you been? How is Anabela?" he asked.

"Oh, you know. Not much changes in Cuba. We're okay. I told her you would be here. She's coming a little later," said Carmen.

"Maura, I see you're sticking it out with this character," said Carmen.

"Somehow we make it work. Don't forget, you're the one responsible for this alliance," she said smiling.

"Here's Agustin with our drinks," said Roberto. "Sit down Carmen, please. What do you want to drink?"

"I'll have whatever he's having, Agustin," said Carmen. "So, you finally got rid of the MG."

"That car was cursed. Although I did make a little profit on her. I have $35,000 pesos to spend on the four paintings we discussed. I had to pay Pedrito the last little bit of what I owed him for the boat and that is all I have left," said Roberto.

"We can make it work. You know, these paintings are the most valuable you will have, Roberto. How do you plan to protect them in the boat?" he asked.

"The boat has a small wheelhouse. I'm going to take all the paintings out of their frames and lay them flat with paper in between each one and then wrap them in several layers of heavy plastic. I plan to hide them in the ceiling of the wheelhouse. I'll put in a false ceiling. Pedrito said no matter how rough it may get they'll stay dry," said Roberto.

"Let me show you the photos. Here, there are two by Evelio Mata, one by Angel Valdes, and one by Antonio Araujo," said Carmen, laying the photos on the table in front of Roberto.

"They are all spectacular, Carmen! Incredible!" whispered Roberto. "I don't know what to say."

"I told you. In the U.S., these four alone may be worth half a million dollars to the right person," said Carmen quietly, deliberately keeping his voice low.

"Where did you find them?" asked Roberto.

"In San Cristobal. An elderly woman whom I've known for many years had contacted me right after you were arrested and wanted to sell some of her late husband's collection. She knew about you from Arturo, in Vinales. I told her you had been arrested and maybe they wouldn't hold you for long," said Carmen.

"But she was willing to wait," said Roberto.

"She was, and is firm on her price, which I think is fair, and besides, she knew there was no one else who had that kind of money in Cuba. Except for Fidel of course, and he's not in the market right now," laughed Carmen.

"Well I'm happy she waited. I think it might be safer if you bring the paintings to my parents' house and pick up the money, rather than me bringing it to you. With my luck lately, the CDR would stop me and then we'd all be screwed," said Roberto.

"I can do that," he said. "Why not tomorrow? I'll come early."

"*Oye*, look who it is," said Roberto when he saw Anabela come through the doorway from the front of the bar. Roberto stood up and walked over to greet Anabela half-way.

Roberto had not seen Anabela in a long time and she looked older. Unexpectedly, he began to feel emotional.

Anabela hugged Roberto and kissed him once on either cheek, then held him by both hands and stepped back for a better look.

"You look amazing," she said. "It must be your new girlfriend." Anabela leaned to the side, looked around Roberto and smiled at Maura.

"Anabela, this is Maura," he said.

"We've already met. At Carmen's. We talk about you all the time. The fact that you're crazy and too independent," laughed Anabela. "Come on, have a seat."

Roberto looked a little confused by the remark and looked to Carmen for some support. "I'm glad you're here, Carmen. This could get ugly," said Roberto.

"Don't worry, Roberto, they love you. Have some rum," said Carmen.

"Agustin," said Anabela, waving to the waiter. "*Un mojito, por favor.* So, Maura has told me you will be leaving soon. How many paintings do you have?"

"I have ten, but I agreed to buy four more from Carmen. So I plan to leave with fourteen," said Roberto.

"Anabela, you remember Ceila, in San Cristobal?" asked Carmen.

"Sure. She and her husband have an amazing collection. Many important works from the early part of this century," she replied.

"Well, her husband passed away and she wanted to sell a number of pieces, so I arranged for Roberto to buy four of the more important ones in the collection. Two by Mata, one by Valdes and one work by Araujo. They're spectacular and should bring good money in the States," said Carmen.

"I hope you have a good plan to protect them when you're in the boat," said Anabela.

"I do. My friend Pedrito, who I bought the boat from, says it should take no more than ten hours to cross. We plan to watch the weather closely the next few days and if there is a window when it is fair and the wind is light, we'll go," said Roberto.

Agustin returned to the table with Anabela's mojito and placed it on a napkin in front of her then rotated the glass so the Havana Club label was facing her. "The conversation tonight looks serious, Anabela," said

Agustin.

"You're very observant, Agustin. That's why you are the best. You know how it is. Difficult times right now in Cuba," she said.

"Yes, I know. I hope none of you are in trouble," he said. "You let me know when you need another drink. Next one is on me." Agustin smiled, tucked the tray he was carrying under his arm and returned to the bar in the front room.

"He's a good guy isn't he," asked Roberto, directing his question to Anabela.

"The best. He's the story of Cuba. Promises made and never fulfilled. If he lived in Miami he would have the best restaurant in the city with the best bar," she said.

"If we had the room I would offer to take him with us," said Roberto.

"He would leave in a heartbeat if you asked him," she said. "And he's trustworthy."

"There's no room, Anabela. We have fourteen people now and the boat is small," said Roberto. "I wish I could help him."

"I understand. The line grows longer every day. Maybe one day when you're settled you can help me to come to America," she said.

"You know I would," replied Roberto.

"We should make a toast, Anabela," said Carmen.

"What shall it be?" she asked.

"To the wonders of art and to the health and safety and a life of freedom for Roberto and Maura," said Carmen raising his glass of rum. "*A tu salud!*"

"Thank you both. You have been truly wonderful to me," said Roberto.

Maura leaned against Roberto, put her arm through his and kissed him on the cheek.

The moment had come quickly and felt painful to Roberto. As the realities of their impending journey had loomed larger in recent days, feelings of sentimentality began to creep into his thoughts which he knew was a danger to his confidence. He realized he needed to remain disciplined and to resist the feelings.

Roberto took another sip of his rum. As he swallowed the rum he could feel inside his chest, the descending warmth which came from the rum's strength, and after, the sweet thick smokey flavor given up by the oak aging barrels. The rum was helping to ease the pain of the moment.

"I feel confident this will not be the end of our friendships," was all Roberto could think to say. "You'll see."

"You're forever the optimist, Roberto," said Anabela. "That's why I know you will be a great success in America."

"It's my intention not to settle for anything less," he said.

"Let's go to the front and find a table close to the music. No more gloomy conversation. That is not how I want to remember tonight. Okay?" suggested Anabela pretending to be cheerful.

"*Vamos!*" said Carmen in agreement.

That evening at La Bodeguita del Medio would be the last time Roberto would ever see Anabela Sobrina. Like countless ordinary Cubans before him—who had fled Cuba over the last thirty years, desperate only for a life of self-determination—Roberto now had to endure the stinging pain of another friendship forever lost. This angered him deeply and he hated the feeling of bitterness he felt that stemmed from the realization of a forced abandonment of friends and family and of the homeland he dearly loved.

He knew the anger he felt was dangerous if it were to take hold and that it could easily lead to a loss of control of the situation and everything he had worked so hard for. If his vision remained clear, he thought, in less than a month everything would be different and the troubles he would face would be good ones.

XXV

Roberto and his two brothers, Lazaro and Pedro had decided they would tell their parents they were leaving the day before they were to leave. The news was going to be especially hard on their mother but better to tell her and leave immediately they thought, then for her to see them for days or weeks knowing they would soon be gone.

More and more in recent weeks, Rosa and Guillermo had to leave home early to take their place and wait in separate food lines which were becoming longer throughout Cuba. The "Special Period," a term coined by the government in a pathetic attempt to fantasize reality, was becoming less and less special for Cubans, especially for the ones without the necessary credentials.

As promised, Carmen arrived early at the home of Roberto's parents with the four paintings, the day after they had met at La Bodeguita. Roberto had reminded Carmen the night before he did not want the paintings in the frames which were too large and would be impossible to store safely in the Rosita II. Roberto's parents were not at home and did not know about the purchase of the paintings which meant he didn't have to answer any questions.

Roberto was waiting outside in the shade of the house, sitting on the stone stoop when he saw Carmen coming with the paintings tucked under his arm in a roll.

The rain that had come during the night had washed the heat out of the limestone steps where Roberto was sitting, leaving them damp and feeling cooler than the air. The street was quiet except for the occasional sound made by one of the resident ring-necked doves when it would call loudly in order to warn the others of an approaching late-migrating pigeon hawk, flying low over the city looking to flush one of the doves high enough above the buildings where it was safe for the falcon to accelerate to a speed sufficient for a clean kill shot.

"*Buenos dias,* my brother," said Carmen. "So this is it. The last ones."

"Maybe not," replied Roberto as he stood up and motioned for Carmen to come inside.

"What do you mean? You haven't changed your mind about leaving?" asked Carmen.

"No, no, of course not. I have been thinking Carmen, once I am established in Miami, why not continue to collect and sell? I could make a good living if there was a way to get the paintings out of Cuba. I have Mariano in Spain and he's told me there are many wealthy Cubans living in Miami. It would be a way for us to keep working together," said Roberto.

"It's interesting, and you know I have a lot of connections," said Carmen.

"Something to keep in mind. Let me see the paintings," said Roberto.

Carmen had laid the paintings flat before rolling them loosely together, being careful to separate them, one from another with brown paper to protect the surface of the paint, then tied the roll on either end with a strong twine made of sisal. He carefully untied the twine that kept the roll together and unrolled the paintings on the floor in front of where Roberto was sitting.

"This one is the Valdes," said Roberto. "I recognize his style. Is it signed?" Roberto looked closely at the signature in the bottom right-hand corner. "I told Carlitos about the paintings. He said that works by Valdes are rare. I wish I had his knowledge, Carmen. He reads all the time, and his mind is like a steel trap."

"Why isn't he going with you?" asked Carmen.

"He's afraid. It seems lately his autism has become more debilitating. I worry about him all the time Carmen," said Roberto, after setting the first painting aside. "And this one is the Araujo? His technique is more *sofisticado*. More precise. I love the rural subject matter. It reminds me so much of my grandparents' farm."

"The other two are the Matas," said Carmen. "They're more like the Valdes in style."

"The colors are more brilliant. I wonder if they knew one another," said Roberto.

"If they did it would have been many years ago. Valdes only lived to be forty-nine. He died in 1957 and Mata fled to America in the sixties," said Carmen.

"Is he still living?" asked Roberto.

"I heard he died maybe eight or ten years ago," replied Carmen.

"If he lived and worked in the U.S. for the last twenty years of his life then for certain his works are in collections outside Cuba," said Roberto.

"Have to be," said Carmen.

"That means he is known and there is probably a market for his work," said Roberto.

"You're going to do well, Roberto," said Carmen smiling.

"I should put these upstairs with the others before anyone sees them. I think my mother knows something is about to happen. She's asking a lot of questions lately," said Roberto. "I'll be right back, and I will give you the money."

"Here is the payment, Carmen," said Roberto proudly after returning to the living room carrying a knapsack containing the thirty-five thousand pesos. "It's a lot of cash so I put it in this *mochila*."

"I will return it to you," he said.

"It's not necessary, Carmen. It's not as though I will be needing it," replied Roberto.

"When do you think Pedrito will want to leave?" asked Carmen.

"He thinks the weather should be good sometime around the sixth," replied Roberto.

"The Feast of the Epiphany," said Carmen. "That's only a few days away."

"Yes, and it's two days after the New Moon so there'll be no light from the moon, which will be better, obviously. The only problem we may have is if Pedrito can't find us in the darkness," said Roberto.

"What do you mean? Why won't you be in the boat?" a surprised Carmen asked.

"If the Coast Guard sees fourteen people in a small boat, what do you think happens? The plan is, Pedrito will take his family in the boat, as though he's going fishing. His wife will hide below deck in the engine compartment in case they get stopped by the Coast Guard. Meanwhile, we leave from the beach in Alamar just to the east. We'll have to start swimming a couple hours before Pedrito leaves in the boat in order to have time to swim far enough offshore where Pedrito won't be seen when he picks us up," explained Roberto.

"What if he can't find you?" asked Carmen in disbelief.

"We'll have a couple small hand lights. When we see the light on the masthead of Pedrito's boat, we'll guide him to us with the lights. I'm not worried," said Roberto.

"Fortune favors the brave, I guess," said Carmen.

"And the crazy," laughed Roberto. "You've been good to me. I will not forget what you have done for me."

The two men stood up, shook hands, and embraced for the last time before walking outside to say their final goodbyes. Roberto watched as Carmen walked to the end of the block, turned the corner and was out of sight.

He now had fourteen paintings and planned to sell all but *El Saxofonista* after he arrived in the U.S. The story of where they had come from and how they had arrived in the United States would be almost as valuable to some people as the paintings' individual values and provenance, he thought.

With only a few days left in Cuba Roberto's priority now was to take all the paintings to Cojimar and hide them aboard the Rosita II.

There was also the matter of telling Rosa and Guillermo, that he and his brothers were planning to flee the country. He was dreading the moment and didn't want to think about it and tried not to.

He had been a disappointment, especially to his mother, many times in recent years and knew this would be yet another devastating blow to her and the family. He worried that there was no way of knowing if the news would take her beyond the limits of her emotional capacities. However, if they were successful and they made it to the U.S., the possibility existed he could find a way for the rest of the family to join him in Florida, and he would tell his mother that.

The day after Carmen delivered the four paintings, Roberto left home before sunrise in order not to be seen by anyone in the neighborhood. He went to Cojimar with the paintings, where, with help from Pedrito, they hid them in a large plastic bag inside the false ceiling of the boat's wheelhouse.

Pedro informed Roberto, as promised, he had managed to secure eight large, truck tire inner tubes from a friend with a tire repair business in Habana del Este, and had safely hidden them in the bush near the point at La Playa Alamar, where Roberto and the others would enter the ocean and swim out beyond the reef to meet Pedro and his family in the boat.

Although few people went to the beach at Alamar in the middle of winter, it worried Roberto that the inner tubes would be there for two days and so he told Pedro he would check at the end of the following day, which was a Sunday, the fifth of January, to make sure no one had taken any of them.

Roberto decided not to take Maura with him when he went to the Alamar Beach to check on the inner tubes the next day, thinking the less she saw and thought about the ocean the less she would worry about having to make the long swim at night to the boat.

The afternoon winter air was cooler than normal, and the sky was cloudless all the way to the horizon. With the deep high pressure continuing to settled in over Cojimar, the wind was gradually lessening and the sea was beginning to flatten out.

This evening would have been a good day to leave, thought Roberto looking out at the ocean. There was no surf line showing, even above the outer edge of the reef where the waves would normally be breaking. Swimming or paddling with an inner tube would be less tiring and they could make good time and it would be easier for Pedro to find them, even in the dark.

In winter, after the leading edge of a norther would pass, the wind would sometimes fall out quickly along the north coast of Cuba. He knew this from experience and knew the window of calm weather that followed would sometimes last for several days and because he knew this to be generally true, he was not worried the weather would turn bad. With a smooth ocean it would take less time and less fuel to make the crossing, unless of course they were unlucky, which he never worried about.

Roberto stayed until he began to feel the breeze slackening. He had wanted to stay and watch the sun set fully, but the sand flies were beginning to bite and he knew they would be worse when it was dusk and the wind was gone entirely and they would no longer be discouraged by the sun.

He walked the short distance down the sand road that ran by the mouth of the river where he flushed a pair of noisy oystercatchers feeding among the rocks on the shoreline, while the tide was still out. The shoreline was fully exposed with the dead low tide so he decided to take the shortest route to the Cojimar bridge, along the edge of the river mouth, back to the harbor to look for Pedro.

As he walked onto the bridge, he stopped to look up at the yellow-crowned night herons—that came out in the evening from their roost in the mangroves along the north edge of the river, to perch and preen. They would sit on top of the iron crosspiece stretching between the two towers in the center of the bridge—never close enough to one another to cause problems—before flying off in search of a nighttime meal. He wondered if they, like the oystercatchers, also lived in Florida.

Walking down the path to the lagoon where Pedro kept the boat, Roberto remembered he had not seen Pedro's friend, Senor Fuentes, in almost two years and hoped he would be with Pedro, enjoying a rum and a cigar by the cabana, like many of the old fishermen in Cojimar did on Sundays.

He regretted not having taken more time to sit with the old man at the dock and listen to his stories as the young men in Cojimar liked to do, or having made time to fish with him on the days when Maykel and the old man would fish together. Even though he was little more than an acquaintance, Roberto admired him greatly and understood completely how important the old man was to the people of the village, especially the fishermen.

When Roberto reached the edge of the clearing where the seagrapes and the almond trees ended and the coconut palms took over, he could see, in the low light from a kerosene lamp hanging under the cabana, his friend Pedro, holding a glass of rum, sitting beside Senor Fuentes, who was smoking a cigar.

"*Buenas noches, grandes pescadores,*" said Roberto, stopping to grab one of the plastic chairs from a stack beside the shed where Pedro kept his fishing tackle.

"*Oye,*" said Pedro, who stood up to greet his friend. "Are you coming from the beach?"

"*Si,* I wanted to see the sun set over the water and enjoy the cool coming in off the ocean. Unfortunately the sand flies had other ideas. If I could find a way to bottle this weather and sell it to the poor bastards in Habana Vieja in July and August, when there is no escaping from the heat, I'm telling you, I could make a killing," laughed Roberto.

"But you would have to give ninety percent of the money to the government, don't forget," said Gregorio. He paused long enough to wink at Roberto, briefly lowering the hand holding the cigar, before striking a match in order to relight it after it had gone out from too much talking and too little smoking.

"Where are you hiding the rum, Pedrito?" asked Roberto.

"Right here," he said reaching under his chair. "You can find a clean glass in the cooler by the shed."

"Not too much," said Roberto as he held out his glass for Pedro. "I promised my mother and father I would be home early for the Sunday meal."

"I'll give you some fish when you leave. I may not fish for a few days," said Pedro.

"With this weather you should be fishing," said the old man. "The bait will be pushed in close to shore with this wind."

"I have some work I need to do on the motor," said Pedro, not wanting to make eye contact with the old man. "Besides, I don't like fishing right after a norther. The pressure is too high. I'll wait a day or two before I go."

Pedro had not told Gregorio about their plan to escape to the U.S. and was uncomfortable keeping the secret from the old man, but knowing if the old man knew, he would worry and would try and talk them out of leaving. Either way he thought, the old man would worry, and it would be hard—although not as hard as the loss the old man endured when his friend, for whom he was so well known, had been forced to flee Cuba in 1959—and so he kept their secret.

"Pedrito tells me you have a passion for old paintings," the old man said to Roberto.

"Yes, I guess you could say that. They saved my life on more than one occasion," said Roberto.

"I won't ask you about that," said Gregorio.

"I don't mind. I see each old work like a window to a world where I am the one controlling how to think. They're liberating. They take me to a place where I feel free," said Roberto.

"I believe I understand," said the old man. "For me it has always been the sea and fishing. Once I had learned the hard lesson of humility, which you must learn to be a good fisherman, and to always do what the sea expects of you, it is the only place I have ever felt truly free."

"I will try and remember your words, Capitan," said Roberto.

"If you forget, your friend here I believe knows something about humility," the old man said. "I remember the day when he learned."

"What happened?" asked Roberto.

"He thought he knew better and went out when he shouldn't have and when I told him not to go. This was several years ago when Pedrito was young and still very foolish and very proud. The wind that day was out of the northeast, blowing a thirty and there was a big *dorado* bite on. The current was pushing hard into the wind with the biggest kind of seas," said the old man.

"I can tell it, Gregorio," said Pedro.

"No, I'll tell it because you're not going to tell the whole story," he said. "Pedrito was trolling down sea and had just hooked up two big *dorado*. I forgot to mention that he was fishing alone—another mistake. When he turned around in order to slow the boat and begin to fight the fish, a wave came over the stern and knocked him down. When he stood up he was facing the bow and didn't see the second, even bigger wave coming. When it broke over the boat, it knocked him into the ocean."

"You obviously made it back to land, but I assume not in the boat," said Roberto.

"The boat was going ahead at trolling speed and was out of sight in seconds. I was maybe a kilometer and a half offshore. Fortunately with the northeast wind I was able to swim into the beach at Bacuranao," said Pedro.

"The other boats that were out that day looked for several hours until one of them saw his boat bottom up and no motor on the beach east of Alamar and figured Pedrito had drowned," said Gregorio.

"I walked the fifteen kilometers back to Cojimar and slept in the shed until Gregorio found me the next morning," said Pedro.

"I can't imagine how you must have felt when you found Pedrito in the shed," said Roberto.

"We were all certain he had drowned that day. Not knowing what happened and thinking you would never know, that was the worst part," said the old man.

Roberto looked over at Pedro who was looking in the direction of the water. He finished his rum and looked back at the old man who was also looking toward the water.

"That's quite a story, Pedrito," said Roberto. "Unless you have one better, I think I should be going. I'm a little late already."

"*Hasta la proxima vez,*" said the old man.

"Yes, until next time, Capitan" said Roberto. "Don't forget, I still want to catch a big blue one someday with you and Maykel.

"I'll remember. Next month, when they start to run," said the old man.

"Take care my friend. We'll go out soon," said Pedro, waving goodbye.

Roberto had already disappeared up the path through the seagrapes where it was dark when Pedro remembered he had promised Roberto some fish to take with him.

"Uh, I forgot the fish for Roberto, Gregorio," he said.

"There's always tomorrow, Pedrito. No need to worry. Have some more rum," he said. The old man took his last cigar from the left breast pocket of his guayabera, lit a match and pulled the air through the cigar until the end glowed red and he could taste the soft sweetness of the smoke in his mouth, then looked out toward the water, and into the darkness.

XXVI

There were few cab drivers working on Sunday in Cojimar, and by the time Roberto walked the half a kilometer into the village from the docks at the river, hailed a cab and traveled the short distance to his parents' home in Santos Suarez, the family had gathered along with Maura, and had not waited for Roberto to arrive to begin the meal.

"Sorry I'm so late, *Madre*," he said, surprising the family who was seated around the table on the terrace.

"There is a place for you next to Maura," said Rosa. "What do you want to drink? I'll get it for you," she said, going into the kitchen.

"If you still have some coconut water from the coconuts I brought from the beach the other day, I'll have some of that. Thank you," he replied.

"I don't know how you ever made it in the military, always being late," said Maura.

"Actually, if you remember, I didn't," said Roberto, smiling.

"That's right, you had the anger management issue. Very happy that phase ended before I met you," Maura said with wry smile.

Rosa returned from the kitchen with a glass of coconut water and a small glass of rum for Roberto and sat down again at the table next to Guillermo, to finish her meal.

"It is not very often the entire family has time for their parents," said Rosa, not looking up from her meal. "Is there something I need to know?"

Maura looked at Roberto for a moment, out of the corner of her eye, then looked away but didn't look at Rosa and said nothing. Rosa knew that Maura had family in Miami and Maura had talked openly about trying to join them one day and didn't want Roberto's mother to think she was responsible for Roberto's decision to leave Cuba.

"You are always worrying, *Madre*," said Roberto.

"That's because you can't seem to stay out of trouble," said Rosa. "At my age it's not as though I have the ability to replace you if something were to happen." Rosa looked at her husband who was unamused by her comment.

"So I'm a little stubborn. That's not a bad quality to have sometimes. I like to think of myself more as ambitious," said Roberto.

"And what are your intentions now?" she asked. "I know you. You're always wanting something more."

"Look, I'm tired of being denied the opportunity to pursue my ambitions. I want the same thing every Cuban with ambition wants," he said.

"And what do Cubans with ambition want?" she asked.

"To make a life of freedom for themselves in America," said Roberto.

Like all Cuban women, Rosa was strong in the places where she needed to be strong and like all Cuban women, when forced to, could face unafraid, the inevitable, with dignity and grace. The unknown was different however, and always the more difficult.

"That is your immediate intention?" she asked.

"Yes," he replied.

"When do you plan to leave?" she asked.

"Tomorrow night," said Roberto.

"The Feast of The Epiphany," said Rosa.

"The weather is right and there is no moon and we're ready to go," said Roberto calmly.

"It seems the only ones who are surprised to hear about this are your parents and your sister. Can I assume anything from this?" asked Rosa.

Lazaro began to speak but was stopped by Roberto. "I am the one responsible, *Madre*," said Roberto. "No one else."

"That's not what I asked," she said sternly. Rosa leaned back in her chair and looked around the table. "How many of my family can I expect to see next weekend for dinner?"

"*Madre*, Lazaro, Pedro, and Maura are coming with me tomorrow. When we are settled...."

Rosa didn't let Roberto finish before interrupting him. "Yes, and what if you don't make it?" she asked. "Do you have any idea how many have been lost between here and Florida?"

"We'll make it. We have a strong boat. Ten or twelve hours and we'll be in the Keys," he said.

"Why didn't you tell me sooner?" asked Rosa.

"We didn't want you to worry," replied Roberto.

"Very considerate. Do you realize how difficult you made the last eight years?" she asked.

"I do realize how hard it's been for you. That's why once we are established in Florida, we'll make arrangements for everyone else to come," said Roberto.

"How many people are going with you?" asked Guillermo.

"Fourteen all together including me," answered Roberto.

"Who is the owner of the boat?" asked Guillermo.

"It's mine. I bought it from my friend Pedrito in Cojimar. He is an experienced captain and fisherman, and he knows the boat well," said Roberto.

"He's also going?" asked Rosa.

"Yes. He and his wife and two children. He'll run the boat," replied Roberto.

"What if you are stopped by the Coast Guard?" asked Guillermo.

"The last patrol each day is at sunset. You remember last month, I was fishing every day until after dark at Alamar Beach?" asked Roberto. "I wanted to know when the last patrol would pass so we would know when it was safe to leave. We plan on leaving in the night."

"Where do you plan on living in Florida?" asked Rosa.

"With my family," said Maura. "They are well established."

"Do they know you're coming?" asked Rosa.

"No, there was no way to tell them," replied Maura.

"I'm sure they will be very happy to see you," said Rosa. She looked down at her food and picked up her fork and pushed the half-eaten meal to one side of the plate, then put the fork down.

"This is not the end, *Madre*, it is the beginning. You'll see. I will make you very proud," said Roberto.

Rosa looked at Guillermo who was sitting next to her, then placed her arm inside his and held his hand tightly with hers. There was nothing else to say and she knew it.

Roberto, although uncomfortable, was relieved the conversation had ended quickly and had not been more difficult and his mother had not blamed Maura for his decision to leave Cuba. But there was no use trying to pretend the rest of the evening or the conversation was going to be normal, so Roberto, thinking his parents needed time alone to process the news, offered to walk Maura to her grandmother's, where she planned to spend her last night in Cuba.

It was late when he returned to his parents' house and found only his brothers, Lazaro and Pedro, still sitting on the terrace, drinking rum. The kerosene lamp was almost out of oil and Lazaro had turned down the wick to extend the life of the flame. Overhead the Big Dipper, inverted and clearly visible, appeared large and bright in the clear moonless January sky.

In the low light of the lamp, Roberto could see the worry in the faces of his brothers and wanted to choose the right words before speaking.

"I hope there are no clouds tomorrow night," said Roberto, sitting down at the table.

"Why do you say that?" asked his brother Pedro.

"You see the Big Dipper, to the northeast?" said Roberto, pointing up at the sky. "It's rotated ninety degrees, with the handle pointing down."

"I can see it. What about it?" asked Lazaro.

"Well, the compass on the boat isn't working. If it's clear tomorrow night we can stay on a northerly course by heading toward Polaris, the North Star," he answered.

"What does that have to do with the Big Dipper and how do you know where the North Star is?" asked Pedro.

"You see the two stars that form the front of the dipper part? Well if you draw an imaginary line from right to left between the two, it always points directly at the North Star, which is always in the same position in the sky. Tomorrow it is supposed to be clear, like tonight," said Roberto.

"And if it's not?" asked Lazaro. "Then what?"

"Pedrito says when you are far out in the Gulf Stream, where the current is strong, and you can no longer see the land, you can tell which way is north because of the current, which always flows from west to east. Of course it would be better if it is clear." said Roberto. He paused for a moment and continued looking up at the night sky. "Pedrito will get us there. Anyway it's going to be clear."

"What do you plan to do, Roberto, when we get to Florida?" asked Lazaro.

"I plan to sell my paintings. Well, all except for the one from Juilo,

El Saxofonista. I have them safely hidden in the boat inside the ceiling of the wheelhouse," replied Roberto.

"We've been talking, Roberto, and I'm worried. We have nothing, no money, and nowhere to live when we arrive. We don't know anybody, and we don't speak English," said Pedro.

"Maura said her family will help us and not to worry about any of that. She told me many people speak Spanish there," said Roberto. "You're both young, and Lazaro, you know the restaurant business and you can cook, and Pedro, you are an experienced auto mechanic. I don't think either of you will have trouble to find a job. It's not like here.

You can do whatever you want, go wherever you like, and there is no one from the CDR watching you."

"You don't understand Roberto. You've never been someone who worries. Besides, no matter what happens, you always come out on top. It's different for us," said Pedro.

"No, I do understand, that's why I don't waste my time worrying about inconveniences," he said. It was growing late and Roberto was losing patience with his brothers. "I would advise against the two of you staying up all night and worrying about tomorrow. We have a long swim tomorrow night to meet Pedrito in the boat, and you need to be ready. I'll see you boys tomorrow evening in Cojimar harbor, by the cabana. I plan to leave the house with Maura, early tomorrow. If we are here all day at the house it will only make it worse for *Madre*. Okay?"

He went upstairs to the bedroom he had always shared with his brother Carlos, where he would spend his last night in Cuba. It was dark and Carlos was asleep lying on his side with a light sheet pulled up over his shoulders, and he could see that he was sleeping, breathing slowly and deeply. The only window in the bedroom was open fully, letting in the cool, damp, late night winter air. Roberto didn't want Carlos to wake from the cold and picked up the blanket that was folded at the foot of his bed to lay over his brother.

After lightly covering Carlos with the blanket he turned around and began to undress, and saw, lying on the bed where the blanket had been, the empty frame that had held the painting of *El Saxofonista*. He sat down again on the bed and picked up the frame and held it in front of him with both hands.

He thought about the day, ten years earlier, when Julio wanted to give them the painting for helping him move, and how disappointed he felt when Julio told them he didn't have the money to pay them, and the painting was all he had and would they please accept it as payment. He remembered too, how excited Carlos was about the painting and how he didn't want to sell it and how he, Roberto, had doubted Julio's story about the painting, only to discover what a great and important painting it was.

Now he was preparing to leave his brother and didn't want to think about it anymore and leaned the frame against the outer leg at the foot of the bed and finished getting undressed.

He laid down on the bed and fell asleep quickly and began to dream about the Rosita II, and the dark blue water of the Gulf Stream, heading north with everyone onboard.

When he awoke it was light and Carlos was gone. The blanket Roberto had placed over his brother when he had come to bed was now covering him and the painting frame was laying on Carlos's bed, against his pillow.

Roberto slept later than he had wanted and dressed quickly and went downstairs to the kitchen. The house was empty but there was a coffee pot on the stove with the flame turned down low. He saw the door to the terrace was open and then heard the sound made by someone placing a coffee cup on a saucer.

"Maura!" he said, surprised to see her. "How long have you been here?"

"I came early to see your mother," she said. "The coffee is hot. I just made it."

"Where is everyone?" he asked nervously.

"Carlitos and your parents went to wait in line for bread and they needed a new *Libreta de Abastecimiento*. It was nearly empty," she replied. "What did you tell Lazaro and Pedro?"

"I told them I wanted to wait in Cojimar, and that we would meet them at the cabana, at sunset. We should be going," he said.

"You're not going to wait to see your mother?" she asked.

"She's upset enough. If we wait it will only make it worse, and I don't need the extra pressure," he replied.

"I packed some bread and fruit," said Maura. "We're leaving now?"

"Yes, let's go. I have enough money to hire a cab and buy something to eat in Cojimar, before we leave," he said. "I hope you didn't pack a lot of food. Pedrito said we don't want too much food or water on board. He said if the Coast Guard stops him and they see extra food they become suspicious."

"Okay, okay, *Vamos*," she said.

When they arrived in Cojimar it was midday and sunset was not for another five hours. Roberto had not eaten anything and suggested they walk into the village by way of the Marti Real, which ran along the edge of the village by the waterfront, to look for a place to eat their last meal in Cuba.

He remembered Senor Fuentes, mentioning in one of his stories about his many years as mate aboard the Pilar, that Papa, after a successful day of fishing, would always insist they end the day at the bar, in La Terazza de Cojimar, overlooking the water at the south end of the river mouth, where the river narrowed and flowed toward the sea from the east.

"That's the place. Ahead on the right," he said, pointing to a large blue sign hanging from the balcony above the entrance to the building. "El Capitan told me about this place. He said he and Senor Hemingway came here often after a good day of fishing, to celebrate a big fish."

"It looks fancy. You have enough money?" she asked.

"You've forgotten already? I am a high-class art collector," he said with a straight face. "Come on, we'll sit by a window so we can look out at the water."

"Happy to see you are so relaxed."

"I'm not really. I'm trying to keep you calm."

"You're talking about the swim."

"Yes. I know you're nervous."

"I am, but I've thought a lot about it and I'm ready now. You don't need to worry about me. Besides, you know I'm a strong swimmer."

"I'd rather sit in the bar if you don't mind Roberto," said Maura, when they walked in.

The restaurant was crowded so they walked through the dining room to the bar in the back of the building and sat at one of the wooden tables by the window that had a clear view out to the sea.

Above the polished mahogany bar and to the right, hung a large painting of a lone straw hatted fisherman in a wooden dinghy, surrounded by a flock of terns diving on a school of pilchard that had surfaced in front of the Torreon Cojimar. Passing the dinghy with the fisherman was a larger vessel with two fishermen returning from the ocean, with the day's catch of billfish proudly displayed across the bow of the boat.

"I like the painting," said Maura.

"It's not really a true work of art. It's more of an illustration," said Roberto, glancing up at the painting and then looking toward the water.

"No need to be condescending," she said. "Here's the waiter. I'll have a mojito and some water."

"*Hola, senor.* May we have two waters, a mojito, and a Havana Club, *Siete Anos?*" asked Roberto.

"What would you like to eat," asked the waiter.

"You have *Pargo Frito Entero?*" asked Maura.

"*Si, senorita,*" said the waiter.

"Two of them please. Thank you," said Roberto.

Maura waited until the waiter was out of earshot before asking Roberto the question. "You think by this time tomorrow we'll be in

Florida?"

"The weather is good and the boat is running well, according to Pedrito. Everything is right. I don't see why not."

"I haven't seen my family in four years. It will be so strange."

"It may be strange for a moment and then you will feel wonderful, and you will only think about how happy you are."

"You're probably right. My younger brother must be very tall by now. Four years is a long time when you are a teenager. I can't wait to see him."

"The waiter is coming. *Gracias, Senor*," said Roberto when the waiter reached the table. The waiter set the two waters on the edge of the table and then placed the mojito in front of Maura, followed by the Havana Club for Roberto.

"Your food is almost ready," he said before turning to walk away.

Maura and Roberto sat looking out the window at the sea without speaking until the waiter came back with their food. The incoming tide flowing in the same direction as the breeze, which was very light from the north, caused a slick to form on the surface of the water in the middle of the channel where the flow was strongest, attracting a handful of least terns, which worked back and forth along the edge of the slick, sometimes stopping mid-flight to dive into the water whenever they spotted a small school of glass minnows.

"Pretty day," said the waiter when he returned to the table with the food. "Nice day to be on the ocean. You ever go on the ocean?"

"A few times with friends. Fishing mostly," said Roberto. He thought it somewhat strange the waiter would ask the question but paid little attention to it and did not react.

"We have a friend who is a fisherman and keeps a boat in the Rio Almendares."

Neither Roberto or Maura said anything about knowing Pedrito, or the boat, or ever having gone out to sea from Cojimar. It was always best not to invite too many questions from anyone in Cuba who isn't family, especially strangers.

"Here's your check. Let me know when you're ready to pay. No hurry," he said.

"If you don't mind, we would like to sit here for a little while," said Roberto.

"You're more than welcome," the waiter replied.

The view to the north from the corner table in the bar where they were sitting, was unobstructed all the way to the horizon. On the eastern edge of the harbor sat the old solar-powered light house on the rock by the cut on the outermost point of land directly across from the Torreon. Alamar Beach was a short distance to the east, where they would begin their swim.

"You see the light on the point? The beach is just around the corner," said Roberto, pointing. "When we start swimming the tide will be ebbing."

"You said Lazaro and Pedro will be at the cabana. What about the others?" asked Maura.

"The plan is to meet them at the beach. Just after dark," he said.

"I hate the waiting," said Maura. "I'd prefer to wait at the cabana if you don't mind."

"*Vamos entonces,*" he replied.

After Roberto thanked the waiter and payed the bill, they walked up the road together to the first intersection and turned left onto the road that lead to the dock where Pedro kept the boat.

When they arrived at the cabana where they were to meet Roberto's two brothers, they saw Pedro, hunched over in the boat, his torso halfway inside the wheelhouse. Because it was a religious holiday none of the other boats were out fishing and they saw no one else but Pedro in the harbor.

"*Oye,* Pedrito," said Roberto when he got to the end of the pier beside the boat.

"You startled me," he said.

"A little nervous, I'm sure," said Roberto.

"I guess. I'm making sure we have everything. I'm taking one five-liter container of water. If the Coast Guard would see a lot of water on board, they would know what's going on," he said. "That should be plenty for everyone."

"You taking a couple of rods so it looks like you're out fishing?" asked Roberto.

"Yes. I don't expect to see the Coast Guard after dark, but you never know," he said. "I'm almost finished. You can wait under the cabana if you'd like."

When Pedro was finished stowing the water and food, he checked the engine oil and fuel levels one last time and walked up the dock to the cabana and sat down with Roberto and Maura.

"You know, there's not much I'm going to miss about Cuba, Roberto. The least of which is knowing I could go to prison at any moment for no God damn reason. But I am going to miss the fishermen of Cojimar, El Capitan, especially. I learned so much from him. He was always so willing to help. Always humble. Just a simple, honest, decent man. Never arrogant. I guess that's why Papa loved him," said Pedro.

"You're fortunate to have him as a friend," said Roberto. "You realize you may never see him again."

"I've thought about, but I don't like to," replied Pedro. "When are your brothers coming?"

"I told them they should arrive by sunset. I was thinking they should carry some hand lines with them when they walk to the beach. That way if someone stops them it looks like they're going fishing," said Roberto.

"That's a good idea. I have a couple hand lines I can give them," said Pedro.

"You have the lights so you can find us in the ocean?" asked Roberto.

"Yes, but you need to remember they are not waterproof," replied Pedro.

"I'm going to give one to Pedro and one to Lazaro. I thought we would swim out maybe two kilometers. Far enough that when you stop, if someone is watching from shore it would be impossible to tell that you had stopped. Then we'll spread out with my brothers maybe sixty meters apart on the outside and the rest of us swimming in between. All you need to do is find one of the lights then you should be able to locate the other, either right or left. What do you think?" asked Roberto.

"That's a good plan. I'll have my masthead light on and my bow lights. Remember the green will be on your left as I am coming toward you. With no wind for a couple days the ocean is a dead calm, so I don't think I'll have any trouble to find you. Without the moon it's difficult to keep your bearings in the ocean at night. The tide will be coming from the west so you need to be swimming into it slightly so when we meet you will be directly north of the inlet. Once you get beyond the drop, the current will increase a little as the near shore water mixes with the Gulf Stream. But it's not as strong this time of year. We'll meet in that area. I'll head a bit to the west and then come northeast along the edge and begin looking when I know I'm in the current," he said.

"Pedrito, I mean, what if you can't find us?" asked Maura.

"I'll find you, Maura, don't worry. It's not that big an area. With the ocean as flat as it is tonight, you'll probably see me first. When Pedro and Lazaro see me they'll shine their lights," replied Pedro.

"She's a bit of a worrier, Pedrito. That's why she's so motivated," said Roberto.

"Roberto, there are Pedro and Lazaro," said Maura.

"Pedrito, *como tu ta?*" said Lazaro when they reached the cabana. "We ready to go?"

"Everything is ready. The others will meet you out at the beach. Roberto thought you should carry a couple hand-lines with you so it looks like you're going night fishing. Here, I have a couple in the shed," said Pedro.

"Grab one for me, Pedrito. Maura, we should leave now," said Roberto. "Lazaro, wait a little while before you and Pedro walk out to the beach. We'll be waiting down the beach a couple hundred meters from the point. I guess this is it, Pedrito."

"Listen, if you start swimming a little after six thirty and it takes you two hours to get out where you need to be, I'll leave the dock at eight. I'll need to go slow so I don't attract attention," he said.

When Roberto and Maura arrived at the beach the sun had set fully, and it was very dark. The others were already waiting by the patch of coppice where Pedro had hidden the inner tubes the week before. Roberto knew everyone but the two fishermen who were friends of Pedro's and lived in Cojimar, Armando and Frank. After brief introductions and confirmation that everyone knew how to swim and was ready to go, Roberto explained the plan and told them as soon as his brothers arrived, they would begin their swim and asked if anyone had any questions.

"How long does Pedrito think it will take to cross?" asked Armando.

"Depending on how the seas are when we are in the middle of the Gulf Stream, he said maybe ten or eleven hours," answered Roberto.

"Roberto, God forbid if someone is bitten by a shark, what should they do?" asked Ernesto, who as an emergency room doctor and had treated shark bite victims several times while working at the Hospital Hermanos Ameijeiras Hospital in Habana Vieja.

"Everyone has to decide for themselves," he replied.

"There are few sharks in the waters close to Havana any longer, Roberto," said Armando. "The shark fisherman have all but wiped them out. That's why they closed the factory in Cojimar."

"Roberto," said Maura, touching his arm. "Your brothers are here."

Roberto walked into the bush where the inner tubes were hidden and began to pass them out one by one until there was one left, then walked out to the edge of the water where the others were waiting.

"Look, we need to stay close to one another. We can only swim as fast as the slowest swimmer," said Roberto, as they began to enter the water. "Maura, stay close."

With the falling tide and a calm sea there was little surf to contend with as they made their way into deeper water toward the outer reef still able to feel bottom. The water felt warmer than the air, which had cooled quickly in the dry January night and made the water feel comfortable.

When they reached the outer edge of the last line of reef, the water was over their heads and everyone was swimming now on their sides and spread out enough so not to break the rhythm of any of the others as they swam. With their legs doing most of the work and one arm in front pulling, the other was free to hold the inner tube above their bodies and to the side.

Pedrito had made sure the tubes were filled with enough air that they would float high in the water, requiring less effort to pull across the water's surface.

Maura was close to Roberto, swimming in front of the others and having little trouble keeping up with him and felt stronger as her body warmed and the muscles began to loosen. Concentrating on maintaining a good rhythm as she swam kept her mind off what she knew lived in the water and what she didn't want to think about.

No one spoke as they swam and once they were beyond the last of the small swells that rose continuously where the ocean water pushed against the deepest part of the reef, they began to make better and steady progress.

Swimming on his left side, Roberto could see the Big Dipper over his shoulder and worked to keep the constellation at the same oblique angle relative to his body position in the water in an effort to maintain a northerly direction.

He remembered what Pedrito had told him about the area where he wanted to rendezvous, and would occasionally slide the tube out of his line of sight as he swam, and look back toward the land, to make sure they were maintaining a northerly course away from the lighthouse. The light from the point was becoming faint but was still visible and he estimated they had covered close to one kilometer when he heard Maura scream.

"Roberto!" yelled Maura, swimming faster and pulling even with him before they both stopped swimming.

"What's the matter?" he yelled.

"I just saw a big fin. There it is again! See it there!" she said loudly.

Roberto didn't see it and Maura was becoming increasingly upset. The others had gathered close to Roberto and Maura and were trying to pull themselves up into their inner tubes.

"There's another one!" she said a little louder.

"I see them now. It's a pod of bottlenose dolphin. That's actually a good sign. They're probably wondering what these crazy humans are doing out in the ocean in the middle of the night. As long as they're around we're safe. They'll kill sharks," he said.

"He's right, Maura," said Armando. "I've seen them follow bull sharks in the shallows by the inlet. Somehow, they know we're vulnerable. You don't have to worry unless you see two fins, one behind the other. The dolphins arch as they swim and their fin has a slight hook to it."

"Everybody okay?" asked Roberto. "We're almost half-way. Lazaro, you keeping the lights dry?"

"Yes. I just checked them. I can turn them on and off inside the plastic. Don't worry," he said.

"We need to keep going. Pedrito is probably leaving about now," said Roberto.

They spread out again and continued swimming to the north. The sea was oil calm and reflected the light from the great silver river, the Milky Way, which gradually increased the farther out they were. Roberto didn't remember having been on the ocean at night when there wasn't a moon and was surprised by how much light there was once his eyes became accustomed to the conditions.

They swam in a loose line with Roberto in the middle, and Lazaro and Pedro on either end. At times someone would see a fin when one of the dolphins that had stayed with them as they swam would surface, and they would tell the others. Knowing the dolphins had stayed with the group was a comfort to everyone and they could relax which helped with endurance.

From time to time when they swam into a warm Gulf Stream eddy, before reaching the edge of the main current, they would see the phosphorescent flashes from marine plankton on the surface, caused by the small splashes from the motion of their swimming. It was unexpected and new.

After another hour or so of steady swimming—with only an occasional break when Roberto would stop to check their position against the lights from Cojimar, and the position of the North Star, and to make sure no one was cramping—Roberto felt a slight warming of the water and knew he had hit the edge of the Gulf Stream.

"This is it," he said, as he stopped swimming. "We're right where Pedrito said he will meet us. I can see a current swirl to the east. We have to be above the drop."

"I can't believe we made it," said Maura.

"I don't see Pedrito, Roberto," said Pedro. "I don't see any boats."

"I'm sure he'll be here soon. Everyone keep looking. Lazaro, I told Pedrito we would spread out in a long semi-circle, with you on one end and Pedro on the other. Check your lights to make sure they're working," said Roberto.

The brothers flashed their light a couple times through the plastic to make sure they were working.

"I think we should spread out now. Lazaro, you swim thirty or forty meters to the southeast and Pedro to the northwest. We'll stay in the middle. Wait until you see the lights from the boat before you turn your light on, and make sure the light doesn't get wet," he said. "Is everyone okay?"

"Yamilet is getting tired, Roberto," said her husband Omar. "I don't think she can go much farther."

"It's okay. This is as far as we need to swim," said Roberto. "Just don't lose your tube. Try and pull yourself into the tube, Yamilet, if you can manage. You can use your arms to paddle if you need to."

"What time do you think it is?" asked Maura.

"It must be at least nine by now. Pedrito should have been here. Unless for some reason he left late," replied Roberto.

Another hour or more went by when Lazaro swam back to where Roberto and the rest of the group were waiting.

"I'm worried, Roberto," he said. "What do you think happened?"

"I don't know. I can't imagine what went wrong. Maybe he was stopped by the Coast Guard," said Roberto.

"What do you want to do?" asked Lazaro.

"What do you mean what do I want to do?" Roberto said.

"I mean what if he doesn't come?" he asked.

"We wait. I'm sure as hell not swimming back to land, if that's what you're thinking. I'm telling you, he'll come," he said. Roberto knew his brother was a doubter and a worrier, but still found it difficult not to be annoyed.

"Okay, okay," said Lazaro. He swam back again to the southeast and continued looking in the direction of Cojimar.

Sometime shortly after eleven o'clock, Pedro, who was farthest to the west, and had remained vigilant and continued looking for the lights of Pedrito's boat, let out a yell.

"I see him, I see him!" he yelled to the others. "I see the light from the masthead!"

"Turn your lights on!" yelled Roberto. "Shit, it looks like he's heading too much in a northerly direction. If he stays on that course, he's going to miss us. Lazaro, come around more to the south so the lights are farther apart. Quickly!"

"Roberto, you need to calm down. He's going to see us," said Maura.

"Come on, Pedrito, turn," said Roberto under his breath.

"Pedrito is a fisherman, Roberto. He'll see us. Not much gets past his eyes," said Armando.

"Roberto!" yelled Pedro, who had swum toward the boat away from the group, in an effort to make it easier for Pedrito to see his light. "He's turning, he's turning. He's coming!"

"Are you sure?" yelled Roberto.

"Yes! The bow light is now in line with the masthead. He's heading straight for us!" he replied.

"Lazaro, keep your light on just in case," said Roberto, loudly, making sure his brother heard him.

Pedro was within one hundred and fifty meters when he flashed a hand light over the bow in the direction of the swimmers, signaling he had seen them. Reaching Pedro first, he gradually slowed to a stop and picked him up, leaving his inner tube behind in the ocean.

Lazaro had already started swimming back to the group, keeping his light on, before Pedrito put the boat back in gear, and with Pedro using his flashlight to guide him, slowly headed toward the others who were now close together.

Nearing the others, Pedrito turned the Rosita II, to the starboard, backed off the throttle, bumped her a couple times in reverse, then slowly let the boat drift to a position where everyone was on the port side, and put her in neutral.

"Pedrito! Man, what happened?" asked Roberto excitedly.

"The Coast Guard was coming from the west just as I made it to the mouth of the inlet. They kept heading east and by the time they passed back to the west and were out of sight it was already ten o'clock," he said. "There was nothing I could do. If they saw me heading offshore, they would have stopped me for sure."

"Ileana, Yamilet, you get on board first," said Roberto.

"Roberto, I need help. My legs are cramping," said Yamilet.

"Pedro, grab her arms. I'll try and lift at her waist. All right, Pedro, go," said Omar.

On the second try, Yamilet was able to get her torso on top of the washboard and balance long enough for Pedro and Pedrito's wife, Magalis to pull her safely into the boat.

Ileana and Maura were lighter and more powerful swimmers and had no trouble propelling themselves high enough with minimal help from Pedro to make it onto the washboard on the first try. Then one by one, the remaining seven men pulled themselves into the boat, with Roberto waiting until everyone was on board. After brief celebration, they checked to make sure everyone was okay, then watched in silence as the last inner tube drifted east with the current into the darkness.

Pedro wasted no time putting the Rosita II in gear and turning around to the north, but with so many people on board and most of the weight aft, he was having trouble getting her on a plane. When she finally got on a plane, they could manage only ten knots. Pedrito had been hoping for more.

Pedrito had the boat going well and making good time in the flat sea. The low ocean swells were coming side to from the west and with a distance of fifty meters or more between them, the ride was smooth and dry. Each of the swimmers had taken some water and despite being tired from the long swim, only Yamilet had trouble with leg cramps and everyone's spirits were high.

The yellow glow from the lights of Havana in the southwest were growing dimmer and they could no longer see the lights in Cojimar, except when one of the larger swells would slide under the boat and the Rosita II would rise high enough to bring the coastline back into view.

They had been traveling for less than half an hour when they saw the lights off the port side.

"Pedrito!" yelled Roberto above the noise of the engine. "Look!"

"I can't believe it! Bastards!" yelled Pedrito.

"You think it's the Coast Guard?" asked Roberto.

"I know it is. I can tell by the lights on the tower. That's a big boat. It's the same one I saw pass the inlet," he said.

"We're screwed, Pedrito," said Roberto. "No way we can out-run them?"

"No. They're probably at least three kilometers away and I'm sure they've seen us. Look, there's enough room below deck for everybody if you go all the way forward to the bow. The smaller people first. It's tight in the bow, but there's room. I'll keep my kids on deck and put out baits on the outriggers. It will look like we're fishing. I can go ahead at trolling speed and head straight for them. We need to get everyone in the bilge, quickly. It' going to be hot next to the engine but it's our only option," said Pedrito.

Pedrito slowly brought the boat down to trolling speed and eased around to a more westerly course and headed straight for the Coast Guard boat which was moving into position to intercept the smaller vessel.

Roberto and Lazaro removed the engine cover in the middle of the deck, and one at a time they lowered themselves into the hold beside the engine, alternating between the port and starboard sides, until Roberto, who was last to go below deck, packed himself, mostly on top of Ernesto. Pedrito slipped the engine cover back over the opening, then slid the large fishing cooler out from under the wheelhouse onto the deck, placing it over the engine cover.

Pedrito quickly rigged the two rods, each with a clear plastic headed rubber skirted trolling lure, which he always had onboard, attached the lines to the outrigger clips, swung the outriggers to a position ninety degrees from either side of the boat, and let the lines play out past the engine wake, then set the drag.

"*Ninos, sientense aqui,*" he said, pointing to the cooler where he wanted the children to sit. "Are you okay? When I talk to the men in this boat, I want you to keep quiet. I'm going to tell them we're out fishing. You understand? I need you to be strong now."

The heat was building in the hold from the engine, and it was difficult breathing, especially for the women who were in the smallest part of the space underneath the bow.

The Coast Guard boat had closed to within fifty meters when one of the men onboard instructed Pedrito, through a megaphone to take his boat out of gear and cut the engine.

As the larger boat pulled alongside, one of the crew members threw a dock line to Pedrito and told him to tie it off to the starboard stern cleat in order to keep the two boats from drifting apart.

Pedrito had already pulled in both fishing lines, swung the outriggers back to a position out of the way parallel to either side, left the lines in the clips, and had each of his children hold one of the trolling lures, now clearly visible to the men on board the government vessel.

In addition to the bridge lights above the pilothouse one of the other crewmen had turned on a large search light and pointed it down into the cockpit of the Rosita II. Because of the brightness and direction of the light it was difficult to see and Pedrito could only make out the silhouettes of the men onboard.

A man came out of the pilothouse and stepped up to the rail at the stern of the Coast Guard boat.

"Captain, I am Commander Lieutenant Hernandez," he said, addressing Pedrito. "It's a bit late at night for you to be this far offshore. Do you have an explanation?"

"Yes Lieutenant. I've been doing a little night fishing with my children," he replied. "Trying to catch a tuna."

Down below with the engine off, Roberto and the others could clearly hear Pedrito's response but were having trouble hearing the man on board the other boat. The heat in the bilge was building and because of the tight positions they had been holding, unable to stretch their legs, they were beginning to cramp from having had so little water. If any of them were to make the slightest noise, it would be over.

"And how has the fishing been, Captain?" the man asked.

"Not what I would have hoped for, Lieutenant. We're on our way in," said Pedrito.

"Where do you fish out of?" he asked.

"Out of Cojimar, sir." he replied.

"I assume you have all your paperwork on board?" asked the lieutenant.

"Yes sir. Would you like to see it?" he asked.

"It's not necessary. I would appreciate it if you would head back to Cojimar," he said.

"Not a problem sir. Like I said we were just about to head in. If you don't mind, I'd like to go slow. I burn less fuel that way," said Pedrito.

"I don't care how fast you go, just head straight in," instructed the lieutenant.

"Thank you, sir. Can I untie the line?" asked Pedrito.

"Go ahead, Captain. Ensign, take the line. We don't need the light anymore," said the lieutenant, motioning for the crewman to turn off the search light.

Before starting the engine, Pedrito unclipped the trolling lures from the lines and then the lines from the outriggers and stowed the rods underneath the washboards on either side. Still visible to the men on the Coast Guard vessel, he casually waved, started the engine, and put her in gear.

Pedrito waited until the government vessel, which had continued on an easterly course, was well away from the Rosita II, before moving the cooler out of the way and removing the engine cover and helping the others back on deck.

"You're pretty slick, Pedrito," said Roberto, who was the first one back on deck.

"I kept my hands in my pockets so they wouldn't see them shaking. I couldn't believe they didn't want to come on board," he said.

"Are you okay?" Roberto asked Maura, who was the last to come back on deck.

"I'm fine, just a little greasy," she said. "Fortunately I don't have any dinner plans for tonight."

"Tomorrow night. I promise," said Roberto, as he helped her out of the bilge.

"What are you thinking, Pedrito?" asked Roberto.

"We need to keep heading toward shore until they're out of sight or at least far enough away they can't see our lights. Maybe another two or three kilometers. When it's safe I'll kill the lights and we'll go as hard as we can go to the north. I don't think anyone is ready to give up," he said. He looked around at the others who were sitting spread out around the edge of the cockpit and waited for a response.

"The thought of spending the rest of my life in Cuba with Fidel is all the motivation I need," said Ernesto. "We may never have this opportunity again."

The others all nodded in agreement. Pedrito looked at Roberto and smiled. "*Es tu barco*, Roberto. What do you want to do?" he asked.

"Yes, it's my boat but you are the captain," he replied, smiling.

Pedrito looked in the direction of the Coast Guard vessel, which was continuing to head to the easter, paralleling the shoreline and nearly out of sight just off Punta de Bacuranao. He looked over again at Roberto, who was standing next to him holding on to the aft edge of the wheelhouse window, then reached down and killed the masthead and bow lights and swung the Rosita II to starboard and slowly brought her up on a plane, taking a northwesterly course away from the Coast Guard boat.

With the two boats traveling almost in opposite directions it was no more than fifteen minutes before they could see only the lights on the highest part of the masthead of other boat, and only then, when a larger swell would lift them for a moment above the rest.

No longer having to worry about the Coast Guard, Pedrito could now focus his attention on steering the Rosita II. It was more difficult to steer a boat at night on the open ocean when there was no moon and you couldn't see what was coming, but the sky was bright with stars and clear almost to the horizon and with the North Star to guide him, Pedrito was having little trouble maintaining a steady course on the still oil calm sea.

The rhythmic motion from the boat rising over the low swells and then easily and softly down again into the following trough together with the low hum of the engine, made it possible and easy for the others, tired from the long swim, to sleep when they wanted.

Because they were able to run parallel to the westerly swells there was no resistance from the sea, and the Rosita II ran smoothly and evenly. Even though it was well past two in the morning, Roberto had felt obligated to stay with Pedrito, who never seemed to tire while steering, or lose concentration.

They were now far out to sea beyond the reach of any light from land and making steady progress when Roberto thought he saw the first faint flash of light on the horizon to the northwest.

"Did you see that, Pedrito?" he asked.

"No, what?" he asked in reply.

"I'm pretty sure I saw a flash of lightning. That way, a little to port," he said pointing.

"The last forecast I heard yesterday right before we left said it would be clear into the afternoon. I heard nothing about a front," he said, pausing. "If the weather holds, we'll be to the Keys in another seven hours."

"There's another one. Right over the bow," said Roberto. "Did you see it?"

"I saw it. It has to be a front. We don't have thunderstorms this time of year unless a front is coming. If it is it could get rough for a bit, Roberto. The weather in a norther doesn't usually last long though and the back side is always clear," he said.

When a norther would sweep out of the Gulf of Mexico in the winter it was usually strong, with a sudden and heavy wind on the leading edge. Pedrito had been caught offshore in many northers and was confident the Rosita II could handle the wind and the waves that would build from the wind, but he had never been this far into the Gulf Stream where the current was strongest and the only option was to try and ride it out.

The first line of wind was light and barely noticeable. It was difficult to feel the breeze because they already had the feeling of the wind from going ahead and only knew something had changed when they saw the surface of the ocean begin to lightly ripple and took the appearance of diamonds.

It was with the second line of wind, when they met the bigger waves, and their direction became more northwesterly, that they felt the sudden drop in temperature along the leading edge of the front.

Wanting to maintain course, Pedrito kept the Rosita II heading into the quartering sea, which made steering more difficult and forced him to slow the boat in order to ease the pounding and prevent her from rolling when she came off the backside of the steepening waves.

As the wind grew heavier the increasing spray thrown up each time the bow met another and bigger wave, would soak the port side of the cockpit and anyone not shielded by the small windshield on top of the wheelhouse.

Pedrito's wife, Magalis, had the children sitting now under the cabin in the bow, wanting to protect them from the ocean spray, which was constant and heavy. But in a position under the bow they were having to endure a greater pounding from the rise and fall of the boat each time it hit another wave, than if they were all the way to the stern.

Only yards before the rain wall hit, the Rosita II was hit by a massive three-meter wave that spun her sideways nearly sending her bottom up. Before Pedrito could bring her bow to, a second wave, bigger than the first, hit her broadside to port with enough force to snap both rudder cables, rendering her steering useless.

Pedrito quickly looked around the cockpit, making sure no one had fallen overboard, before pushing down on the throttle, hoping the rudder was frozen slightly to port, making it possible to bring the Rosita II back around enough that they could take the next wave bow to, lessening the risk of a rollover. It worked but only just, and then the rain hit.

The wind was now howling at a steady forty-five making it impossible to hear one another even when someone would yell something. The sea had built to four meters and visibility was little more than the length of the boat. There was nothing Pedrito could do, and he knew it.

Wave after wave poured into the cockpit threatening to swamp the boat, sending everyone into the ocean. Pedrito had never encountered conditions anywhere near this extreme and there was no way of knowing if the bilge pump would keep up. He knew it would continue to pump as long as there was enough fuel to keep her running and the batteries charged, but what he couldn't know was how long the conditions would last.

When the steering went out, Roberto, wanting to make additional room forward, underneath the wheelhouse, slid the large wooden cooler up against the stern, giving Maura, Yamilet, and Ileana some protection from the direct force of the waves as they broke over the bow and into the cockpit. It was then, when he moved the cooler, that he noticed the water jug was gone and must have been washed out of the boat by one of the larger waves.

The worst of the storm lasted no more than fifteen minutes, but the damage was done. Unable to steer, they were now at the mercy of the easterly flowing Gulf Stream current, and without knowing exactly how far they had come it was impossible to know what land lay to the east and how far.

As the sky cleared the wind began to fall out and the sky began to fill once more with stars. The relentless pounding from the waves breaking across the bow had blown out the window on the port side of the windshield, letting even more water into the cockpit, helping to overwhelm the deck scuppers and filling the cockpit to a depth of twenty centimeters. Pedrito had kept the engine running at idle speed to maintain a charge in the batteries keeping the bilge pump running, which somehow managed to stay ahead of the water below deck.

As the sea began to flatten Maura was the first to emerge from under the wheelhouse. A large welt had formed on the right side of her face from having been thrown against one of the uprights supporting the bow deck, and it had not yet begun to darken. She sat down next to Roberto who was sitting in the starboard corner of the cockpit along the stern, rested her headed against Roberto's shoulder and held his arm tight against her body.

Although no one seemed to be seriously injured, the experience had left everyone, even Pedrito, the most experienced seaman, in a mild state of shock. There was no need to speak, and everyone knew they were in serious trouble.

"Magalis, how are the children?" Pedrito asked, looking under the bow deck for the first time since the storm began.

"We're okay, Pedrito. Just a little beat up," she said.

"Pedrito, we lost the drinking water overboard in the storm," was all Roberto said.

"You're sure? It's not under the bow?" he asked.

"I'm sure," he replied.

"Ernesto, how long can we make it without water?" asked Pedrito.

"Three days perhaps. Maybe a little longer if you stay out of the sun. It depends on the individual. Everyone is different," he replied. "If we're lucky maybe we'll see some more rain."

"The front was too strong to see any rain the next few days," said Armando. "It will be clear for at least three days, maybe longer." Pedrito knew Armando well and that he had spent many years on the ocean and knew the patterns of the weather in the north of Cuba in winter as well as any fisherman from Cojimar, and didn't question him.

"What direction you think we're drifting, Armando?" asked Pedrito.

"You have something I can throw overboard? A small piece of wood, anything," he said.

"Here, you can use this cutting board, Armando. It will float. Magalis, hand me the light. It's in the box behind the steering wall," said Pedrito.

"You see the North Star, Pedrito?" asked Armando.

"Yes, it's almost directly off the port side. Here's the light," he said. Pedrito turned the light on and handed it to Armando. Pedrito then took the pine bait board from Armando, and using the sharp edge of the apron on top of the wash board, split a narrow piece off along the grain line that paralleled the edge of the board. "I don't want to throw the whole thing in. I'm sure we'll need to check our drift again," he said when he was finished.

Armando threw the small piece of wood off the port side and followed it with the light as it drifted away from the boat off the stern until he could no longer see it with the light.

"Looks like we're drifting a little bit to the northeast," said Armando. "For now."

"Better that than southeast I suppose," said Pedrito. "If we're half-way across and continue drifting in this direction we have at least two hundred kilometers until we hit the Great Bahama Bank. I don't think we're drifting more than a knot or two, even in this current. Which means we wouldn't make it to the bank for almost three days."

"Isn't this a shipping lane, Pedrito?" asked Roberto.

"Yes, but unless a ship is within four or five kilometers of us they'll never see us. Especially in the dark. That's when it is most dangerous," he said.

"Still, we should have someone watching all the time," said Roberto.

"For sure, it's our best hope," said Pedrito.

"How much food do we have, Pedrito?" asked Ernesto.

"Only what is in the cooler, and it isn't much," he answered. "If we're lucky the boat will attract some fish. We have the two fishing rods and I have a couple hand lines."

Pedrito had not heard the bilge pump cut on for some time and decided to check the water level below deck. Sliding the engine cover off enough to shine the light into the bilge, he saw that the water had gone down to a level below the stringers and the keel and decided to turn the engine off to conserve fuel.

"Pedrito, I'll watch until sunrise. You should rest," said Roberto. "You were at the helm for many hours."

"We need two people watching," said Pedrito.

"I'll keep watch with you," said Maura, as she stood up.

The pulsing drone coming from the diesel engine as it idled helplessly in the open ocean, was replaced now by the sound of the swells—that continued to diminish in size as the wind lessened—when they would break weakly against the stern then quickly die out as they washed under the Rosita II, then roll down sea beyond the bow without a sound.

Roberto looked up at the night sky which had cleared completely except for the clouds on the backside of the front—still visible in the southeast—and saw the lights from a jet heading north, probably to an airport in Florida, backlit by the brilliant light of the Milky Way, and wondered what it must be like to fly. From that altitude, he thought, the passengers could see the lights both from Havana and Miami. Two cities separated by a formidable but negotiable physical boundary was easy for Roberto to understand. It was the unnecessarily cruel and absurdly artificial nature of the political boundary that was not.

Container ships and oil tankers must travel the Florida Straits on their way to and from the Panama Canal, he thought. Surely it was only a matter of time before they would be spotted. He knew the American Coast Guard regularly patrolled these waters and had rescued thousands of people who had fled Cuba, many of whom for whatever reason never made it all the way across.

He looked at Maura who was standing next to him with her hands on top of the windshield of the wheelhouse for balance. "Are you frightened?" he asked.

"No. I mean not really. I was kind of expecting something to go wrong," she said. "It's the story of my life. At least up to this point."

"You and ten million other Cubans. I like that you're still optimistic, though," he said.

"When things are this bad, I don't think you have the option not to be. Things will change when we get to Florida," she said.

"Why do you think that?" he asked.

"Because I'm with you, and every time you fall over backwards into a pile of horse shit, you come up smelling like a flor de mariposa," she said smiling. "It hurts when I smile."

"It's starting to turn blue," he said.

"Do I look as bad as I feel?" she asked.

"I'll let you know when I can't stand to look at you anymore. If it gets too bad I may have to throw you overboard," he said smiling.

"You're hysterical, Roberto. I can tell you this, Alexis Valdes has nothing to worry about," she said confidently.

"Look," he said pointing to the east. "It's beautiful."

The predawn light was faint and faded quickly up into the bank of eastern stars which still dominated the sky. In winter the sunrise came slowly. Because the angle of the sunrise was lower in winter, even in the northern tropics, it took more time for the sun to show itself. The fishermen in Cojimar always said when you had a clear view of the sunrise in winter from the ocean, it was always more beautiful than in summer.

"I've never seen the sunrise from a boat," said Maura.

"This one will be memorable," said Roberto, not taking his eyes off the horizon.

"You have a profound grasp of the obvious, Roberto."

"Is that a good thing?"

"Let's just say it's endearing," said Maura. She looked again toward the horizon, and watched in silence until the sun broke free of the ocean's surface, then looked away when the glare was fully on the water.

XXVII

With the passing of the front the air had turned cooler and dryer and the sun was very bright. The watch was shared by everyone throughout the day, taking turns whenever someone had become too tired to concentrate. Pedrito and Magalis were careful to keep the children out of the direct sun under the bow deck of the wheelhouse. But for the others, there was little chance escaping the sun, especially at midday when the light was more direct and the intensity was greatest.

Once, late in the afternoon, Armando shouted out when he saw the very top of the pilothouse of a passing oil tanker, barely visible above the horizon. So far away though the only part of the ship they could see was the radar on top of the light tower. At such a great distance it appeared not to be moving, which frustrated everyone.

As afternoon gave way to evening and the sun went low, there was little conversation and they knew the chance of being seen that day was lessening as quickly as the the light was fading, and that they would have to wait again until morning. It had been almost a full day now without water and they were beginning to suffer, but no one spoke about it.

Roberto stayed up with Maura through most of the night until just before the sun rose. They preferred keeping watch at night when there was no glare on the water and they didn't have to work as hard to see and it was easier to see a great distance.

The weather on the second day was like the first and there were no clouds and it was still cool. Roberto's brother Pedro seemed to be struggling more than any of the others and he was becoming increasingly dehydrated.

Occasionally, when the nausea was greatest, he would throw up mostly small amounts of bright mustard colored bile over the side of the boat, prompting the small bait fish that had collected under the Rosita II, to dart out and frantically pick out any solid pieces before returning to the safety of the underside of the hull.

Unable to remove the false ceiling under the bow deck without the proper tools, Roberto couldn't know for sure if the paintings hidden above had been damaged by the storm. There was nothing he could do which made him worry more, but he saw no sign water had penetrated the bow and the pine boards holding the plastic bag in place containing the paintings, still seemed dry and tight. He thought of it as a small consolation, considering the situation, when Maura reminded him they were still alive and for that alone he should be grateful.

When Armando and Frank took the watch shortly after sunrise, Roberto was able to briefly fall asleep lying in the shade of the starboard wall against the side of the cockpit. The sleep was a brief but a welcome relief as he was beginning to weaken and his legs were now cramping involuntarily.

When he awoke, Maura was lying next to him mostly in the sun and she was asleep. The bruise that covered the entire right side of her face, where she had been thrown against the side of the boat under the bow deck, had turned a greenish yellow color, bordered around the edges by a deep purple.

Looking down at her he thought about how fearless she had been when they swam out to meet Pedrito and how she had bravely faced the storm and had not complained or afterwards voiced a single regret. He knew she was remarkable but knew it to be truer now than before. Moving around to the other side of Maura, he carefully slid her out of the sun into the shade where he had been sleeping. She opened her eyes slightly and smiled and then closed them again.

It was January and it was not hot during the day, but the many hours spent under a cloudless sky were slowly and relentlessly robbing their bodies of precious moisture. Toward evening as the sun was setting and the air began to cool again, Roberto noticed his brother Pedro was sweating and asked Ernesto why his brother continued to sweat in the cooling air.

"Your brother is very dehydrated, Roberto. He may only last one more day, two at the most, and that's if he's lucky. We need to keep him out of the sun as much as possible," said Ernesto.

"His eyes are sunken. They look terrible, Ernesto and his breathing is becoming more rapid," said Roberto.

"That's because his heart rate is increasing. It's likely his blood pressure is dropping also," he said. "It's very serious, Roberto."

"Is there anything we can do for him?" asked Roberto. "I've heard of people drinking urine to stay alive."

"I know of cases where that has happened and the people survived, but I wouldn't recommend it. Those people would have survived anyway," said the doctor. "It's getting cooler now. He should be more comfortable overnight. Let's see how he is in the morning."

Roberto sat with his brother Pedro until it was dark and then began the overnight watch once again with Maura. The breeze, as it had in the previous two nights, had fallen out to a flat calm and the ocean once more took on the appearance of pond water covered in oil. They had for two days continued to drift slowly bow first to the northeast with the current.

Earlier in the day Pedrito had briefly run the engine, wanting to maintain a charge in the battery in order to keep the bilge pump operating in case they encountered another storm, but after several minutes the fuel ran out. They were entering their third day and had now run out of food, water, and fuel, and had not seen any other boats, even at a distance, in two days.

Standing in the cockpit with his back against the steering wheel, Roberto leaned against the port side wall. Staring into the dark he thought about his parents and his brother Carlos and the trouble he put on them and how he didn't want things to end this way and how he had endured terrible suffering in prison and that he knew he was capable of worse suffering and didn't care or worry how it would end for him. It was the suffering of the others that he hated and that he couldn't take much longer.

He thought about the famous quote from *A Farewell to Arms*, which he remembered reading many years ago and never forgotten, that read, "The world breaks everyone and afterwards many are strong at the broken places. But those that will not break it kills. It kills the very good and the very gentle and the very brave impartially. If you are none of these, you can be sure it will kill you too but there will be no special hurry." He wondered if Fidel had read those lines and if he had, what was his interpretation and what he thought it said about him and the people of Cuba.

Roberto could tell Maura was losing strength and was having difficulty standing but was determined to hang on through the night to keep watch with Roberto. He tried to get her to lie down but she refused, cheerfully reminding him that her vision was better than his and she was going to be the one to see the first boat.

Sometime after midnight they drifted through a large mat of sargasso weed that had built along the edge of one of the stronger current seams. In the center of the mat, resting on top of the weed in the thickest part, Roberto noticed a small loggerhead turtle of no more than five kilos and after waiting to drift within range, tried to gaff it with the long gaff, but managed only a glancing blow off the back of the shell. He tried for it again, but the turtle was too quick and after paddling a short distance across the top of the mat, disappeared underneath the weed and was gone.

"The blood from that turtle might have meant the difference between life and death for Pedro," said Roberto. Disappointed with himself for not gaffing the turtle, he leaned with both hands on the washboard and looked down at the sargasso weed as it slowly drifted under the boat.

"Stop talking that way, Roberto. Pedro is not going die," said Maura.

"Ernesto said he may only have one more day," he said.

"Something will happen tomorrow, after it is light," she said.

Suddenly they heard Pedro's voice. He was sitting on the deck and pointing excitedly toward the west behind the stern.

"Pedro, take it easy," said Roberto. He couldn't see anything but kept looking in the direction Pedro had pointed. "What did you see?"

"It was a boat, and it was very near. I could see the light on the masthead," said Pedro, who was having trouble speaking.

"I don't see anything. Are you sure?" asked Roberto, who was now kneeling beside his brother.

"I'm sure I saw it," he said, pointing once more. "Look! There it is again. There is the light."

Roberto saw only a bright star low on the horizon in the direction Pedro was pointing that appeared and disappeared as the Rosita II rose and fell on the low swells.

"Pedro, you're seeing things. There is no ship. Please, you need to lie down," he said. Roberto carefully cupped the back of Pedro's head and then with his other hand eased his brother's upper body back onto the deck.

Pedro briefly looked up at Roberto before his eyes closed and his head slowly rolled to the side.

He's worse now," said Roberto. "If we could only catch some fish."

"Pedrito and Armando have been looking. Nothing has come close enough," said Maura.

"We need to find a patch of grass during the day like the one we just passed," he said.

"You mean to find another turtle?" she asked.

"No, I was thinking of the *dorado* and wahoo that sometimes hide under the Sargasso. We don't have any bait, but they'll sometimes bite a bare hook," he said.

"Do you think we've drifted any closer to the Keys?" she asked.

"Pedrito is certain we are still heading northeast, so we must be getting closer. We may not be out of Cuban waters though," he replied.

"Does that mean if the U.S. Coast Guard were to spot us, even if we're just south of the maritime border, they couldn't help us?" she asked.

"Something like that," he said. "The sun is coming again, Maura." Roberto was looking east at the thin yellow line just beginning to appear above the line of the water. "Let's hope this is our last sunrise on the Rosita II."

It had been a long night and Roberto's legs had started to cramp more as the dehydration worsened, making it difficult to stand now for more than a few minutes at a time. By the time the sun was fully clear of the horizon and Ernesto and Armando had taken the morning watch, he was all but done. Maura was sitting on the stern next to Pedro, who hadn't changed position overnight and who's condition had continued to deteriorate.

Several times during the night he had thought about his conversation with Ernesto about the possibility of Pedro drinking urine. He was watching his brother die and couldn't take it and had made a decision.

"Ernesto," said Roberto.

Ernesto turned around to face Roberto, who was sitting on the deck next to Pedro.

"I want Pedro to drink some urine. He isn't going to last much longer."

"You could make his condition worse," said Ernesto.

"I want to try," he said. "That's my decision."

"He's your brother and it's your conscience," replied Ernesto.

"I'm trying not to think about my conscience, Ernesto. I've never known it to be helpful," said Roberto.

After three days without water, it was difficult for anyone to produce even the smallest amount of urine, but everyone agreed to help. Pedrito remembered he kept a plastic bleach bottle in the tool bin behind the wheelhouse bulkhead to use as a hand bailer in case the bilge pump went out and gave it to Roberto. Pedrito had cut the top off just above the handle to make the mouth of the bottle larger for bailing.

Roberto took the bottle from Pedrito and dipped it several times in the ocean before filling it half-way with sea water then held the bottle on top of the washboard and ran his free hand around the inside in an effort to remove the dirt and grease that had collected in the bottom of the bottle.

When it was as clean as he could make it, he tried urinating into the plastic bottle, but his body was only able to produce about thirty milliliters of urine. After passing the bottle around to the others it contained less than three hundred milliliters total, barely enough to fill an average size coffee cup.

Roberto knelt beside his brother who was struggling to remain conscious, and with help from Ernesto, who had lifted Pedro's torso and head off the deck to a position high enough that he could swallow, partially filled Pedro's mouth with the still foamy yellow liquid, then waited.

Pedro tried swallowing but began to choke on the salty liquid, causing most of it to run out of his mouth and down the side of his face, soaking the collar of his shirt and staining it a dark greenish yellow color. After waiting until Pedro was no longer coughing, and with a little more than half the urine remaining, Roberto tried again. This time, Pedro managed to swallow a small mouthful. He waited for a few minutes, looking for a response from his brother, but nothing came, and he gave Pedro the remaining urine.

"Pedro needs to rest, Roberto," said Ernesto. "There's nothing more we can do for him now."

Roberto looked at Maura who was kneeling beside him. He stood up and leaned over the side of the boat and filled the bailer several times with sea water to clean it and handed it back to Pedrito who had been standing by the helm watching and sat down again next to his brother.

"He's going to make it," said Maura.

"I'd rather it was me," he said.

"We're all going to make it," she said.

"Pedrito! Pedrito!" yelled Armando. "There is a freighter! Look, right over the bow."

Pedrito had turned around and was looking hard in the direction Armando was pointing, his hands cupped around the side of his eyes, trying to reduce the glare from the low angle of the morning sun on the water, but was having trouble.

"I can't see her, Armando!" he said loudly.

"Directly over the bow light. Do you see her now? I can just see the front of the pilothouse. It looks like she's coming straight for us," he said.

Everyone but Roberto's brother Pedro was standing on deck now looking to the east, straining to see the freighter which was still four or five kilometers distant.

"I see her now, Armando," said Pedrito. "I think you're right. She's coming straight for us."

"Let me have one of the rods, Pedrito," said Armando. "I want to tie my shirt onto the rod and stand on the bow deck. I believe she'll pass very close."

Pedrito quickly grabbed the longer of the two rods from under the bow deck and disconnected the heavy Penn 12/0 reel from the rod seat, making it lighter, before handing it to Armando who had already climbed onto the bow deck.

"Do you see her, Roberto," asked Maura.

"I think so. She's far, far though," he said.

"I told you, I told you," she said excitedly.

"I believe she'll pass a little to port, Pedrito," said Armando. "They'll see us, easy."

Slowly the hull of the freighter came into view, and like Armando had predicted appeared to be on a course that would take her no more than a couple hundred meters to port.

Armando had already begun to wave the fishing rod with his shirt attached when the freighter appeared to make a slight turn to its port in the direction of the Rosita II.

"She's turning, she's turning, Pedrito!" yelled Armando, looking back and still waving the rod.

"She's flying an American flag! *Ella se llama la* Naches!" yelled Roberto. "*Ella es Americana!*"

As the freighter came closer, they could see some of her crew members gathered along the port bow rail, waving down at them and were close enough now to hear the diesel engines when they began to idle down. As the freighter slowed the sound from the engines increased again when the captain put her in reverse in order to bring her to a stop, causing a large foaming boil to appear at her stern that was easily heard aboard the Rosita II.

One of the crewmen on the Naches had a megaphone and began speaking in English. "Where are you from?" he asked.

Between Ernesto and Maura, they were able to understand English well enough to respond.

"*Nos somos de Cuba!*" yelled Ernesto. "*No hablo Ingles.*"

"Okay, *espere*," said the crewman, who then handed the megaphone to one of the other crewmen who began speaking in Spanish.

"*Estamos llmando a la Guardia Costera de EE. UU.,*" he said.

"We need water!" yelled Ernesto in Spanish.

"How many are on board?" asked the crewman.

"Fourteen!" yelled Pedrito. "We have one that is very sick."

"Have you lost all power?" the man asked.

"Yes, we have no steering and we've run out of fuel," said Pedrito.

"Okay. We'll throw you an end of rope," he said. "We can attach a bucket with water bottles to the other end and lower it just above the water. Then you pull the bucket on board. Don't let it hit the water. When you have the bucket, take the water bottles out and we'll pull it back onboard and refill it."

"When we have the water, we need to be careful and not drink too fast," said Ernesto. "A small amount at a time in order to keep it down."

Signaling they were ready aboard the Rosita II, one of the crewmen, aided by the calm sea, managed to land the rope perfectly across the cockpit of the Rosita II, on the first attempt.

Pedrito quickly handed the rope up to Armando on the bow deck, who was in a better position of leverage to handle the rope and pull the bucket on board.

Working together with the crewman on the other end of the rope, Armando kept the bucket from dragging in the water, preventing the loss of any of the water bottles in the ocean. Quickly he pulled the bucket up over the side of the bow, took out one bottle and handed the rest to Pedrito over the top of the windshield then let out his end of the rope allowing the crewman to pull the bucket back aboard the freighter.

Roberto opened his bottle, and after taking a small sip and swallowing slowly, he took in another small amount and held it inside his mouth for a moment letting the sweet coolness of the liquid fill the inside of his mouth. Closing his eyes and swallowing once more he could feel the water cooling his chest as it tracked downward.

He then knelt down next to his brother and with one hand between Pedro's shoulder blades, he carefully supported his head with his forearm and raised his body off the deck into an upright position and held the water bottle to his lips.

Pedro opened his eyes slightly and tried to move his lips, but the words wouldn't come.

"Maura, I need some help," said Roberto. "Take the water and open his mouth. Just a little. Not too much."

Realizing what was happening, Pedro immediately tried reaching for the water bottle Maura was holding. By now Ernesto was kneeling beside Roberto and helping to hold Pedro.

"Small amounts, Pedro," said Ernesto.

After a few minutes, his mouth now moist from the water, Pedro was able to speak.

"What is happening, Roberto?" he whispered.

"The American Coast Guard is coming Pedro," Roberto replied. "We'll be in Florida before sunset."

"*Es verdad?*" asked Pedro.

"*Es verdad, hermano,*" said Roberto.

"Pedrito!" yelled Armando from the bow deck. "More water coming. The red bottles are some kind of drink for hydration. They said it would help Pedro more than the water."

"Ask them how long before the Coast Guard arrives," said Pedrito.

"He says no more than one hour. They have a small boat, but he told me she is fast," said Armando. "He said American law will not allow them to take us on board and that we have to wait for the Coast Guard."

"I don't care who takes us. As long as he's sure they're coming," replied Pedrito.

"Pedrito, they have to tow us in. I have my paintings," said Roberto.

"They may have other ideas, Roberto," he said.

"Pedrito!" said Armando, who had to speak louder now after the captain restarted the freighters diesel engines. "The captain says they have to continue on to port."

"Ask them if they can send down some food before they leave," said Pedrito.

"I already asked them," replied Armando.

Once Armando had emptied the last bucket and the crewman on the other end of the rope had pulled the empty bucket back aboard the Naches, Armando threw the rest of the rope in the water and stepped back down into the cockpit of the Rosita II.

"How is Pedro?" asked Armando.

"He's coming around," answered Roberto. "Did the captain say how big the Coast Guard boat was?"

"He said was it was big enough for all of us," replied Armando.

"We're going to need a tow," said Roberto.

"Did the captain tell you our position, Armando?" asked Roberto.

"He said we're just inside U.S. waters, not far from Cay Sal Bank where the three maritime borders come together," said Armando.

"Let's hope we stay in U.S. waters until the Coast Guard arrives," said Roberto. "We need to keep watch, Pedrito. What direction did he say they're coming from?" asked Roberto.

"The captain said northeast," replied Armando.

"I think I see another freighter!" said Maura suddenly who was not looking in the same direction as the others.

"Where are you looking?" asked Pedrito.

"To the south. You see it?" she asked.

Armando, who had the best eyes of anyone, saw it first. "That's not a freighter Maura," he said, raising his voice. "You see it, Pedrito?"

"I see it! It's the fucking Cuban Coast Guard!" he yelled.

"What?" said Roberto loudly. "Are you sure?"

"I'm certain. I can see her flag. She looks like the same boat that stopped us the night we left. They probably found the inner tubes. I guarantee they've been looking for us," said Pedrito.

"There's no God damn way I'm going back to Cuba. They'll have to kill me first," said Roberto.

"They may not have to, Roberto," said Ernesto who had continued watching for the American Coast Guard. "Look!"

Coming straight for the Rosita II, at full throttle was a U.S. Coast Guard Utility Boat. The smaller American boat was farther away but appeared much faster than the older and much larger steel hulled Cuban vessel that was now within two kilometers.

"If we're in American waters there's nothing the Cubans can do," said Pedrito. "The Americans are going to reach us first."

"Yeah, like that would stop them. I'm sure they have more fire power than the Americans," said Roberto. "Remember, you're dealing with Fidel."

The American Coast Guard vessel was closing fast and no more than four hundred meters from the Rosita II when they saw the Cuban cutter slowly start to turn away, and head to the southwest, toward Cuba. It was then they knew their ordeal was finally over. They were safe.

"Your family is not going to believe it when they see you, Maura," said Roberto.

Maura put her arms around Roberto and began to cry. "I can't believe it. I think about all the ones that didn't make it."

One hundred meters out the American boat began to slow and as she came off a plane, her stern dropped and then her bow, finally leveling-out as she eased toward the Rosita II, coming in bow first. The man at the helm briefly put the boat in reverse to prevent her from drifting past the Rosita II, then turned the wheel to port bringing her stern around next to the bow of the smaller boat, cut the engines and stepped out from behind the wheel.

"Do any of you speak English?" he asked.

"*Solo un poquito, Capitan,*" said Pedrito. "*Lo siento.*"

"*No hay problema,*" he answered. "Ivan," said the captain to the man in the bow.

"You need to explain to them what the procedure is."

The crewman, who had been holding a coil of heavy rope, motioned to Roberto, whom he was closest to, to catch the rope. "Tie it off to the stern cleat," he said in Spanish after he threw the rope to Roberto.

"Have them tie the bow off, Eddie," said the captain to the other crewman in the stern.

Pedrito knew what needed to be done and was already standing on the bow waiting for the man to throw him the second rope.

"*De donde eres?*" Roberto asked the man he had taken the rope from.

"*Soy de Ponce. En el sur de Puerto Rico,*" he replied. "*Cuál es su nombre?*"

"Roberto. Roberto Ramos. *De la Habana,*" he answered.

"Ivan, tell them they are now in the custody of the United States and are to come aboard," said the captain.

"Did you understand anything he said?" asked the man in Spanish.

"*No, senor,*" replied Roberto.

"Roberto, I think he said we are to come with them in their boat," said Ernesto.

"Once you are aboard our orders are to sink your vessel," the crewman from Puerto Rico explained in Spanish.

"What?" yelled Roberto. "*No! No puede hacer eso!*" exclaimed Roberto.

"Those are our orders," replied the Puerto Rican. "I'm sorry, our orders are to sink all refugee boats."

"*No! no! Tengo una valiosa colección de arte a bordo,*" yelled Roberto.

"What?" replied the crewman in disbelief. "Captain, uh, he says he has an art collection on board."

"A what?" asked the captain loudly in disbelief.

"Sir, I'm sorry," said the crewman to Roberto.

"I have a million dollars worth of paintings stowed under the bow deck! You have to tow us in," said Roberto, becoming more agitated.

The captain and the other crewman had begun to help the others aboard the Coast Guard vessel and only Roberto, Pedrito, and Maura were still on board the Rosita II.

"*Senor*," said the Puerto Rican. "You need to come with us. Please."

"I'm not leaving this boat. You need to tow me in or I will die with my collection," said Roberto.

"Captain, he says he would rather die than lose his collection. He says it's stowed under the bow deck," said the crewman.

"Tell him to bring it with him," said the captain.

"*Puedes traer las pinturas contigo?* he asked.

"*No, no puedo.* The paintings are in plastic and built into the ceiling under the bow deck," replied Roberto.

"He said it's not possible, sir," said the crewman.

"Jesus! This is unbelievable. All right, look, Ivan tell him I am going to radio for permission to tow his boat. He'd better be telling the truth," said the captain.

While the captain radioed his superior for permission to tow the Rosita II, Maura climbed aboard the Coast Guard boat with the others to help Ernesto tend to Pedro, whose condition had improved but was still very weak and needed more fluids.

"Ivan," said the captain as he placed the VHF handset back in its clip. "Lieutenant said we can tow them in. Free the ropes and we'll get turned around, then we can attach the tow bridle."

"You're very lucky, *Senor* Ramos," said the crewman. "We never do this."

Roberto untied the rope from the stern and handed it to the crewman, then motioned for Pedrito to do the same from the bow. After taking the rope from Pedrito the crewman in the stern of the Coast Guard boat clipped the heavy nylon towing bridle to the tow rings on either side of the stern of the American boat and waited for the captain to bring her around. When the two boats were stern to bow, the crewman then handed the loose end to Pedrito, who clipped it into the bow ring on the Rosita II.

"Ivan. I'll keep her here so they can step aboard. Tell them they need to come now," said the captain.

"Roberto, you need to come aboard. We need to get going," said the crewman.

"I'm staying here," said Roberto, who was now standing on the bow of the Rosita II.

"Captain, he says he wants to stay aboard his boat," said the crewman.

"What for? He got what he wanted. I want him on board, Ivan," he said.

"Roberto, the captain wants you to come aboard now," he said.

"I'm staying with my paintings. If I come with you what's to prevent the captain from cutting my boat loose?" asked Roberto. "*Lo siento, senor.*"

"Sir. He says he won't come aboard. He thinks you'll cut his boat loose if he does," he said.

"*Senor, por favor,*" said Maura, to the crewman. "*Que se quede con su barco.*"

"Jesus this guy's persistent, Ivan. It's a God damn first for me, I can tell you," said the Captain. "Ivan, tell him he needs to be read his rights. We have to do it before we take up."

"*Senor,* the captain says before we return to port we are required to read you your rights," said the crewman to Roberto. "You are now in the custody of the Untied States of America and you're entitled to certain legal rights. Do you understand?"

Roberto stared at the man in disbelief. He had heard the man's words clearly but couldn't believe what he had heard and was unable to respond.

"Do you understand, Roberto?" he asked again.

Exhausted, Roberto fell to his knees. Slumped over—his arms quivered as he held himself with his hands braced on the deck—he began to cry.

"Roberto. *Senor*," said the crewman softly.

Roberto looked up at the man who was holding open a small black book. "*Senor*, I'm sorry, but this is the first time in my life I have been told I have rights," he said.

"Well then today is a good day for you, my friend. I'll read them now?" he asked.

"*Si Senor*," replied Roberto. Summoning his last bit of energy Roberto came to his feet. Now barely able to stand, he wanted to show the man respect and faced him directly, staring into the man's eyes. His breathing was deep and measured.

"*Senor* Ramos. *Usted tiene de derecho de guardar silencio. . . .*"

Acknowledgements:

I would like to thank, Roberto Ramos, for allowing me to tell his remarkable story, and above all for his sincere friendship and help during the writing process. I would also like to thank, Deborah Reid, Ash Nichols and Chuck Garrettson for their love, encouragement, and unwavering support throughout this improbable adventure. And lastly, John Probst, Pamela Michael, and Kimberly Nichols for helping to make the telling of Roberto's story a reality.

About the Author:

The author, Michael Reid, lives in the Bitterroot Valley of western Montana with his wife Deborah, and their elderly rescue dog, Punkin. When not fishing for wild trout in the rivers of Idaho and Montana, or blue marlin in the waters of the Bahamas, he can occasionally be spotted in CubaOcho, in Little Havana, Miami, in the company of Roberto Ramos, enjoying a glass of premium rum and a hand-rolled cigar.